A Deal Undone

A DEAL UNDONE

THE MAKING
AND BREAKING
OF THE
MEECH LAKE
ACCORD

ANDREW COHEN

Andrew Cohen

Douglas & McIntyre
Vancouver/Toronto

Douglas & McIntyre, 1615 Venables Street, Vancouver, BC V5L 2H1

Canadian Cataloguing in Publication Data
Cohen, Andrew, 1955–
    A deal undone
    ISBN 0-88894-704-6
        1. Canada — Constitutional law — Amendments.   2. Canada.
Constitution Act, 1982.   3. Canada — Politics and government —
1984–   4. Federal-provincial relations — Canada.   I. Title.
JL65 1990.C64 1990   342.71'03   C90-091393-2

Editing by Jennifer Glossop
Design by Alexandra Hass
Front cover photograph by Montizambert Photography
Typeset by The Typeworks
Printed and bound in Canada by D. W. Friesen & Sons Ltd.
Printed on acid-free paper ∞

Excerpt from "The Love Song of J. Alfred Prufrock" by T. S. Eliot, reprinted by permission of his literary executors and Faber and Faber.

Contents

To my parents, Ruth and Edgar Cohen

Preface

THE IDEA FOR THIS BOOK CAME TO ME ON 1 MAY 1987, THE MORNING AF-
ter the first ministers signed the Meech Lake Accord. Although the
events of the patriation debate had been well mined, I contemplated a
book on the making of the Meech Lake Accord. At the time, the
meeting at Meech Lake seemed like the end of the story. As things
turned out, it was the beginning.

My interest in the constitution began in 1980, when I was parliamentary reporter for United Press International in Ottawa. Because
everyone else in our modest bureau considered the constitution to be
a contagion, I was assigned to the story. That fall, I covered the joint
committee that had begun studying the proposed Charter of Rights.
It was there, in a carnival of participatory democracy, that the Charter was shaped. Subsequently, I followed the constitutional issue as it
was debated in Parliament, argued before the Supreme Court and, ultimately, decided by the first ministers at a dramatic conference. It
was, perhaps, because of that experience that I was so struck by the
process that led to the Meech Lake Accord. It had transpired so
quickly, yet was so consequential. I watched it unfold, then as political writer for the *Financial Post,* and I was strangely fascinated.

Deciding to write the story was one thing, finding a publisher was
another. While excellent books have been written on the constitution
in Canada, it is not a sexy issue. Jean Marchand, the former Liberal cabinet minister, said people do not stay up all night
thinking about the constitution, and he may have been right. Indeed,
the glories of the amending formula are more likely to inspire somno-
lence than poetry.

When I broached the subject with Beverley Slopen, one of the country's leading literary agents, she was enthusiastic. She always believed there was a story there, even when I had doubts. Throughout this exercise, particularly daunting for a first-time author, she was attentive and clear-sighted.

So were Rob Sanders and Scotty McIntyre of Douglas & McIntyre. While other publishers were offering polite refusals, they embraced the idea. Moreover, they took on the book long before the subject was topical, the real measure of their commitment.

A book of this type, which is no more than a rough draft of history, is only as good as its subjects. Scores of politicians, federal and provincial officials, and constitutional experts made themselves available, many of them with nothing to gain. All the premiers willingly gave of their time, some on two or three occasions. Frank McKenna, David Peterson, Howard Pawley, Joe Ghiz and Clyde Wells were particularly generous in sharing their thoughts. Ian Scott, the attorney general of Ontario, and Hershell Ezrin, the former principal secretary to Premier Peterson, were also expansive. In shedding light on constitutional law as well as on their personal involvement with the accord, Professor Peter Hogg of Osgoode Hall and Professor Bryan Schwartz of the University of Manitoba were helpful.

If this book achieves any recognition, it will be due in part to the efforts of John Fraser and George Galt, editor and associate editor of *Saturday Night*. Fraser suggested I write an adaptation for his magazine and, accomplished salesman that he is, made sure the country knew about it. Galt used his light touch to condense and focus unwieldy prose.

In researching this book, I was helped by the gracious staff of the Library of Parliament, one of this country's treasures. I am also grateful to Professor Ron Watts and Dwight Herperger at the Institute of Intergovernmental Relations at Queen's University, who kindly made their superb collection available.

Others played important roles in completing this book. Neville Nankivell, the publisher of the *Financial Post,* and John Godfrey, its editor, granted me leave of absence to undertake this project and then extended it. Both make the *Post* the civilized organization it is.

Patrick Gossage, former press secretary to Pierre Trudeau, provided a convivial place to work in his firm's offices. His unfailing humour and boyish mischief helped lighten the burden of incarceration. His associates, Martha Durdin and Jim Maclean, showed enormous tolerance for unsolicited advice from a restless writer-in-residence.

My special appreciation goes to those who shaped the content of this book. My editor, Jennifer Glossop, superbly organized, focussed and pared a manuscript on a subject that changed often. Her patience and cheerfulness were especially admirable when cascading events broadened the task while narrowing the time. She was ably assisted by Beverley Beetham Endersby, who copy-edited the manuscript with precision and care.

Andrew Coyne, a columnist with the *Financial Post*, and Martin Cohn, an editorial writer with the Toronto *Star* gave the manuscript a careful and constructive reading, and, remarkably, claimed to enjoy doing it. As two journalists who followed the debate closely, they offered insights, made suggestions, and issued stern remonstrances. Their eye for detail and ear for style brought a measure of balance and continuity.

Lastly, this project would have been well-nigh unbearable without the unflagging support of Mary Gooderham, a reporter at the *Globe and Mail*. Mary — who can skin a fish, tend a garden and name every tree in the forest — compiled the index and the chronology and made valuable suggestions on the text. She treated the project as her own, bringing to it her customary dedication and affection.

Prologue

ON THE NIGHT OF 20 MAY 1980, THE ARMY OF INDÉPENDENTISTES GATH-
ered at the Paul Sauvé Arena in Montreal. It was there that the Parti
Québécois always awaited victory or defeat, and this night its leaders
and followers assembled to watch the returns from the provincial referendum. On this, the occasion of his worst defeat, René Lévesque,
the rumpled premier, was almost alone on stage. With him stood
only his wife, Corinne, who held a long-stemmed rose, and Lise
Payette, one of his ministers. Lévesque talked of the pain of losing
("This hurts more than any election," he said) and conceded that
Quebeckers had voted to give federalism a chance. In the crowd, partisans were crying. At the end of his remarks, Lévesque forced a
smile, managed a wave and said wistfully, *"A la prochaine."* Until
next time.

In that sepia-coloured spring of 1980, Quebec had agonized deeply
over its future. The soul-searching had played itself out in church
basements and committee rooms, in community halls, lecture halls
and union halls. The referendum was to decide not just the place of
Quebec in Canada, but also the place of Canada in Quebec. When it
was over, Quebec chose Canada and the fundamental question
seemed resolved, for at least a generation. Still, the uneasiness between the two founding peoples lingered. The cheering stopped, but
the crowd never left.

But the referendum in 1980 was only a way station on a longer
journey. The Canadian constitutional train had been travelling since
1927, when Great Britain proposed legal autonomy for its domin-
ions, but the provinces and the federal government could not agree
on a domestic amending formula. For the next half a century, the

country's founding charter, the British North America Act, resided abroad and caused division at home. When federal governments attempted to free it from British trusteeship, the provinces demanded powers in return. Indeed, it was in 1927 that the premiers of Ontario and Quebec propounded "the compact theory" of Confederation, by which provinces would delegate powers to the dominion government. The struggles for jurisdiction have been the hallmark of federal-provincial relations ever since. They have become, in a sense, Canada's Constitutional Wars. Between 1980 and 1990, there were two more battles for constitutional reform: the "Patriation Round," from 1980 to 1982, which finally saw the arrival of the BNA Act and the entrenchment of the Charter of Rights; and the "Quebec Round," from 1986 to 1990, which produced the Meech Lake Accord. The first left out Quebec, when it refused to sign. The second sought to accommodate the province, and it did sign.

A constitution is the soul of a nation. It is a repository of values. Changing one is not easy anywhere, particularly in Canada. In the sixteenth century, Niccoló Machiavelli warned: "It should be borne in mind that nothing is more difficult to arrange, more doubtful of success, and more dangerous to carry through than initiating change to a state's constitution." His world was Florence, during a regime of poison and intrigue, but his dictum holds true in contemporary Canada.

The Quebec Round initially seemed free from Machiavelli's curse. At the start of its short, unhappy life, the Meech Lake Accord was greeted with indifference. Within a year, however, it was no longer seen as a symbol of unity. Instead, it had become a sword of division.

To the players in the story, it was more than a piece of paper. For Brian Mulroney, Meech Lake promised a place in history; for Pierre Trudeau, the repudiation of a legacy; for John Turner, a return to power. For Robert Bourassa, it meant a stronger Quebec; for Gary Filmon, the survival of his government; for Clyde Wells, the end of a vision; for the rest of the premiers, more powers and profile. In political terms, the accord united the Conservatives in the beginning and divided them in the end, leaving their Quebec strategy in ruins. It also divided the Liberals and cost them an election. At the outset, people wondered what the accord would do for Canada; by its end, they wondered what it had done to Canada.

Now, ten years after the referendum that was supposed to settle the question, Canada finds itself in another constitutional crisis. Once again, Quebec feels rejected. Once again, a referendum looms. Once again, the future of Canada is in doubt. *La fin de siècle* threatens to bring *la fin du pays*.

When the premiers gathered at Meech Lake that spring day in 1987, they wanted less to make history than to rectify it. But they, too, would soon be caught up in the malaise, both captains and casualties in the Constitutional Wars.

The Miracle at Meech Lake

THE PREMIERS AND THE PRIME MINISTER CAME EARLY TO MEECH LAKE, A footprint of water in the Gatineau hills of Quebec. The mercurial Richard Hatfield of New Brunswick arrived first, to discuss strategy with federal officials. The rest of the first ministers appeared by late morning. Brian Mulroney, the presidential prime minister, was ferried to the retreat in the back of a chauffeur-driven Cadillac, second in a three-car motorcade; Howard Pawley, the socialist premier, rode in the front of a rented van with a clutch of advisers. Despite his protests, they forbade him to drive.

One by one, they sped up Highway 5, through the hamlet of Old Chelsea and on to Meech Lake. They passed through the stone gateposts marking the entrance to the dirt-strewn road that hugs the western shore. While the Manitobans parked the van and walked up the hill, most of the limousines bearing the other premiers swung around the semicircular driveway and stopped in front of Willson House, an imposing pink-granite mansion ringed by ten provincial flags that snapped in the wind. Shunning the order of precedence that usually determines everything at these meetings, down to the serving of dessert, the first ministers arrived without ceremony. From British Columbia and Alberta came William Vander Zalm and Donald Getty. From Saskatchewan came Grant Devine. From Ontario and Quebec came David Peterson and Robert Bourassa. From Prince Edward Island came Joe Ghiz; then the three most senior first ministers: Brian Peckford of Newfoundland, John Buchanan of Nova Scotia and Richard Hatfield, the dean of them all. Accompanying them was a coterie of courtiers and cosmeticians, though a far smaller one than usual. Peterson and those who took this exercise most seriously brought their closest advisers. Vander Zalm, on the other hand, brought only two, one of whom left early. In affairs of state, the premier believed austerity was more important than advice.

As is their custom, the premiers and the prime minister answered questions from reporters outside. Then they turned, mounted the stone steps, crossed the broad wooden verandah and entered the house. When they removed their coats, it became apparent that all were wearing dark suits, except Robert Bourassa, who had on a light spring suit. Fitting, someone mused, that the black sheep would wear white. Around noon, when the bells of the Peace Tower were murmuring on Parliament Hill, the nation-builders went to work upstairs. Downstairs, in a sprawling panelled room, their ministers and advisers waited hopefully. Outside, reporters shuffled and gossiped. Down the hill, in a coach house, chauffeurs, bodyguards and footmen settled in for the afternoon. In the nearby woods, sharpshooters took up position.

A curious place to summon the first ministers, this wooded, lakeside estate. Intergovernmental meetings were usually held in the Government Conference Centre in Ottawa, the old, cavernous railway station that had been the battleground during so many of the Constitutional Wars. Although the cabinet and deputy-ministers met often at Meech Lake, the place was better known for the consideration of the human constitution than of any other kind. Truth be told, it was a mecca for nudists. On hot days, Ottawans would crowd its slender public beaches. In more secluded areas, beneath the trees, sunbathers would disrobe, oil their bodies, and lie on the rocks and indentations of the shoreline, looking for a kind of littoral truth. This celebration of nudity was something of an embarrassment to cottagers. The park posted signs ("Nude bathing prohibited"), and poker-faced Mounties were said to hand out tickets to naked offenders. As things would turn out, the nudists had more in common with the visiting premiers than they thought. When the accord began to crumble, it appeared that these emperors, too, had no clothes.

Meech Lake is one of about two million lakes in Canada. However pleasant, the attention it has attracted since that meeting on 30 April 1987 is far out of proportion to its size, beauty or history. While it was generally unknown in the nation at large, in the capital it was a favoured spot. Situated about thirty-two kilometres north of Ottawa in the Gatineau hills, the lake adjoins Lac Philippe and Harrington

Lake, where the prime minister has his weekend residence. The lake is two kilometres long and a third of a kilometre wide, typical of the blue lakes in Gatineau Park, an enclave of forest, hills and water in western Quebec owned by the federal government. Meech Lake is named after Asa Meech, an American minister who fled to the area in the late eighteenth century because, it is said, he abhorred the fractious politics of the day. On his grave are the words: "I ask not to stay where storm after storm rises o'er the way."

The government bought Willson House and the surrounding 186 hectares in 1979. Distinguished by its gable roof and dormer windows, it was built by Thomas Leopold Willson, an inventor and industrialist, in the architectural style of Queen Anne Revival, in vogue among displaced aristocrats at the turn of the century. The mansion sits on a windblown bluff that offers a commanding view of the lake. A path from its front door falls sharply to the shore several metres below. At the water's edge, beavers and deer munch greedily on the foliage, creating what biologists call "a browse line."

Willson House is an unlikely place in which to write a constitution. Those who watch Ottawa the way Kremlinologists watch the Politburo were convinced that nothing would come of the meeting because serious talks had never taken place there. Too small, too remote, too far from the bureaucracy. Meeting at Meech Lake was thought to be Mulroney's idea, but no one is certain. In the preceding months, there had been a sense in government circles that the only way to get agreement on the constitution was to follow "the Camp David Formula" — the one President Jimmy Carter used to bring peace to the Middle East in 1977. As one senior federal official put it, "You put them in a sylvan setting, lock them in, throw the advisers out, and keep them there until you get a deal."

But Meech Lake is not "Canada's Camp David," nor is it Bretton Woods or Dumbarton Oaks, legendary places that gave their names to historic agreements. It is simply a modest stone-and-wood pile on a pretty spot, without grandeur or pretence, a millionaire's country house that would stumble into history.

If the place did not suggest success, neither did the season. On that wooded promontory, high above the stands of white pine, it was overcast and chilly that day. The lake was still frozen. There was scarcely a hint of a political spring. For months the national agenda had been dominated by free trade, the deficit and the purchase of nuclear submarines. Even Quebec was distracted by its forthcoming budget. The only sign of spring was the arrival of playoff hockey and the midnight deadline for filing personal income-tax returns.

Few of the first ministers had gone to Meech Lake with any expectation of success. Indeed, even the idea of meeting left some of the provinces skeptical. If there seemed so little chance of reaching an agreement, why bother? But when Brian Mulroney wrote the premiers in March, they were in no position to refuse. Months of intergovernmental negotiations on Quebec's five proposals, first put forward the previous May, had taken the matter as far as it could go. If there was to be progress, it would have to come from the first ministers themselves. Hence, Mulroney's invitation to gather at Meech Lake. Roland Penner, Manitoba's attorney general, had no idea where the discussions would lead. He doesn't recall any consultation. "Mulroney just wrote us and said, 'Come down to Meech Lake for a little chat,' said the spider to the fly." And so Penner and the rest of them did.

One of those who feared the talks might succeed had been reassured that very day. Donald Johnston, a Quebec MP who had served in the Trudeau cabinet, had run into Pawley on the plane from Winnipeg to Ottawa. Pawley assured him nothing would happen. "I was happy about that," says Johnston, who would later wage something of a holy war against the accord. "The most I expected was a working paper, a task force, the usual bullshit. I didn't expect the premiers would emerge with a signed document. It was inconceivable that they would walk out with something that would change the country."

The second floor of Willson House, where the premiers met, was simply furnished. It housed a few small offices, occupied by federal officials, but was dominated by a large, airy room, with windows looking out on the grounds. The room was panelled in oak and had two fireplaces, one of which was obscured by a large translation booth. There were black-and-white photographs of early twentieth-century Canada on the wall, and a row of light fixtures. Padded chairs were placed around eight tables arranged in a tight rectangle. Strangely, in the heart of the Canadian Shield, the tables were veneered in ersatz wood. The place could have been a bingo hall in Moose Jaw.

The premiers took their seats, their places arranged in order of each province's entry into Confederation. Robert Bourassa and David Peterson sat on either side of Mulroney, who was at the head of the table. This arrangement was nicely symbolic. A Conservative flanked by two Liberals, representing the country's heartland, most of its people, most of its land, most of its wealth. The three might clash on other questions, but here they would find a common cause. The younger the province, the farther its premier from Mulroney. On Peterson's right sat the premiers of Nova Scotia, Manitoba, Prince Edward Island and Alberta (the penultimate province to enter Confederation). Facing them, on Bourassa's left, sat the premiers from New Brunswick, British Columbia, Saskatchewan and New-foundland (the last province to enter Confederation). History, how-ever, would explain only so much at these meetings. Each province had only one vote. Influence was often a product of personality. Brian Peckford represented the poorest and newest province, but he always presented a strong case. John Buchanan came from a founding province and Don Getty from a wealthy province but were less forceful.

Uncharacteristically for such meetings, the premiers were virtually alone in the room on that chilly afternoon. The only other persons there were two public servants. One was Norman Spector, the secre-tary to the cabinet for federal-provincial relations, and Ottawa's lead-ing bureaucrat on the constitution. Spector had joined the govern-ment in 1986. He had come from British Columbia where he had worked for former premier William Bennett. Fluent in French and Hebrew, he was wily, masterful and occasionally abrasive. In this constitutional campaign he was the choreographer. He sat near Mul-roney. The other person was Oryssia Lennie, an assistant deputy minister from Alberta. Because Getty had been chairman of the Pre-miers' Conference in 1986, Alberta provided the provincial represen-tative. Lennie had been involved in constitutional questions since 1971, shortly after the Victoria Charter. In Alberta they called her "the Mother of the Constitution." She sat near Getty.

Both Spector and Lennie would take notes at the meeting, though no formal minutes would be kept. No official record exists. Their real role was to summarize the consensus, put the ideas into general language, and send them out for drafting and typing by a battery of officials in another room. In addition to senior civil servants from the Justice Department, these included Senator Lowell Murray, minister of state for federal-provincial relations; Bernard Roy, principal secretary to the prime minister; L. Ian MacDonald and André Burelle, two key speechwriters; and Senator Arthur Tremblay, a constitutional expert. When the proposals came back, they were discussed by the premiers again. This process repeated itself all day long as the first ministers grappled with principles. "We were waiting for the doctors to deliver the child," says Tremblay of the mood of anticipation during the marathon session.

The subject of the discussions at Meech Lake — a series of amendments to the constitution — was based on the proposals Quebec had unveiled in May 1986 at a conference at Mont Gabriel, Quebec. At that time, Quebec had made five general proposals. The province wanted a role in selecting judges to the Supreme Court; greater powers over immigration; a veto over constitutional amendments; a limitation on federal spending power in areas of provincial jurisdiction; and explicit recognition as a "distinct society." Other matters — Senate reform and jurisdiction over the fishery — would come up in the talks. Though not on Quebec's shopping list, they would find their way into the agreement.

At their annual meeting in Edmonton in August 1986, the premiers had agreed to put aside their own constitutional agendas and deal only with Quebec's five conditions. That fall and winter, federal and provincial officials held a series of private meetings to find common ground. The meeting at Meech Lake did not just happen; it was the culmination of intensive cross-country negotiation. By the time the invitations to Meech Lake were delivered, the broad outlines of an agreement were in place. The premiers had summaries of the negotiations of previous months. They had a list of Quebec's demands, a suggested solution, and their own responses. Throughout the day at Meech Lake, however, Mulroney and Spector would be calling the plays.

In the absence of a formal record or transcript, it is hard to know precisely how the talks unfolded. The reason no official minutes were kept is uncertain. Although there were thirteen people in the room, many were unable to recall the precise sequence of events. One first minister often contradicted the recollections of others, particularly if doing so enhanced his role. While there is general agreement on the tone of the talks and the order of business, there is no agreement on the controversial areas.

To the federal officials, some of whom were closeted on the third floor, the key to success was to make early progress on the least contentious points. If the premiers could agree on some issues, they might do so on the final ones. Richard Hatfield, a veteran of so many of these talks, took Mulroney aside before the meeting opened and advised: "Try to get three of five proposals by six o'clock, and if you do, tell them to come back the next day. Whatever price you have to pay, get them to come back the next day. I'm convinced we can get the three. But don't drive us all night."

The talks did not begin well. Mulroney and Spector wanted to deal first with Quebec's demands relating to the Supreme Court. Their plan was to get quick agreement and build momentum. No opposition was expected to Quebec's demand to entrench three judges from Quebec on the high court. This situation already existed in practice but Quebec wanted it written into the constitution. (Some legal experts argued that it already was.) In addition, Quebec wanted a say in the selection and appointing of the judges. Quite unexpectedly, however, the premiers began to talk about each of the provinces having a judge. They suggested expanding the court from nine to eleven or fifteen judges. This kind of discussion had not been anticipated, and it worried Spector. Would the debate on all the conditions be this long and laborious? Finally, after two hours, the premiers agreed to entrench Quebec's three judges. Moreover, Quebec would have a say in the selection of judges. But so would the other provinces. In the event of a vacancy, the provinces would submit lists of nominees and the federal government would choose one. Immediately, an important principle had been established: all provinces would be treated the same.

Because the first ministers had spent so long on one item, which it was assumed would be dealt with quickly, Spector and his officials realized they could be in for a long day. They were encouraged, though, that there had been progress. Immigration, the next item, went smoothly. The Cullen-Couture Agreement of 1978, an arrangement between Quebec and the federal government on selecting immigrants, was enshrined in the constitution. Quebec was also guaranteed a proportion of immigrants to Canada in relation to the province's population, a guarantee that its leading constitutional adviser called Quebec's biggest gain in the accord. Other provinces won the right to negotiate similar agreements.

On the spending-power issue, Quebec had wanted a limitation on the right of the federal government to launch shared-cost programs in areas of exclusive provincial jurisdiction. At Meech Lake, Mulroney suggested making the establishment of any of these new social programs conditional on the approval of seven provinces and 50 percent of the population. Pawley and Peckford objected to that suggestion on the grounds that it would then be too hard to launch any programs. That condition was dropped, but the language was loosened. The accord would compel the federal government to provide "reasonable compensation" to a province if it chose not to participate in a program, provided it undertook "its own initiative on programs compatible with national objectives." Originally, "objectives" had read "norms" but never "standards" — a term that made the document more precise. The discussion of spending power took about an hour. It was not a terribly controversial question. Only later would Pawley question the ability of the federal government to establish new programs if a province could "opt out," or refuse to take part in the program, while still getting its share of the money allotted for it.

Curiously, the recognition of Quebec as a distinct society was not hotly debated at Meech Lake. The first ministers talked about the meaning of "distinct society" but were convinced it merely recognized a sociological and historical reality. When David Peterson made an eloquent plea to accommodate Quebec, one premier wondered why he was bothering. He and others were already sold. Ironically, it was Peterson who would later question the point most vigorously. At Meech Lake, though, he was not terribly concerned. His reservations, and those of Pawley on the spending-power issue, were not strong enough to derail the talks. The fireworks over both matters would come later.

By late afternoon, the broad shape of an agreement was emerging. "I don't think we were into the meeting longer than three or four hours before we all felt that we were making more progress than we thought [we would]," recalls Brian Peckford. "Someone remarked, 'Holy gosh, what are we doing here? Making progress? This is a strange piece of business.'"

At Meech Lake there were no misgivings and no misrepresentations. The mood was buoyant. Vander Zalm, with his boundless enthusiasm for things big and small, described it this way: "It was a long meeting, a good meeting, a great meeting! A good feeling! A great spirit! There was enthusiasm for the process! So much so that some of my earlier concerns were, in fact, secondary to the spirit which led one to believe that all things could be accomplished when people of goodwill came together." The first ministers happily went about cutting and pasting. Encouraged by the prospect of accommodating Quebec, delighted with the opportunity to enhance their role in Confederation, they set themselves to the task of nation-building. For every concession Quebec won, the other provinces won one too. When one of the premiers balked, Mulroney looked for a way to accommodate his concerns. If he saw a premier wavering, he paid him special attention. His skillful handling of the issues, in the manner of a labour negotiator, dazzled and amused his colleagues.

"I was impressed by the PM's style, the way he was able to bring the consensus," recalls Joe Ghiz. "By gosh, he had a smooth style. He'd say, 'Now look. Let's deal with Question A first. I have a piece of paper here. Norman [Spector], why don't you pass that piece of paper around. Just have a look at this piece of paper. I know it's complicated, but just have a look at it, and if you want to make a change in it . . . Norman, there's someone outside, isn't there? We can get the paper changed. How does that grab you? Don, you have a question about it?' 'Yes,' says Getty. 'Well, then why don't we just put the piece of paper aside, and we'll get this other piece of paper dealing with Question B. Norman, Norman, we'll pass that around. I understand you don't like the word. While we're looking at B, I'll ask Norman to take that piece of paper out and have our people have a look at it and we'll come up with another word. Now let's deal with B.' Then he would get A back and ask Don how it looked. And that's how he carried that thing from start to finish."

At the meeting almost a year earlier at Edmonton, the premiers had agreed to deal only with Quebec's five proposals. But something happened at Meech Lake: the Quebec Round, which was to address only the concerns of Quebec, became the Provincial Round. What Quebec wanted on immigration, the Supreme Court, the veto and spending power, the other provinces wanted too. The only concession the other provinces did not seek at Meech Lake was recognition as a distinct society. (Some time later, however, British Columbia suggested they share this recognition as well.) The provinces made much of the spirit of co-operation and compromise at Meech Lake, but, shortly before the meeting, Alberta had signalled its intention to win a concession on Senate reform or scuttle the deal. Peckford announced that he needed something on fisheries, and Hatfield wanted the entrenchment of property rights. The solemn promise to address only Quebec's conditions had faded like a soft summer mist.

At Meech Lake, the linkage of the other provinces' concerns and Quebec's concerns began with Senate reform. Getty had arrived at Meech Lake with a surprise demand: any agreement would have to include a clause establishing annual federal-provincial constitutional conferences on Senate reform. It looked like a small concession to keep him happy. The proposal was drafted by Alberta and presented to the provinces the night before the meeting. An Ontario official found it slipped under the door of his hotel room. Given Getty's vague threats, his proposal was a relief. Alberta would trade substance for process; it would not hold up the round for the "Triple E Senate" (elected, effective and equal). But there was still no assurance Getty would not ask for something else. He could not be seen to be giving and not getting, whatever promise he and the other premiers had made in Edmonton. "We had to have something," said one of his advisers. "Absolutely."

If Alberta was going to get a concession, so was Newfoundland. Peckford saw Getty's prize and wanted one of his own. As a symbol, he argued, fish was as important to Newfoundland as the Senate was to Alberta. He now says he did not necessarily want jurisdiction over the fishery, though Hatfield, Buchanan and Ghiz insist he did. When all three objected, he settled for a commitment to discuss "roles and responsibilities" in managing the fishery. "Brian needed that for political consumption at home," recalls Ghiz, "and if that was needed to get his signature on the piece of paper, fine. But he's never going to get jurisdiction. Never." Peckford eventually came around. "Okay, that will do," he said. Vander Zalm was tempted to raise the issue of property rights. Three years earlier, the B.C. Legislature under former premier William Bennett had endorsed the idea of a constitutional amendment to entrench the principle. But neither Vander Zalm nor Hatfield pushed it, probably because they knew that Peterson would put up a fight. "The women of Ontario would revolt over marital property rights," he told Hatfield.

Over the course of the day at Meech Lake, the premiers dealt with the concerns of Bourassa, Getty and Peckford. At one point during the discussion of Senate reform, Mulroney introduced a little business of his own. "How many of you are in favour of abolishing the Senate, like I am?" he asked. Just like that. The question stunned the premiers. Ghiz didn't think he was serious. Pawley and Vander Zalm raised their hands. That Pawley would agree was predictable, but Vander Zalm's enthusiasm here was puzzling. Pawley stared across the table in disbelief, incredulous that the conservative Vander Zalm would agree to something so radical. Peckford, who supported the idea, remembers Mulroney saying, "Look, if we're going to get into a big debate on this, I am prepared to go out of here tonight and make a statement that the Senate will be abolished. How's that? Now, you're all here pissing on the Senate, you're all saying that it's no good. Let's do something about it."

The discussion of the Senate punctuated the talks for much of the ten hours they lasted and formed a tangled web that ensnared a host of other issues. Those most in favour of Senate reform, such as Don Getty, worried that if they got rid of the Senate holus-bolus it would be hard to replace. Getty preferred to wait. But the question, which seemed to come out of the blue, showed the premiers that Mulroney was prepared to deal. "Yes, sir," recalls Peckford. "That helped. People began to see that Mulroney was really serious and well prepared. What surprised us was that the government was serious about finalizing this. They had done their homework to the nth degree." The question of eliminating the Senate was debated briefly and dropped. Robert Bourassa does not even remember talking about it. But, for a moment at Meech Lake, Mulroney could lay claim to being a modern-day abolitionist.

If doing away with the Senate came as a surprise, so did a related proposal from Mulroney to give the provinces a role in choosing senators. The proposal originated in Alberta. Norman Spector and Senator Lowell Murray sensed Alberta was thinking about it. Ten days earlier, the two constitutional troubleshooters had visited Medicine Hat to confer with Alberta's minister of federal and intergovernmental affairs, James Horsman. Horsman had talked about asking the government to stop making appointments until the Senate was reformed. Murray rejected the idea out of hand. "That's crazy," he said. "Here I am, Government House leader in the Senate. We're outnumbered three to one. And you're telling me not to appoint any more, to tie our hands. Better to abolish it and start with a clean sheet of paper."

It was during this discussion, when Alberta was holding fast, that Mulroney suggested that they do for the Senate what they had done for the Supreme Court: allow the provinces to submit lists of candidates. This proposal surprised some of the premiers, largely because it had not been one of Quebec's demands. "It came out of nowhere," said one premier. "No one had asked for it." In fact, Alberta had raised the issue and Mulroney had thrown it on the table to break the impasse. Peterson and the rest were willing to accept it as an interim measure until the Senate was reformed. The symbolic effect of this offer was significant. It would not go unnoticed that Bourassa got more than he demanded. He had come with five proposals and would go home with seven. The offer would haunt Mulroney, who would be accused of making a gratuitous concession. As he saw it, however, interim appointments were a timely, ingenious way to save the talks.

Some premiers now suspect that Mulroney was trying to co-opt them into sharing the burdens of patronage. Hatfield, for his part, argues that appointing senators is unpleasant and troublesome. "You don't get anything out of it," he says. "The sure way of committing political suicide in this country is the exclusive authority to appoint senators. It's an awful thing to go through. No one ever got any personal or political satisfaction out of it. If somebody is appointed, only one person will care: the appointee." Ghiz suggests that Mulroney pulled a fast one. "He got himself off the hook," he says. "He was getting in trouble with his party." If both explanations are true, they represented a change of heart for Mulroney. After all, he had run for his party's leadership on the promise to spread out patronage appointments and had seemingly been prepared to enjoy doing it. "I see a judge there, a senator there," he once told a Tory crowd. As the premiers had it, he now found dispensing this largesse distasteful.

The issue of Senate reform was linked to another of Quebec's demands: the right to a veto over constitutional amendments. Quebec had originally asked for the Victoria Formula for constitutional changes. The formula, which had been agreed to at the Victoria Conference on constitutional reform in 1971, required that any amendment have the support of Quebec, Ontario and any two provinces in Atlantic Canada and any two in western Canada representing at least 50 percent of the population of the region. Now Quebec had compromised, agreeing to accept the power of veto solely over changes to federal institutions. As the session wore on, it appeared that here, too, a veto for Quebec would be a veto for everyone. The veto would apply to changes to all federal institutions — the monarchy, the Supreme Court, the House of Commons and the Senate. In addition, the provinces would now have a say in the creation of new provinces. The extension of the veto was welcomed by the premiers, though some wondered why Don Getty agreed to it. Wouldn't Senate reform be *harder* if all provinces had to approve? Getty shrugged. He conceded that unanimity would not make Senate reform any easier, but at least it would prevent the rest of the country from imposing upon him a Senate he rejected. Devine and Vander Zalm shook their heads in disbelief.

Downstairs, the minions were getting restless. They had been sitting around for hours in cushioned rattan chairs, talking, reading, playing cards. A fire was lit, and the television rigged with a coat hanger aerial to pick up the hockey game. Ministers tended to talk to ministers, officials to officials; one sensitive soul called this social divide a form of apartheid. Many of the senior advisers — Peter Meekison of Alberta and Gary Posen of Ontario — were veterans of the circuit and knew each other well.

No one could leave the house for fear the premiers might need some help, though the first ministers seldom emerged. For some officials, the lack of news on the talks was frustrating. Roland Penner decided to go upstairs and intercept Pawley on his way to the bathroom. As he tried to mount the stairs to the second floor, a security guard stopped him. "Where do you think you're going?" he asked Penner, turning him away. Penner was incensed; he was the attorney general of Manitoba and he had a right to see his premier. Rebuffed, he returned to his colleagues.

If officials could not enter the room at will, they could send in notes and a premier could come out, although he was unlikely to do so as the talks would continue in his absence. There was little doubt Mulroney wanted to keep the premiers away from the Penners and the Posens and the Meekisons. Without advisers, there would be less posturing and grandstanding; it would be easier to get a deal. But, as a consequence, this lakeside conclave took on an aura of secretiveness that would afterwards undermine its public legitimacy.

For the mandarins, even going for a walk outside was hazardous. If the mud or the chill did not drive them inside, the hordes of reporters eager for progress reports would. Moreover, everyone was hungry. Willson House had run out of food, a sure sign the meeting was lasting longer than its organizers had expected. For the assembled ministers, aides and advisers, food was becoming something of an obsession. Barry Toole of New Brunswick invited Gerry Steele of Prince Edward Island — both old constitutional hands — to join him for a little Québécois cuisine in Old Chelsea. Steele was reluctant; Premier Ghiz might need him. "Look, Gerry," said Toole, "I've been in this business for thirteen years. I was only asked my opinion once — and the premier didn't even follow it. Now, let's go to supper." The two left. Meanwhile, Hershell Ezrin, David Peterson's principal secretary, surveyed the limp celery, soggy sandwiches and lukewarm soup. Ezrin, a gourmet cook, mused about calling for pizza or ordering in from Nate's Delicatessen, Ottawa's fabled smoked-meat emporium. A kind of delirium was setting in. Finally, tourtières and sugar pie arrived from the village.

While some officials worried about food, others were taking care of business. Jim Eldridge, a top civil servant from Manitoba, was huddling with his colleagues when he was tapped on the shoulder by a burly Mountie. Eldridge had driven the van carrying the Manitoba delegation, which made him the province's official chauffeur. The Mountie barked: "Meeting of all the drivers in fifteen minutes. Gonna talk about picking up the premiers." "I'm busy," protested Eldridge, and returned to the discussion. The Mountie was unmoved. "You're coming," he said. Eldridge went to the meeting. He asked if Pawley could walk down to his van and leave from there, which was seen as terribly unorthodox. The Mounties, he recalled, did not like his attitude.

Actually, food had even greater significance for the premiers than their staff. Once the premiers decided to stay for a supper of poached salmon, it was clear they were making progress. They would have gone home otherwise. Hatfield, for his part, knew a deal had been reached in principle by six o'clock. Gordon Coles, an adviser to Buchanan, knew that with each passing hour the prospects for an agreement improved. "I thought it was like a jury," he remembers. "The longer it was out, the more hope for the defendant."

Upstairs, the premiers had been busy. The agenda was shrinking. The Supreme Court, done. Immigration, done. Spending power, done. Then the veto, the distinct society and Senate reform fell into place. Because the discussion was about principles rather than wording, it was less likely to founder. The ambiguity that would cause grievous problems over the next three years was welcome here. Some of the premiers, particularly Peterson, Pawley and Bourassa, were at home with constitutional discussion and were helped by having large delegations, even at arm's length. Vander Zalm, on the other hand, was virtually alone. "A cheap bugger for not bringing more help," sniffed one of the Ontarians. Reluctant to run up a travel bill and wary of civil servants bearing advice, the premier brought only David Poole, his principal secretary. His attorney general, Brian Smith, was at Meech Lake only because he happened to be in Ottawa on other business. Vander Zalm, unlike most of the premiers, was not a lawyer and had no background in constitutional talks. Yet he saw no need to compensate for his inexperience. He had advisers but refused to bring them; he had a thick briefing book but refused to read it.

In mid-evening, a tired Brian Smith checked with Poole to see if he was needed, and left. A little later the premiers emerged to consult their officials one last time. It was a critical moment in the discussion. The premiers were on the cusp of an agreement. But Vander Zalm had reservations and no legal adviser when he most needed one. Like all the other premiers, he alone could make or break the agreement. While each of the others was conferring with his officials, Vander Zalm was pacing the verandah alone. One official saw him and asked his premier if he should offer advice or information; the premier replied that that would be inappropriate. As Vander Zalm was joined by Poole, himself no constitutional expert, others watching began to question a process that invested so much authority in someone who knew so little. As one minister put it: "My God, this thing that I thought was never going to happen was going to happen. We were all excited and moved by how close we were to success. And there is poor old Vander Zalm, not a lawyer, hardly a scholar, perhaps not even very sophisticated, alone. It was quite shattering." Earlier, Vander Zalm had placed calls to his advisers in Victoria. In this — a flustered premier, fumbling at a pay phone, seeking counsel from associates far from the talks — there is one of the enduring images of the session at Meech Lake: the innocent in search of the impotent.

Because Vander Zalm was new to the process, he was a concern to his colleagues. Left to his own devices, they thought, he might overcome his natural suspicions. But if he was allowed to get advice, he might resist. No wonder a senior civil servant had warned the premier's handlers: "Never let him go in [the room] alone because they'll make a decision." Earlier, Vander Zalm had wanted to know how much more power the distinct-society clause would give "the French." The other premiers had argued it meant no new distribution of powers. Unconvinced, Vander Zalm said he would speak to his

officials. As the premier rose to leave the room, Mulroney urged caution. "Do that, Bill, but I want you to know that this is absolutely
key to making this go." Vander Zalm stopped in mid-step, decided
to stay put and replied, "If you are telling me you need this, Prime
Minister, I'm prepared to accept it." When Vander Zalm returned to
the table, Hatfield leaned towards his seatmate and whispered: "Bill,
you are your own man. I have a higher regard for you now than I did
a minute ago."

Around nine o'clock, minutes after Brian Smith had left, Vander
Zalm was in a quandary. The nine other premiers and the prime minister were for the deal. He was the lone dissenter. The sticking point
was Senate reform. He had spoken to Getty earlier in the day about
demanding a concession on Senate reform. "My view was that it had
to be a commitment sufficiently binding so that we could go home
and give our people some assurance that it would in fact become a reality," he recalls. But at Meech Lake he was disappointed that Getty
was willing to accept the promise of future discussion, as well as the
unanimity rule. It bothered him terribly. He argued for the "seven
and fifty" rule, and it made him a self-described hold-out. "This is
where, in fact, things became somewhat difficult for me," he remembers. "I was almost very unpopular for a time." At the final break, in
front of a bay window overlooking the lake, he told Poole that Getty
had capitulated.

"I'm all alone," he said. "All the rest are ready to go. But I can't."
Poole said initially that if that was how he felt he should walk away.
He offered to get some advice, but Vander Zalm declined, saying the
two of them would work it out.

"Premier, you can't be the only one," said Poole.

"I don't want to be the only one," replied Vander Zalm.

"Then if you don't want to be the odd man out," said Poole,
"you'll have to sign. For all the things we want to do, we will pay too
great a price if B.C. is the stumbling block."

As Vander Zalm and his advisers recalled later, the premier paused,
thought about the implications of saying no and decided to go along.
The decision did not turn on Canada or Quebec or the constitution. It
was about the impact on the province of an angry federal government. Afterwards, his associates said he regretted the decision. Later
Poole received a letter from Diane Wilhelmy, a senior Quebec official, thanking him for his role in bringing along the premier. She and
others had seen the two men talking in front of the window, and had

known Vander Zalm was holding out. She told Poole he was more important than he knew to the sealing of the deal at Meech Lake.

During the course of the evening, there was another moment of high anxiety. At one point, a distraught Bernard Roy burst into the room. Hatfield thought the deal was collapsing. "He had an end-of-the-world look on his face," he recalls. "I thought, my God, what has happened? We had agreed to three or four items. I thought one had come unravelled when it went to the lawyers. Bourassa said, 'I have to leave. I have a budget leak in Quebec.' I thought that was the end of Meech Lake." Bourassa left the room and telephoned his finance minister, Gérard Levesque. He authorized him to release the budget immediately. Then, coolly, he returned to the talks.

By ten o'clock that night, the deal was done. Such was the feeling in the room that there was no vote, no head count. Mulroney, who had led long sessions in search of consensus in labour negotiations, just seemed to know. Perhaps he could tell by the mood. By all accounts, the tone of the ten hours of discussion was warm and conciliatory. Unlike other meetings of this kind, there was virtually no acrimony. The first ministers wanted a deal, and with an accommodating prime minister, they had got one. The agenda had been handled with relative ease. Everyone in the room had won. Quebec had its five demands. Alberta and Newfoundland had promises to talk about the Senate and the fishery, ad infinitum, in the next round. The rest of the provinces had won the same concessions as Quebec — including the right of veto. What they said they did not necessarily want they were pleased to accept. The federal government, for its part, had won Quebec's acceptance of the constitution. Why wouldn't everyone be happy?

Mulroney left the room to confer with his officials in a makeshift office on the third floor. L. Ian MacDonald wrote the English statement, and André Burelle the French statement. A jubilant Arthur Tremblay, who had spent many of his sixty-nine years in federal-provincial diplomacy, hugged Mulroney. He recalls, "I never thought at my age I'd see a moment like that." Mulroney returned a few minutes later with the final document. Suddenly, spontaneously, all ten premiers rose and clapped. Mulroney accepted their applause with appreciation. "I'll never forget that," says Hatfield. "It was an important moment, a moving moment, a very, very emotional moment. Very few damn politicians get the recognition he got then. We look for a standing ovation from the mob, but don't expect it from our peers." The mood was euphoric. On the floor below, the exhausted advisers were ebullient. Those who remembered the bitterness in 1981, who had been there when Quebec walked away from the table, were overjoyed. They, too, exchanged hugs and congratulations. To them, this was an historic reconciliation.

Having saluted the prime minister, the premiers congratulated each other. All shook hands; some even embraced. They rushed around asking each other to autograph their copies of the agreement. Pawley was frantically looking for a pen and paper, worried because he had all signatures but Brian Mulroney's. His boyish excitement, caught by television camers, embarrassed him later. Vander Zalm even got several lunch menus signed, which he auctioned off at party fundraisers for a few thousand dollars each. A couple of veteran Quebec journalists who were among the crowd of reporters led into the room were teary-eyed. The tables had been pushed aside except for one in the centre, where Mulroney sat. With the smiling first ministers ranged behind him, he declared the rebirth of a nation. "What you have now is a whole country as opposed to a part of a country," he said. "I am profoundly convinced that as a result of today's discussions that the bonds of Confederation will be strengthened and the unity of our people will be enhanced."

Afterwards, the nation-builders emerged into the crisp night air. One by one, they fixed their leaden feet to the stone stairs and faced the battery of microphones. From each, the refrain was the same: the country was united because Quebec had chosen Canada. None had the eloquence to part the waters or bend the trees, but each tried in his way to evoke a sense of occasion. They had forged an unlikely compromise, and they believed that something strange and wonderful had happened here. The little questions — about price, process and power — would come another day. So would the cries and fears that would ultimately bring their house down. But, for now, as they heralded the new Articles of Confederation, they revelled in their triumph. It was their day, this miracle at Meech Lake, and it seemed that nothing could dim the incandescent moment.

We, the Premiers

THE MAKING OF THE MEECH LAKE ACCORD WAS AS MUCH ABOUT POLITICS
and personality as about powers and principles. The byword of constitutional reform in Canada is consensus. The provinces speak for
themselves, Ottawa speaks for Canada. The province of the dominion government is the country; the province of the province is the
province. There has always been tension between levels of government in the federal system, and from this comes creativity. What surprised everyone at Meech Lake was that the warring parties had come
to an agreement so easily. Suddenly either something was very right
in federal-provincial relations or something was very wrong.

The first ministers said they were successful because everyone was
willing to compromise. Times had changed; priorities had changed;
people had changed. New faces meant new chemistry. This explanation was true in part. Such a deal would have been improbable under
Pierre Trudeau and the first ministers of 1981. But, in 1986, the
world was different. The political map of Canada had been redrawn.
Pierre Trudeau and René Lévesque — the warring titans of Confederation — were gone. A Conservative government, led by an English
Quebecker embraced in western Canada, had replaced a Liberal government led by a French Quebecker rejected in western Canada. A
federalist government had displaced a separatist government in Quebec. Moreover, the Conservative dominance in the hinterland had
been broken. In 1981, there were seven Conservative premiers and no
Liberals. Five years later, there were three Liberals. Here was the
quirky logic of the Canadian voter at work: install a national government of one party in Ottawa and elect strong governments of other
parties in the provinces. Then let them strike a balance.

No doubt the old order was changing. New leaders were emerging at the centre and in the regions. New blood brought new ideas. The Trudeaus, Lougheeds and Lévesques in the 1960s and 1970s had shaped the debate over the central questions of contemporary Canada: nationalism, separatism and regionalism. By the second half of the 1980s, the most eloquent voices of these divergent visions had fallen silent. The departure of either Trudeau or Lévesque alone would have facilitated constitutional change. In fact, their leaving within a year of each other created a vacuum. It was as if guards on the watchtowers on either side of the frontier had abandoned their posts. Suddenly, the border was open.

The change went even deeper than that. Premiers who were fixtures in the 1970s were gone too. Peter Lougheed of Alberta, William Davis of Ontario and Allan Blakeney of Saskatchewan had been elected in 1971. William Bennett of British Columbia came to office in 1975. All had been spokesmen for their regions, and all had left public life before the start of the new round. During the debate, another two left: Richard Hatfield and Brian Peckford, elected in 1970 and 1979, would also retire. By 1990, when the Quebec Round ended, only John Buchanan of Nova Scotia remained from the old circle.

New did not necessarily mean better. In fact, an argument could be made that, in savvy, experience and intelligence, the old crowd was superior. Could anyone say that Brian Mulroney was more interested in the constitutional issue than Pierre Trudeau had been? That Grant Devine was more cerebral than Allan Blakeney? That Don Getty was more effective than Peter Lougheed? That Robert Bourassa was more passionate than René Lévesque? That Bill Vander Zalm was shrewder than Bill Bennett? Yet all that did not seem to matter at Meech Lake. There, intellect and passion mattered less than endurance and persistence. In some ways, the Quebec Round of the Constitutional Wars was not a battle at all. If Mulroney did not know the constitution the way Trudeau did, it mattered less: neither did most of his colleagues. Besides, intellectual one-upmanship was not Mulroney's style. He was not going to be an *agent provocateur*.

When the first shoots of reform began to appear a year before Meech Lake, the landscape of federal-provincial relations had already changed. The five-year interlude between the end of the Patriation Round in 1981 and the beginning of the Quebec Round in 1986 had reaped a harvest of anticipation. It was clear at Meech Lake that each premier was prepared to bring an agenda to the table. Each had his prejudices, his priorities, his price. Deny as they would, rage as they might, most knew that they had to get something in the constitutional game. It was true that some provinces never wanted constitutional talks, and some that did came with no demands. But once the process began, they reminded the country that they were once and always premiers — and premiers are provincial.

In the events that shaped the constitutional debate in the 1980s, some premiers and provinces were more important than others. At the outset, Quebec and Ontario were the critical players, as were Manitoba and Alberta. Prince Edward Island, Newfoundland and New Brunswick, by virtue of their premiers, made a sound contribution. Saskatchewan, British Columbia and Nova Scotia were largely insignificant; the Yukon and the Northwest Territories, absolutely irrelevant. A province's role was influenced by size, wealth and history, which explained the prominence of Quebec and Ontario. Its role also depended on its political philosophy — Manitoba's social democracy or Alberta's free enterprise. In the end, though, the Meech Lake Accord was largely the work of eleven men in a room, each with his own vision and style.

Belgium, in the winter of 1977. A lone, slender figure makes his way across a windblown boulevard in Brussels. His black hair askew, his body wrapped in a long topcoat, Robert Bourassa longs to come in from the cold. From across the street, Pierre Pettigrew, a fellow Quebecker living in Brussels, recognizes the former premier. Pettigrew would like to introduce himself, but hesitates out of politeness. Later, when he knew Bourassa better, Pettigrew would tell him of his reluctance to approach him that day. "But I wish you had," Bourassa would say, wearing the pained expression of a fallen politician.

Bourassa's mood that winter was understandable. His Liberal government had been defeated by René Lévesque and the Parti Québécois the previous November. He had fled Quebec to study and to teach economics in Brussels and Paris. It was something of an exile, a place to lick his wounds and contemplate his defeat. But the sojourn in Europe would be brief. For Bourassa, like the Corsican corporal, there was to be a triumphant return.

Bourassa had been the boy-wonder of Canadian politics. A lawyer and professor, he was a provincial representative at age thirty-three and premier at thirty-six, the youngest in the province's history. He

won huge majorities in 1970 and 1973. *Time* magazine had picked
him as one of the world's 150 Leaders of the Future. However,
shaken by scandal and labour unrest, his government fell in 1976. In
the process, Bourassa lost some self-esteem. "The most hated man in
Quebec," spat a member of his caucus. "A *mangeur de* hot dogs,"
sniffed Pierre Trudeau. In the last days of his government, his popularity was so low that passengers aboard cruise ships on the St. Lawrence River would jeer as they passed his summer residence near
Sorel.

Bourassa seemed to invite this kind of repudiation. His enduring
problem was his inability to establish a rapport with les Québécois.
He was never able to transmit his personal charm and sense of humour to more than a small group of people. Here was a politician
who hated to go to cocktail parties and, when he did, talked only to
those he knew. In his early days as premier, his fortified office, called
"the bunker," fostered an image of aloofness. He was foremost a
technocrat. He saw himself as a manager, a fixer, a doer. He did not
have the populism of Lévesque, the bonhomie of Daniel Johnson, the
bearing of Jean Lesage. He could leave the bunker but the bunker
would not leave him; Bourassa remained clinical, cool, bloodless.
While his fondness for power was obvious — he never stopped be-
lieving he would be premier again — it would be wrong to call
Bourassa unimaginative, unprincipled and treacherous, as English
Canada was wont to do. In fact, he was arguably the most sophisticated, shrewd and refined of the premiers. He envisioned Quebec as a
highly developed state, with an economy based on trade, investment,
technology, education and a generous social system. Although he
could not bring that vision to life through politics, he pursued it in
policy.

"You know," he said one day, "I am a man of numbers." Ultimately, he was. Votes, dollars, megawatts, contracts — it was all a
matter of numbers. The figures on hydroelectric power at James Bay,
he once allowed, were like pornography to him. "He is continuously
concerned about the economic welfare of Quebec," says Richard
French, who served in his cabinet as minister of communications.
"He thinks about it at night and in the morning, when he goes swim-
ming and when he shaves. Many Quebeckers, without ever articulat-
ing it, recognize that as a tremendous asset." Beyond economics,
Bourassa's lone passion in life was politics. Sports, the arts and travel
held little interest for him.

He acquired his taste for politics early and developed it quickly. As a Liberal campaigner in the 1956 election, he was sent out to debate the future premier, Paul Sauvé, and a little-known iconoclast from the CCF named Pierre Trudeau. Sauvé and Bourassa conspired to keep Trudeau from speaking, something Trudeau never forgot. Bourassa, who was born on Bastille Day, 14 July 1933, had followed Trudeau to Collège Jean-de-Brébeuf, where he, too, learned well the rigorous catechism. Like Trudeau and Lévesque, he lost his father at an early age. Unlike Trudeau, he was born into a modest working-class family. He went to law school at the University of Montreal, consistently leading his class, and did graduate studies in economics and political science at Oxford. Afterwards, he pursued a second graduate degree at Harvard, in international tax law and corporate law. In the early 1960s, Bourassa acted as an adviser in the Department of National Revenue and taught at the University of Ottawa. Later while he was secretary and research director to a commission on tax reform, he was recruited to run for the Liberals.

As a politician, the young Bourassa seemed irresolute and remote. The image took form during the October Crisis of 1970, when he seemed uncertain of how to handle the violence, and later at the Victoria Conference in 1971, when he agreed conditionally to a constitutional deal and backed out ten days later. Among journalists, the premier became known as "Bou-Bou," or simply, "The Bou." The moniker was not an affectionate one. When the debate over Meech Lake reached fever pitch in 1990, Bourassa's *froideur* did not endear him to English Canadians. From him came no declarations of love of country, and they resented it. When Eric Kierans, his erstwhile colleague, challenged him to say, "I am a Canadian," Bourassa shrugged and said in so many words, "Of course, I am a Canadian. It's obvious. Can't you see? If I weren't, why would I have asked so little at Meech Lake?" Maybe so, but he never seemed to understand the value of the symbolic gesture.

Bourassa was the accountant of Canada. For him, federalism was a ledger, a balance sheet, an abacus. If Quebec had more debits than credits, he would try to balance the books. Co-operative federalism was fine as long as it was profitable federalism. In demanding his fair share from Ottawa, Bourassa was no different from any other premier. With Bourassa, though, one always suspected that this arrangement would last only as long as it was good for Quebec. The implicit message — expressed in the waning days of the Quebec Round, first sotto voce, then in a stage whisper and finally in full roar — was that if Quebec did not get its way on Meech Lake, it would pick up and leave. The attachment to Canada was conditional. "You know, Quebec's loyalty to Canada is not unlimited," Bourassa warned in 1989. He went to Europe later, mused slyly about an emerging "political superstructure" in Canada and said no more about it. The point was made; if the accord fell apart, Quebec would look at new options of economic and political association with Canada. It seemed his year in Europe in 1977 may have been more instructive than anyone knew. John Kennedy implored Americans to ask what they could do for their country, not what their country could do for them. Robert Bourassa urged Quebeckers to ask what their country could do for them, and if it wasn't enough, to leave it.

Was Bourassa a fair-weather federalist? Perhaps. Those who thought Bourassa was sympathetic to independence pointed to his flirtation in 1967 with Lévesque and the separatist wing of the Liberal party, which later became the Parti Québécois. Claude Morin, a Quebec civil servant and then a minister in the PQ government, remembers that Bourassa's reservations were over the party's proposed monetary policy — it couldn't work — and his political career. When he thought he could become Liberal leader, the story went, he refused the invitation to join the new party. But the accusation that Bourassa was never committed to the idea of Canada would dog him throughout his career, surfacing again during the 1989 provincial election campaign. The word was that Bourassa had let slip that if Meech Lake failed and Quebeckers seemed prepared to embrace the separatism of the Parti Québécois, he would pre-empt them. He, not Jacques Parizeau, would lead Quebec out of Canada. It was hard to know who Bourassa really was. He may not have known himself. To the separatists he was a *vendu,* having sold out to Ottawa; to federalists, he was a *vendu,* having sold out to Quebec City. "Bourassa?" asks Senator Jacques Hébert. "He is a Bourassa-ist. He is nothing. He has no ideology. He wants power. He could be a nationalist or a federalist, whatever serves his purpose. Right now he is a nationalist."

If one believes Hébert — one of Trudeau's closest friends and an unrepentant federalist — Bourassa is a chameleon. The theory is not farfetched. Richard French, one of Bourassa's former ministers, is probably closer to the mark: "He is a federalist if he can be, but he will not sacrifice his political career for the federal link. He is hoping to get through but preparing for the possibility that it might not be the case. Bourassa's allegiance to Canada would not pass muster with the Imperial Order Daughters of the Empire. But that's true of a very large majority of francophone Quebeckers. 'Canada if possible, but not necessarily Canada.' If circumstances force him to take Quebec out of Canada, he will do it."

Bourassa is what he has to be. In 1980, during the Quebec referendum, he was a federalist. He campaigned vigorously for the "Non" side. There was nowhere he would not go to sell the cause. Maybe he was pursuing his own political rehabilitation, but his colleagues applauded his energy and commitment. As a member of the "B" team, he was sent to the university campuses and the labour halls, ready to take on lions in the dens of nationalism. Whatever his motives, he was there. "There is no doubt that Bourassa is a federalist," says Pettigrew, who was then executive assistant to Claude Ryan, the Liberal leader. "I always thought he was. During the referendum campaign, he would speak to the most hostile crowds. He wanted to win to keep the country together." Pettigrew places Bourassa in the context of Quebec, where there are limitations on how much federalism a leader can practise. All premiers there have to be Quebec nationalists; the highest identification must be with Quebec. "Remember, Bourassa cannot be more federalist than the prime minister," says Pettigrew. "His first loyalty is to Quebec, but he's an ardent federalist. It's true he never gets excited about Canada. Then again, he never gets excited about anything."

In 1983, looking younger than he did the day he left Quebec City after six years as premier, Bourassa regained the leadership of the Liberal party. Two years later, he won the election, again by a large majority, vanquishing the Parti Québécois after its two terms in office. But, as if voters wanted to register their personal disaffection, they denied him his seat in Montreal, as they had in 1976. Nonetheless he was back after nine years in the political wilderness, and his return was hailed as the reconciliation of Quebec and Canada. The new Bourassa, the manager of prosperity, was seen as the right man for the new Quebec. In 1985, separatism was in eclipse. Enterprise was in vogue. The economy was more important than the constitution.

Still, Quebec had not accepted the 1982 constitution. With a federalist government in place, it seemed a good time to reopen talks. When Quebec announced its five proposals in 1986, Bourassa was showing a willingness to make a fresh start. Quebec was offering a new, modest agenda. No one paid much attention at the time and no one dreamed the issue would push the country to the abyss four years later. No one envisioned that in 1990 a disconsolate premier, feeling rejected by Canada, would retreat to Quebec to study his options. No one foresaw the division and bitterness. In its hour of crisis, English Canada would yearn for the bicultural patriotism of Henri Bourassa. Instead, in the eye of the hurricane, it would find the flinty pragmatism of Robert Bourassa.

Shortly before Bourassa returned to office in Quebec, the Liberals came to power in Ontario. Their arrival, only nine months after the Conservatives had won a majority in Ottawa, brought three new players to the Constitutional Wars. As preliminary talks laying the groundwork for the Meech Lake Accord opened in the summer of 1986, Ontario and Ottawa led the effort to accommodate Quebec. For the fledgling government at Queen's Park, here was a chance to restore the old alliance between the two provinces that had flourished in the 1960s. It had died a while ago. William Davis, the phlegmatic, pipe-smoking Rotarian who had run Ontario since 1971, never seemed to understand Quebec. When he retired in 1985 and was replaced by the folksy Frank Miller, the Liberals saw an opening; they played on the desire for change and toppled the government in June 1985. Although the Tories won more seats in the May election, the Liberals formed an alliance with the New Democrats and ended forty-two years of Conservative reign. It was the end of the longest modern political dynasty in the Western World and led to the revival of the old axis of central Canada.

The face of the new Ontario was David Peterson, the young, stylish arriviste. Elected in 1975, he become party leader in 1982. Peterson was born in 1943 to a well-heeled family in London, Ontario. His father, Clarence, had signed the Regina Manifesto. Peterson studied philosophy at the University of Western Ontario and law at the University of Toronto. He was a boxer in university and a teacher at Frontier College. Before entering politics, he had managed the family's electronics business, which was later sold at a large profit. In the 1960s, it was said, Peterson and Brian Mulroney, two young men on the make, used to carouse together in Montreal. Neither spoke much about their association after they entered politics, though Mulroney does say he tried to make Peterson into a Tory.

In 1985, Peterson represented a meeting of the man and the moment. He was the urban professional who understood the multicultural society of Ontario; the organization man who understood the needs of business; the charming campaigner of earthiness and sophistication. He had the good fortune to arrive on the political scene when the economy was booming and the provinces were wielding more influence over economic policy and institutional reform. His rise to power still astounds observers. His performance in opposition was mediocre and his party was a divided, conservative rump. The Big Blue Machine, as the Conservatives were known in Ontario, was preparing to anoint one of its four seemingly invincible successors to Davis. Moreover, the federal Liberals had just been decimated in the 1984 election. That autumn was not a good time to be a Liberal. Yet Peterson, tutored by Hershell Ezrin and other Liberals from Ottawa, saw the opening left by Davis. The Tories had chosen Miller, a lodge-owner, engineer and veteran minister who opposed the minimum wage and pay equity. Recognizing the new demographics of Ontario — the province was no longer white, Protestant and Anglo-Saxon — Peterson pulled his ragtag caucus to the left, brought down a progressive platform that borrowed heavily from the New Democrats and mounted a well-organized campaign. In Ontario, he and the Liberals were the greatest surprise since the Toronto Maple Leafs won the Stanley Cup.

More than his predecessors, Peterson reached out to Quebec. The Conservatives were also committed to good relations with Quebec, but not on the personal level. It helped that Peterson spoke passable French, that he had spent two summers in Trois-Pistoles, that he had assembled advisers who understood Quebec. He opened a permanent provincial office in Quebec City and extended French-language services in Ontario. (Like the Conservatives, however, he refused to make the province officially bilingual, fearing a backlash among rock-ribbed, rural Ontarians.) Moreover, he began to court Bourassa. He had invited Bourassa to speak in his native city of London when he was opposition leader. Two days after Bourassa was elected, he invited Peterson to dinner at the Beaver Club in Montreal. It was a public place and their meeting was a statement of the new *entente liberale*. From then on, the two saw more of each other. In Quebec, Peterson joined Bourassa on an open-line radio talk show in French and English. In Toronto, Bourassa lunched with Peterson at Cibo's, a toney Italian restaurant. Bourassa could never get the name right ("I like that Chico's," he said), but the new solidarity looked good. Those were heady days: two new leaders of the 1980s, both

Liberals, speaking each other's language, at home talking business or politics. They seemed to like each other. When Bourassa arrived in Toronto, Peterson would send a quart of milk, Bourassa's favourite drink, to his hotel room in a champagne bucket. Bourassa would send Peterson a bottle of Scotch when he came to Quebec. This was an unusual relationship. "Bourassa saw in Peterson someone who didn't treat Quebec with disdain and fear," says one of Peterson's associates. "Davis could never have done that with Lévesque."

The relationship was not without tensions. Sometimes it did not suit Peterson's purposes to be too close to Bourassa, and he was urged to step back. But Bourassa would not attack Peterson for failing to embrace official bilingualism, and Peterson was careful about what he said about minority language rights in Quebec. Occasionally, though, there was anxiety over who got what from the federal treasury. When, for example, Bourassa claimed that Ontario got far more in contracts than did Quebec — the old refrain — Peterson's advisers were livid. They urged him to respond. But the premier refused, arguing that it would not be helpful to get into a war of words with Quebec. Ontario did not like it either when Ottawa chose to locate the new space agency in Quebec — a decision it thought more political than economic — but the province declined to make political hay of it.

Peterson, it was clear, wanted to improve relations with Quebec and become the broker of Confederation. But the constitution was not on his agenda in 1986. Halfway through his two-year accord with the New Democrats, he was more concerned with establishing a young government in a minority Parliament, guiding an inexperienced cabinet and caucus, managing a burgeoning economy and dealing with striking doctors. Still, he also wanted to end Ontario's isolation in Confederation, a product of its independent positions, earlier in the decade, on energy pricing and the constitution. So when Quebec decided to present its proposals, Peterson supported them and agreed to act as intermediary. While his reservations grew during talks after Meech Lake — he once almost scuttled the deal — Peterson backed Quebec in the beginning and at the end.

More than any other province, Ontario could claim that it had the least to gain from a new round of constitutional talks. Ontario had long identified with the federal government more than did any other region. (In a poll in *Maclean's* in January 1990, 78 percent of Ontarians identified with the federal government, the highest percentage of any province.) Ontario was the heartland of Canada, the most industrial-ized, the most diversified, the most populous, the wealthiest. It was the least regional of the regions; in fact, some said Ontario was not a region at all. It had little reason to welcome new talks. With twenty-four seats in the Senate — a number equalled only by Quebec — Ontario had no interest in seeking an institution with more equitable provincial representation. With three justices on the Supreme Court, Ontario did not need a say in choosing judges. With a de facto veto because of Quebec's refusal to participate in constitutional talks, it had none of the complaints of the smaller provinces. With reason, Ontario could argue that it went into the Quebec Round for the sake of Quebec. "Ontario wanted Quebec to sign on the dotted line," says Hershell Ezrin. "Ontario did not want anything for itself. We were, in fact, giving up our leverage, our veto power and a bunch of other things. The question for us was, how much do we give up? Not, do we get something? I honestly believe, I will always believe, that what we did was altruistic. It may have been misguided to some people but it was done with the best of intentions."

Just as Ontarians looked more to Ottawa than to Toronto, Ontario's provincial government was more national in outlook. Its interest in completing the unfinished business of 1981 was similar to Ottawa's — but without the prospect of political advantage that so attracted the federal Conservatives in Quebec. The challenges of the global economy, the demand to be competitive, the strain on social services — all would demand a united, effective national government in the next century. Peterson, the yuppie premier, liked the buzzwords of the new age of globalization and competitiveness. He feared that if Canada continued to bicker on the constitution it would be left behind. "Ontario wanted to take the tension out of Confedera-tion," said one of his advisers. "It wanted to change the focus to so-cial and economic adjustment. To do that Quebec had to be in. We were conscious of going through a decade when traditional relations between us had been broken. There was no need to carry on that way."

Peterson also knew that Ontario was in a position of maximum au-thority because Quebec had refused to sit at the table. Under the 1982 amending formula, changing the constitution required seven prov-inces with half the population. With Quebec in, it was possible to ex-clude Ontario. With Quebec out, it wasn't. As one senior provincial minister noted: "We were running the country in those days. No amendment to the constitution, no matter how trivial, could be made without Ontario. Our dominance was established." There was also a sense of history in Ontario's calculations. Thoughtful people around Peterson knew that the major moments of crisis in Canadian unity — the Manitoba School question, the hanging of Louis Riel, the conscription issue — arose when English and French Canada were apart. They did not want that to happen this time. Ultimately, Ontario would stand with Quebec. It would never bolt. Peterson, tormented in the final hours of the meeting after Meech Lake at the Langevin Block, would apologize for his persistence and Bourassa would console him. Bourassa would later urge Peterson to run for the Liberal leadership. Their awkward friendship would not ensure the accord would pass, or calm fears that arose when it collapsed. But it would make picking up the pieces afterwards a little easier.

When Quebec came calling that spring of 1986, Manitoba did not want to answer the door. Although it was important in shaping the accord at Meech Lake and Langevin, Manitoba originally wanted no part of it. There were good political and historical reasons for a cautious response to Quebec's initiative. While the time may have been right for Ottawa, Ontario and Quebec, a new round of negotiations was anathema to Manitoba. Constitutional reform had never been a big winner in the province, even less so a round dedicated exclusively to Quebec. In fact, the government had just been re-elected because it had managed to distract public attention from minority-language rights to the economy. With a razor-thin majority in the provincial legislature, the New Democrats were reluctant to revive the issue that had nearly cost them power.

To understand the premier and his province at the outset of the Quebec Round, consider the furor over the extension of French language rights. In 1983, the New Democrats had introduced a bill making French and English official languages in Manitoba, ordering the translation of laws, and offering more government services in French. Public hostility was fanned by old prejudices exploited by the opposition Conservatives, led by Gary Filmon. The imbroglio became a national issue. Parliament passed a resolution in 1984 supporting the extension of language rights. Brian Mulroney, the newly elected Conservative leader, gained stature by standing against Manitoba Conservatives. But he never forgot the hostility of one visit to Winnipeg, where he was denounced, and his wife, Mila, was called a whore. John Turner, seeking the Liberal leadership in 1984, lost stature when he retreated from his party's traditional support for minority rights. In the end, the antipathy to its new bill was so great that the Manitoba government withdrew it. The whole episode opened wounds in a province sensitive about its history of intolerance. It also scarred the New Democrats. "What we did was right in principle, right in law, right in finance, right in common sense," says Howard Pawley. "It was terribly wrong politically."

Pawley's government spent the rest of its mandate trying to recover. Its strategy was to focus on the economy, where the NDP had done well. But long before the minority-language explosion, it knew the dangers of the constitutional issue in Manitoba. In 1981, Pawley had actually campaigned against the constitution. While Sterling Lyon, the Tory premier, was in Ottawa amending the British North America Act, Pawley was at home working the bread-and-butter issues. "Let's patriate our sons and daughters back to Manitoba," Pawley said, decrying the exodus from the province. "It's more important than patriating the constitution." While the austere, humourless Lyon talked powers and prerogatives, Pawley talked prosperity. Manitoba was reeling from the economic recession of 1981–82 and the New Democrats capitalized on it. Lyon, who was to Manitoba what Bourassa was to Quebec — the man everyone liked to hate — became a one-term premier. Few shed any tears over his departure.

Pawley approached the constitution with trepidation in 1986. During the election campaign that winter, he barely mentioned the subject. "It was not in our platform," he recalls. "We avoided it like the plague. We saw the disaster which had overtaken Sterling Lyon because of his obsession with it. We'd had our fingers burnt on the French-language thing. We had misjudged the intensity of the furor it had unleashed before. We were very, very naive. This time, we knew there was nothing in it politically for us." Grateful for his re-election, Pawley had learned his lesson. It would take some selling to convince him to reopen the debate on its agenda. At the same time, he knew that he could not avoid responding to Quebec. "I realized the forces that could be unleashed in Manitoba and western Canada," Pawley says. "But, on the other hand, I knew it was right to accommodate Quebec. And even with my reservations, it would be totally wrong for us not to participate. . . . Who were we, all alone, to say that we would walk out of the process?" That Pawley should take a risk on this may have shown bad judgement, but it was consistent with his deeply held belief that government must try to improve the social condition. If one region was alienated or impoverished, the rest of the country would have to try to redress the imbalance. Such was the conviction of a social democrat.

Howard Russell Pawley had felt that kind of need to do right since he was a student at Manitoba Teachers College and Manitoba Law School in Winnipeg. He had moved out west as a child from Brampton, Ontario — also the home town of William Davis — where he was born in 1934. He entered provincial politics in 1969 and held a string of key cabinet jobs under Edward Schreyer, including attorney general and House leader. He was responsible for the public automobile insurance scheme that eventually brought his government down. When Schreyer left to become governor general in 1979, Pawley became party leader and, in 1981, the province's eighteenth premier. Pawley was not a natural politician. Despite his success, he was plodding, flat and uninspiring. Physically, his movements were fitful and awkward. There was no doubt Pawley was warm, cordial and decent. But he was a listless speaker with the charisma of a china cup. Pawley was more steak than sizzle. The joke was that a good time for Pawley was going to Eaton's on Friday night and trying on gloves.

By 1986, Pawley had been premier for five years. Although he had missed the Patriation Round, he was more experienced in federal-provincial relations than were most of the other premiers. He was not popular with the others, which may have said more about his colleagues than about him. "Howard was a hand-wringer," allows one of his fellow first ministers. "He was an intellectual pantywaist," says another. No doubt that Pawley was "the odd man out." At the myriad meetings at which premiers gather, Pawley stood alone in advocating economic intervention or promoting self-government for aboriginal peoples. As the leader of the only NDP government in Canada, he was ideologically different. To the Vander Zalms, Gettys and Devines, who represented something of a cashew coalition of the West, this social democrat was a nuisance. Devine, in particular, had no use for his neighbour. When Pawley made his opening statement at conferences, Devine made a habit of going for coffee. The snub was so predictable that Pawley's staff began to take bets on it. For Pawley, independence meant isolation and ridicule. "He really didn't like going to those meetings," remembers Ginny Devine, one of his assistants. "He really didn't care in the end what they thought about him. But when you have to spend two days with them, trying to get your agenda across, it's pretty hopeless."

If Pawley's relations with the premiers were frosty when the Quebec Round opened in 1986, they were icy with the prime minister. In the wake of the dispute over minority-language rights, Pawley was already handling the constitutional question gingerly. By that October, he had yet another reason: the federal government awarded the contract to build the CF-18 fighter plane to Quebec rather than to Manitoba even though the bid from the Winnipeg company had been lower than that made by the Montreal company. Manitobans were outraged; this was another concession to Quebec. An angry Pawley denounced the decision and led a delegation of municipal leaders and labour representatives to Ottawa. He was already annoyed Mulroney had not given him warning of the decision, as Pawley said he had promised. "I can't trust this man," he told his staff.

The meeting was a debacle. As soon as they sat down, Mulroney lit into the premier. "Mr. Pawley, I found your remarks to be vulgar," he said. "I have taken due note of them." Mulroney then turned to Mayor William Norrie of Winnipeg and asked him to make the presentation. This, of course, was an insult to Pawley, who reminded Mulroney that, as the premier, he should speak for the province. Pawley said that regardless of what Mulroney thought of him personally, the prime minister would have to explain his decision to Manitobans. As Clifford Scotton, an adviser to Pawley tells it, Mulroney tried three times to leave the room. At Scotton's insistence, Pawley implored Mulroney each time to listen to another member of the delegation. The bad blood lingered for some time. In November, Pawley clashed with Mulroney at the annual federal-provincial conference on the economy in Vancouver.

The issue did not enhance the climate of federal-provincial relations in general, nor Manitoba's view of Quebec in particular. "I was in no mood to talk about the constitution after that," says Pawley. The real impact of the CF-18 episode was less on relations between Mulroney and Pawley — they would improve by the time the two met at Meech Lake — than on Manitoba's perception of Quebec. It helped tap a vein of prejudice in the province. In 1986, people were unlikely to extend an olive branch to Quebec. Pawley rose above that, made peace with Mulroney and signed the deal. But public skepticism —

some called it racism — was never far from the surface. At the first
pretext, it emerged again, and Pawley's successor would reap the
whirlwind.

While Alberta did not share Manitoba's reluctance to open talks, it
did approach them with suspicion. The question was timely for Premier Donald Getty because he was chairman of the annual premiers'
conference that year. In August 1986, in Edmonton, the premiers
agreed to put aside their individual concerns and deal only with
Quebec's. Chairing the conference flattered Getty, who had been
elected only the previous year. Heir to the mantle of Peter Lougheed,
who was something of a demigod in Alberta, Getty had little of his
predecessor's substance or savvy. He did know that the constitution
could redress regional alienation, still a grievance among Albertans,
despite the election of a federal Conservative government with
twenty-one members from Alberta, some of them in senior cabinet
posts. The answer was a reformed Senate. By having representation
at the centre, Alberta would have as much voice for its interests as did
Quebec and Ontario. As the talks opened, Alberta made much of a
"Triple E Senate" — elected, effective and equal among the provinces — that would finally bring the regions to the centre. "Our
number one constitutional objective was to have a properly functioning second chamber," recalls James Horsman, Alberta's minister of
intergovernmental affairs. "It was always our goal."

The trouble with Alberta's commitment to an elected Senate was
that it was not one of Quebec's five proposals, which were driving
this exercise. When Quebec came calling, Alberta listened and agreed
to talk. Nonetheless, it never abandoned Senate reform, an ambition
that generated little interest in Manitoba and Ontario. And if pursuing Senate reform meant reneging on the promise made at Edmonton
to limit the agenda to Quebec's items or threatening to scuttle the accord, so be it. There would be no deal without progress on institutional reform.

In Donald Ross Getty, Alberta had an untested voice at the table.
Getty had been in and out of politics. He had helped Lougheed build
the provincial Tories in 1967 and take power in 1971. He had served
in Energy and in Intergovernmental Affairs and had emerged as a key
minister. Then he left politics in 1979 to see more of his family and
make some money. Like John Turner, who was frustrated waiting
for Trudeau to leave, Getty planned to secure his financial future and

return to public life. When King Peter abdicated in 1985, Getty was ready. The leadership race was his coronation.

Getty was born to an affluent family in 1933 in Westmount, Quebec. He studied business administration at the University of Western Ontario and played quarterback for the Edmonton Eskimos. His admirers called him the best in the league. One of his teammates was Peter Lougheed. When things got rough later in life, he found inspiration from his years on the gridiron. "My whole life has prepared me for what I am doing now," he said in an interview in 1987. "A Canadian cannot get to be starting quarterback for the Grey Cup without encountering tough times." Tough times he got. Oil and wheat prices collapsed, his caucus started to rumble, he lost his own seat in the legislature, his son was convicted on drug charges. But football had taught him about perseverance, loyalty and teamwork. "Getty isn't necessarily a brain surgeon," says one provincial official. "But he is a straight-shooter and an honourable man."

It wasn't Getty's fault that Alberta's economy soured in the mid-1980s. The boom had ended before he succeeded Lougheed. His problem was that he could never match Lougheed in intelligence or energy. Getty was physically imposing — six foot two, lean, rugged — but his style was aloof. He talked a lot about being a team player but was unwilling to call the plays. Unlike the indefatigable Lougheed, who worked seven days a week, Getty liked hunting and visiting Hawaii. Added to his image problems, sumptuous office renovations he authorized and his coolness toward the press suggested an air of regal indifference.

At the outset of the new round, Getty was sensitive to Quebec's demands. The two provinces had long had a special relationship, largely because they were the strongest advocates of provincial rights. That alone was reason for Alberta to listen to Quebec that spring. As chairman of the conference, Getty agreed to push for the reopening of negotiations at Edmonton. But, in the subsequent talks, he still needed a commitment to Senate reform. Whatever the promise in Edmonton to end Quebec's isolation, one thing was clear: without that commitment, there would be no deal.

East of Alberta, Grant Devine was convinced of the need for national reconciliation that spring of 1986. He had been troubled about the unfinished business of the Patriation Round ever since he took office days after Queen Elizabeth proclaimed the new constitution in 1982.

His view of the country had been shaped by his sojourn in Ottawa as a young civil servant during the October Crisis of 1970. Struck by the implacable antagonism he later saw between Lévesque and Trudeau, he wanted Canadians to stop bickering and start building. While he liked both Lévesque and Trudueau, he knew there would be no constitutional reform until both departed. Devine recalls that he once tried to make peace between them.

At a particularly unpleasant dinner for the premiers at 24 Sussex Drive, he thought he would break the tension by playing the piano. He sat down and pounded out a little honky-tonk. Trudeau danced, Lévesque clapped, the other premiers watched — and then they resumed their quarrelling. So much for Devine's career as conciliator. (Devine has a picture of himself, Trudeau and Lévesque in this *pas de trois*. On it, Trudeau wrote: "Dear Grant. Thanks for playing at my party. Hope you can do it again soon. Pierre." Underneath, Lévesque added: "Ditto. And I don't often agree with the SOB. Love, René.")

When Quebec began to talk about talks, Saskatchewan did not hesitate. "We thought there might be some hope, with a PM working on reconciliation, with a western premier taking the lead," says Devine. "It would be a good place to start. I really endorsed it. I thought we could do it now. You needed new faces at the table and we had them." No one knew if Devine genuinely felt that way or if he just wanted to please Brian Mulroney. It really didn't matter. The knock against Devine, a plucky, pugnacious farmer, was that he listened to the prime minister too much. No premier was more loyal to Mulroney. "He's bought and paid for," said one. "He's a fierce partisan." It paid off for Devine. When he needed help running for re-election in 1986, Ottawa was happy to oblige with $1 billion in farm aid. Every little bit helped. Two years later, the province ravaged by drought, Mulroney again found some money. No one could prove that it was a *quid pro quo,* but it did not hurt that Devine had been on the right side of both the Meech Lake Accord and the free-trade debate.

Over the years, in a political sense, Devine became both remittance man and point man. He always seemed prepared to do Mulroney's bidding. "Devine was viewed as a lackey of the prime minister, the whipping boy, the bearer of trial balloons," says a provincial official. The view was shared by the premiers. At one meeting Devine got so frustrated with this perception that he threw up his arms and said: "Look, you guys, you think I'm calling the PM and reporting to him and everything. It's not true."

The outburst was typical Devine. He said exactly what he meant. If candour meant denouncing homosexuality, opposing abortion or sacking civil servants, so be it. Bashing gays, defending the unborn and firing bureaucrats were popular in some quarters. Meanwhile, Devine liked to be seen as the family man; the patriarch of the large, wholesome brood; the defender of down-home values of family, religion and thrift. His speeches were sprinkled with reference to solidarity, love and God. His favourite pastime was home life with the family, playing ball with the kids. His favourite snack was sardines on dry toast.

For someone who affected the hick, Donald Grant Devine was no fool. If the cerebral Allan Blakeney wore a three-piece suit on the hustings, Devine shed his tie and rolled up his sleeves. The hayseed humour and colloquial English came easily to him. Born in Regina in 1944, he grew up on the family farm. He cherished his intimacy with the land. "I'm the only premier in Canada with a wheat-board quota book," he once boasted, a claim none of his confrères could dispute. He had studied farming at the University of Saskatchewan (Bachelor of Science), University of Alberta (Masters degree in agricultural economics and Master of Business Administration in marketing), and Ohio State University (doctorate in agricultural economics). Between 1975 and 1979, he taught agricultural economics at the University of Saskatchewan while running the family farm with his brother and father. There were also stints with the federal Food Prices Review Board and the Department of Agriculture. He became leader of the Tories in 1979 and premier three years later. When he finally won a seat in the legislature in 1982, it was his third try. The election ended eleven years of New Democratic rule. Dr. Devine was thirty-eight, the father of five children and the winner of the Vanier Award as one of "Canada's outstanding young leaders."

On the constitutional issue, Saskatchewan fell between the eagerness of Alberta and the indifference of Manitoba. It welcomed the opening of talks in 1986 but did not take a big part in them. Devine's priority was simply to ensure a say for his province in future constitutional change. "We wanted more equal power in the administration of the country," he recalls. "That's why the veto was very, very important to us. We could have comparable power to a larger province like Ontario or Quebec. It was about equality. You have to have balance." That veto would prevent Senate reform from going ahead without his approval. (If the amending formula spelled out in the

1982 constitution continued to call for changes to be approved by
seven of ten provinces with half the population, amendments could
go ahead without Saskatchewan. With the requirement of unanimity,
as spelled out in the accord, they could not.) Devine said he wanted a
veto on Senate reform, but, beyond that, he had nothing else on his
agenda.

From the western edge of the country, British Columbia watched the
constitutional carousel with detachment. When the premiers sat
down in Edmonton in August, its harried premier arrived just in time
to pull up a chair. For the first time in ten years, British Columbia
was not represented by William Bennett. His successor, chosen by his
party only days earlier, was William Vander Zalm. The newest Father of Confederation brought little interest to the question and made
little contribution to the efforts to solve it. In the past, when the
provinces had no influence beyond their borders, that would not have
mattered. But federal-provincial conferences had become a branch of
government. In 1986, Vander Zalm was premier and his view of
things suddenly mattered. National reconciliation would now have
to contemplate a premier who had called René Lévesque "a frog,"
railed about French on cornflakes boxes and referred to Quebeckers
as "the French." He meant no harm, but that was the man himself.

It has been said that politics is a religion in Quebec, a business in
Ontario and entertainment in British Columbia. Purists could argue
that things had changed in Canada. Bourassa was no more Maurice
Duplessis than Peterson was John Robarts. But in British Columbia,
the rule held. Like his predecessors, Vander Zalm was a showman. A
tulip grower and a theme park owner, he was the consummate enter-
tainer. His critics thought him detached and unhinged. In his failure
to win respect, he became the Rodney Dangerfield of Canadian politics. Still, nothing seemed to bother Vander Zalm, who had an un-
canny ability to speak his mind, ignore his critics and soldier on.

The self-reliance probably came from his self-made success.
Vander Zalm was born in 1934 in Noordwykerhout, Holland. As the
story went, he was so poor during the war that he gathered wood and
ate tulip bulbs. It was there he learned the work ethic. (In one of his
more celebrated comments, Vander Zalm urged recipients of welfare
to get a shovel. He then auctioned off the shovels.) Vander Zalm emi-
grated to Canada in 1947 and went to secondary school in Ab-
botsford, B.C. Beyond that he had no formal education. In 1956, he

bought a nursery, displaying a fondness for horticulture and a commercial instinct. Eventually he owned a chain of nurseries in southern B.C. In 1983, he opened his biggest business venture: Fantasy Garden World, a theme park of castles and drawbridges. In this, a dominion of make-believe, Vander Zalm spent weekends, greeting visitors in the gardens, talking and tilling. The premier made his home on the grounds in an apartment on the second floor of an ersatz mediaeval town. When the criticism of his leadership reached full howl at the end of 1989, he retreated behind its thin walls and raised the drawbridge. Five weeks later, having fostered a sense of anticipation, he said he was staying after all. The knight had come out to fight.

Like other self-made businessmen, Vander Zalm wanted the rules of the market to apply to government. He became an alderman in the city of Surrey in 1965 and mayor in 1969. In between, he ran unsuccessfully for a federal seat as a Liberal, revealing an admiration for Pierre Trudeau. "I ran with him," he says today. "And I still think he was a great politician. He was a pretty bright guy, but philosophically, he left me." Vander Zalm entered the legislature in 1975, held several cabinet portfolios, and left eight years later. His megawatt smile and engaging manner helped Vander Zalm win the leadership of the Social Credit party in 1986. A few months later, he was elected premier.

Vander Zalm is a natural politician, everyman's everyman. "I think of myself as an individual who really is very much involved in government, with government, but who doesn't really like government that much," he says. He is open and polite, offering homilies and pleasantries in a honeyed voice with a hint of a Dutch accent. He is handsome and charming. His rudddy complexion highlights the whiteness of his teeth, which often seem to clench a wooden pipestem. With his solid frame and broad grin, Vander Zalm looks as if he could be slicing smoked meat on Montreal's St. Lawrence Boulevard.

In the world according to Bill Vander Zalm, there would be no abortion, less welfare, limited birth control. His honeymoon with British Columbians ended when he tried to impose his conservative views on them. They recoiled and he recanted. But his principles were unyielding. "You explain things to him and he still doesn't believe you," said one frustrated premier. In the language of the stock market, he would be called a contrarian. Nonetheless, it gave him independence, made him different and inspired loyalty.

The constitution did not hold great interest for Vander Zalm. His agenda was economic development and public service reform. In 1986, he was more worried about free trade and softwood lumber. The attitude in Victoria was: "Why should we care?" Like Manitoba, British Columbia was not enthusiastic about reopening talks. Vander Zalm's senior officials spent little time on the issue and gave little direction to the bureaucracy. The low priority accorded the issue bothered civil servants such as Mel Smith, the province's veteran constitutional hand who had a personal interest in the dossier. "You have to remember that B.C. came into this with a huge chip on its shoulder," recalls one of Vander Zalm's advisers. "We felt, 'You don't care about us anyway.' The feeling was simply that we would go along because we had to." When Vander Zalm did speak up, it was usually about the need for Senate reform. Most of the time, he was dazed and uninterested, more a curiosity than an impediment.

As the western premiers brought their own intelligence or irrelevance to the table, so did their counterparts in Atlantic Canada. None was more aggressive in advancing the regional interest than Brian Peckford of Newfoundland. What distinguished him from the other premiers, though not necessarily from his predecessors, was his modus operandi. Peckford did not observe the niceties or subtleties. In Peckford's Rules of Order, anything went. "The Bad Boy of Confederation," *Maclean's* called him in 1981. He abhorred the epithet, but it stuck. "My style was forceful," he observes today. "One had to be dramatic to capture attention, to get ideas on the national stage. But I wasn't out to destroy the country."

No one ever accused Peckford of wanting to destroy Canada, just to turn it upside down. He established his reputation early as a formidable combatant in the Constitutional Wars. His rows with Pierre Trudeau were legion. There were a lot of reasons for the two to dislike each other — both were obstinate, persistent and independent — but Peckford went out of his way to antagonize Trudeau. On the night of the referendum in Quebec, he referred to the federal government as "the agency of the provinces, not the other way around," a declaration certain to arouse hostility in Ottawa. (Afterwards, he said he meant "creation.") Later that year, at the disastrous federal-provincial conference, Peckford listened as René Lévesque enumerated all the things he wanted in a new constitution, a shopping list that would have emasculated the central government. When his turn came, Peckford allowed that he preferred Lévesque's vision of Canada to Trudeau's. Jean Chrétien, sitting beside Trudeau, said he wanted to vomit. The declaration confirmed Trudeau's view that the premiers were vain, petty and parochial. "It just came out," Peckford remembers. "I still believe it. I completely refuted the Trudeau vision because it would lead to a strong centralized government over time. I could sympathize with a lot of what Lévesque said behind closed doors, particularly about the regional nature of the country."

The animosity poisoned the talks. It raised Peckford's profile but diminished his stature. Trudeau resented Peckford's willingness to trade rights for fish. He shuddered that a Charter of Rights and Freedoms could be set against a demand for offshore resources. But that is what Peckford wanted in return for his support for other items on the agenda. No wonder they loathed each other. "All Peckford wants is all the fish and all the oil," Peckford quoted Trudeau as saying, and then denied it. "Trudeau would make simplistic, provocative comments," he recalls. "I would tell him he was lying. One night, after his verbal gymnastics with Lévesque, I really got into it with him: I said, 'Prime Minister, either you believe what you said or you're just trying to have fun by being provocative. If you believe what you said, then you really fail as prime minister because you don't understand one part of the country. And if you're being coy, you're acting like a spoiled child.'"

By the time the Quebec Round opened, Peckford was the constitutional prizefighter. By 1986, having sparred a few rounds with Ottawa, he had less hair on his crown. The rimless glasses, which he now wore more often, did little to soften his countenance. Nor did they hide the eyes, which flashed a look of crazed conviction. In a land of moderation, Peckford lived on the margins. He was a hard shot to the solar plexus, a spray of iced water in the morning, a dash of iodine on a wound. He was cocky, bright and ambitious, a rough-and-tumble romantic who liked poetry and history. He would quote Ulysses and fight like him too. He had always been that way. A story is told of Peckford at seventeen, skinny and frail, walking home in the early morning with forty dollars in his pocket. He had finished work at a supermarket and had just been paid. Three young toughs set upon him, one landing a kick below the belt. He dropped to his knees, clenched his fists and told them, "You want it, you're going to have to come and get it."

Alfred Brian Peckford was born in 1942 in Whitbourne, Newfoundland, a tiny community on the Avalon Peninsula. At Memorial

University, he was disturbed that so many of his generation in the 1960s wanted to leave the province. They did not share his pride of place, a regional chauvinism that would shape his attitude and his manner. As an English teacher on the province's north coast, he began questioning Premier Joey Smallwood's approach to economic development. He thought the province had given away too much of its forestry, fishing and mining industries. It was time to get rid of Smallwood, he thought, to bring in new ideas and new people.

Peckford worked unsucessfully to unseat Smallwood in 1969. He decided then to enter politics himself, winning election to the provincial assembly in 1972, the first Tory from the district of Green Bay. Premier Frank Moores made Peckford his special assistant and appointed him minister of municipal affairs and housing. In 1977, he became minister of mines and energy, and made a reputation for ordering oil companies to meet provincial demands on labour, goods and services. Two years later, Peckford won the leadership over nine other candidiates. He called a snap election and won it, too, defeating Don Jamieson. At thirty-six, the same age as Bourassa when he took office, Peckford became the third premier of Newfoundland.

After the Tories came to power in 1984, Peckford struck a deal giving him control over offshore resources under conditions the Liberals had refused. Now, in the Quebec Round, Peckford wanted fish. His desire for control and jurisdiction was clear from the moment Quebec made its five demands. When the talks began in 1986, Peckford said he was ready to put aside his interests and to try to accommodate Quebec. "We were breaking new ground," he says. "We were doing something correct." But as the talks advanced, the temptation to push the fisheries was irresistible. If Getty got something, so would he.

Peckford, like Hatfield and Pawley, was not destined to be around at the end of the day. Beset by scandal over a harebrained scheme to raise cucumbers, down in the polls and bored with the job, he resigned in 1989. In one of the ironies of this saga, his successor showed the same kind of bloody-mindedness on a wholly different mission. As much as Brian Peckford was a provincialist, Clyde Wells was a federalist. The first provincial demand Wells discarded was jurisdiction over the fishery, which must have pained Peckford. The constitutional voyage had carried Peckford far from the Avalon Peninsula and given him a national profile. But when he returned home, he had left no tracks.

Peckford liked to think of Newfoundland as different from the rest of Atlantic Canada. Psychologically he had so detached his province from the region that geographically Newfoundland did not seem part of it. And as the other eastern premiers assessed their position at the outset of the Quebec Round, they detached themselves from him. This estrangement was in part a matter of style, in part a matter of substance.

Consider John Buchanan of Nova Scotia. By 1986, Buchanan was a decorated veteran of the Constitutional Wars. He had been around for the skirmishes of the late 1970s and, of course, the Patriation Round of the early 1980s. Next to the venerable Richard Hatfield, he had the most seniority. Experience had not made Buchanan more knowledgeable, effective or important to the process. By and large, he remained irrelevant. He wanted little from constitutional reform — which made him different from Getty and Peckford — and he offered little — which made him different from Pawley and Peterson. There was a consistency in this. Nova Scotia, whatever its historical stature in Confederation, was not a big player in the Patriation Round, nor would it be in the Quebec Round. The reason was Buchanan.

The best explanation is that Buchanan was uninterested in this constitutional stuff. Amiable, avuncular and impassive, the premier seemed bored by the numbing detail and countless meetings. He preferred to break into a Cape Breton folk song, tuck into a plate of mussels, or warm up a crowd with a shopworn story. A natural ham and a seasoned raconteur, the premier never met a microphone he didn't like. The constitution was not his issue in the way it was Peckford's. His attitude infected the sleepy bureaucrats in Halifax, who did not seem to know what the province wanted in the Quebec Round or how it would get it. Their fondest hope was that it would all go away. "The constitution just isn't much of an issue here," sighed one adviser after much dissembling. "No one really cares that much about it."

Buchanan says all he wanted from Meech Lake was to satisfy Quebec. "We really don't have any axe to grind, other than keeping the country together," he recalls. "As one of the founding members of Confederation, we have more of an interest in keeping the country together than other provinces. Historically, we have felt that way." The premier says in 1986 there was not deep alienation in Nova Scotia, as there was in western Canada. He knew that something had to be done to break the constitutional impasse. "It couldn't continue forever. It was just a matter of time and timing." Buchanan, for his part, was prepared to go along to get along.

The fishery? Peckford could carp about it but it wasn't that important to Buchanan. If it had been, he would not have resisted Newfoundland's bid for jurisdiction. In fact, it was he who suggested at Meech Lake that the future constitutional talks discuss "roles and responsibilities" in the fishery. "It's a fallacy to think there would be a change of jurisdiction in the fishing industry," says the premier. "Fish respect no provincial boundaries. It is a natural asset, not a provincial one. Peckford always thought that Newfoundland should have jurisdiction and set quotas, but that's nonsense. It's just not going to happen." On the other matters, he was all ears. The Senate? Of course. Spending power? No problem. Immigration? Why not? "By the time we got to Meech Lake, we were on side," said Buchanan. Indeed he was. The premier wanted not and asked not. He rose from his slumber when Peckford stirred him, and retired when the agenda turned to anything else. This was the politics of ennui.

At Meech Lake, as elsewhere, Buchanan was as nebulous as fog over Halifax harbour. His critics would accuse him of speaking baffle-gab and turning in circles. He would demur, defer and dawdle, and the good citizens of Nova Scotia would elect, elect and elect. He was seen as "a nice man," as they used to say of Gerald Ford, as if bad things could not happen in the kingdom of a nice man. They could. Whether it was breaking the union at the Michelin Tire plant, or bungling the case of Donald Marshall, the Micmac Indian, or appointing maladroit ministers, unpleasant things did happen in Buchanan's Nova Scotia. The way he chose to handle them was to ignore them.

John MacLennan Buchanan was born in Sydney, Nova Scotia, in 1931. Both his grandfathers were coal miners. Buchanan put himself through Mount Allison University, earning a degree in science and a certificate in engineering, and then studied at Dalhousie Law School, from which Joe Ghiz, Frank McKenna and Clyde Wells also graduated. Buchanan was elected as a Conservative in 1967, and became minister of fisheries in 1969. He won the leadership in 1971. After seven years in opposition, he became premier. One reason for his success is that Buchanan had the look and the touch of a politician. He lived in a modest house in a working-class district where he raised five children. On his desk a sign read: "It's hard being a perfect Dad." Buchanan liked this kind of campiness. He fit the stereotype of the provincial politician. He was a man of church and community: the Canadian Legion, the Canadian Red Cross, the Boy Scouts, the Masonic Lodge and the Shriners.

By the end of the debate over Meech Lake, Buchanan would be "Dean of the Premiers," a title he disliked. His seniority, though, did not bring wisdom or respect. Buchanan remained Buchanan, hail-fellow-well-met. Did he lead the negotiations? Did the others look to him for guidance? "I suspect not," says Gordon Coles, his senior constitutional adviser. "They showed him a great deference, though. They did want to know his position."

Across the Northumberland Strait, Joe Ghiz shared Buchanan's sense of history in 1986. After all, it was in Charlottetown that Confederation was born. Islanders might be insular but they are not ignorant. They know they rely heavily on the federal government for their economic well-being. It was natural that Ghiz talked of loyalty and patriotism when contemplating the country. He stressed the strong identification among Islanders with Canada and the need to make it whole again by accommodating Quebec. Ghiz brought to Meech Lake a sharp mind, abundant energy and a familiarity with constitutional law. He endorsed the accord early and never wavered. Although he came from the smallest province in Canada, he showed that, in this exercise, personality counted more than geography. It had been a while since anyone had taken a premier of Prince Edward Island seriously. Ghiz had stature. His colleagues knew who he was, where he came from, what he stood for.

Ghiz had a firm grasp of the issues. As a lawyer, he had served on a committee of the Canadian Bar Association that had proposed a set of constitutional proposals in 1978. (The representative from Newfoundland on that committee was Clyde Wells.) In 1980, Ghiz went to Harvard University for a Master's degree in law. The subject of his thesis was the constitutional impasse over oil and gas in Canada. "I didn't have to be briefed to the wall on it," he said of the constitution in 1990. "I was aware of the concepts and understood them and I had firmly held beliefs on the way the country was governed and some of the changes which should take place." Ghiz, like Buchanan and Hatfield, believed in the need for a strong central government. "I was a centrist then and I am now," he says. "I don't believe that would have distinguished me from my colleagues. Of course, then it becomes a question of definition. What is a strong central government for you may be a weak central government for me." At the same time, he says more decentralization would be harmful. But in the spring of 1986 he saw nothing in Quebec's proposals — nor would he later in the Meech Lake Accord — that suggested a weakening of the centre. Rather, he thought the deal would strengthen it.

As important to Ghiz as the idea of the centre was an awareness that his was the smallest province in the country. Prince Edward Island, green and bountiful, had always been a curiosity. No one really understood why it was a province. In population it was no bigger than a good-sized suburb; in area it was a generous county. Yet, it still had all the features of a major political system, and a storied history to boot. In constitutional talks, the challenge for its representatives was less what the Island might gain than what it might lose. It was no surprise, then, that Ghiz championed the governing principle of Meech Lake: the equality of provinces. Bringing in Quebec was fine with Prince Edward Island as long as the change did not jeopardize what the province already had. Ghiz knew well that his province, with 130,000 residents, had four members of Parliament and four senators. British Columbia, with almost three million people, then had twenty-eight members and six senators. That infuriated Vander Zalm. Ghiz recognized this inequity but still had to resist any encroachment on the Island's powers. That was what being premier was all about. At the same time, Ghiz knew the consequences of failure. At the height of the debate, when the air was heavy with threats and taunts, his words were laden with prophecy. "I really believe in my heart that unless Quebec is reconciled, it will go. It's not scaremongering. Any reasonable interpretation of our history cannot lead to any other conclusion."

Next to Vander Zalm, Ghiz was the newest face at the table. He became premier in May 1986, days before Quebec announced its conditions. Ghiz was new but assertive. His election had just ended eight years of Conservative rule. As is so often the case in politics, his rise to the top was predictable. Joseph Atallah Ghiz was the classic ethnic success story in Canada, an achievement all the more remarkable because he had succeeded in the homogeneous Prince Edward Island. He was born in Charlottetown in 1945, the year after his father, Atallah Ghiz, had arrived from Lebanon. The senior Ghiz opened a grocery store, as had other Lebanese immigrants. Joe worked there on afternoons and weekends, studied hard and put himself through university. At Dalhousie, he took an undergraduate degree in commerce before going on to law school. He returned to the Island in 1970 to practise law as a senior partner with his own firm, and also as a Crown prosecutor. He became president of the Liberal party in 1977 and leader in 1981, the year he was elected to the legislature. Opposition was a holiday, he said, after the time he had put into his law practice.

Ghiz was an oddity on the Island: an ethnic Canadian in a white Anglo-Saxon sea. The issue surfaced in the 1986 election campaign, and Ghiz met it head on. His firm denunciation of his critics was reminiscent of John Kennedy's dispelling of doubts about his Catholicism in 1960. Ghiz's background became an issue again when a Tory called him a "black boy" in the provincial legislature. Ghiz rose, demanded an apology and got it. Still, Ghiz does not consider himself "ethnic." He is proud of his heritage but knows its limited political value. More likely, Ghiz has succeeded because he has assimilated. There is about him a studied effort to fit, to be as comfortable as a pair of old shoes in the Island's red earth. If he lost his chance to become premier in 1982 because he used too many five-dollar words, Ghiz learned the next time around to refuse to use the past tense of the verb "to come" and to sprinkle his conversation with "ehs." It isn't surprising that Buchanan, the lawyer, and Devine, the doctor, talk the same way. Ghiz, the Harvard graduate, says he does not know who Franz Kafka is.

When he discusses the constitution, he simply says: "It comes natural to me." What also comes natural to Ghiz is a penchant for the theatrical. He is a good speaker, quick and agile, with an infectious sense of humour. He paces, bobs, weaves and turns. His head moves about like a ball on a tether, eyes darting and shining. He has a down-home quality about him. He is the kind of guy who spends a night in a gymnasium to register his child for French immersion classes, who is as comfortable discussing his recipe for Caesar salad as his recipe for nation-building. Above all, Ghiz knows the importance of never straying too far from the people. Talk about the constitution if you must, but don't make it an obsession. It's not a big winner in the blueberry patch.

Whatever his commitment to the ideal of accommodating Quebec, Ghiz showed later that he could play politics with the constitution as well as could any other premier. When the federal government announced it was closing the military base at Summerside in 1989, Ghiz kicked, screamed and shouted. What was surprising, after all the affirmations of statesmanship, was his threat to make an issue of the closing at the next first ministers' conference on the constitution. "How can you talk about the constitution when your bellies are empty?" he raged. The threat was bluster, and quickly dropped. But it surprised those who thought that Ghiz, this fresh breeze from the Gulf, was different from the rest of them. Such were the requirements of being a premier and a nation-builder.

The most senior of the premiers in 1986 was Richard Hatfield of New Brunswick. Because he had been around the longest, Hatfield had seen the most constitutional history. He had been at Victoria, when the first ministers had almost reached a deal in 1971; he had seen the renewal of negotiations in 1977 and 1978; he had played a key role in the Patriation Round in 1980 and 1981. By the time the provinces and the federal government were ready to try again in 1986, he had been a player for a decade and a half. Four terms in office had taught him much about federal-provincial diplomacy — the hard bargaining, awkward compromises and endless bickering. It also helped him understand Quebec. Hatfield had been there before. He had sided with the provinces and he had sided with the federal government. His province was a microcosm of linguistic Canada, the only one in the country to be officially bilingual. If anyone carried the credentials of influence, it was Hatfield.

When Hatfield first saw Quebec's five proposals, he doubted they would work. Still, he saw the willingness to compromise and pushed for new talks. "I really was a crusader at that point," he says of the early efforts in 1986. "I wanted this to happen very badly. My argument was that we had been at this for years and we have got to settle this. We must put this behind us. We must deal with it. I sensed there was a chance." At the same time, for his own agenda, Hatfield saw the reopening of constitutional talks as an opportunity to secure property rights. Like British Columbia's, his legislature had urged entrenchment. The idea had been explored in the intergovernmental negotiations that fall but dropped because there was not enough support for it. The other issue of interest to Hatfield was aboriginal rights. It remained unresolved largely because Quebec refused to take part in aboriginal conferences. (Under the 1982 agreement, there were to be three such conferences to define aboriginal rights. The last one ended in failure a few weeks before Meech Lake.) "I wanted self-determination for aboriginal people," he says. "Canadians had no idea how much that issue was a wart on our nose around the world. There was no way to move that issue forward until Quebec was in." Beyond those two issues, Hatfield had no other priorities. More than anything, he wanted to seize the day. His sense of history suggested that this was the right place, the right time and the right terms for a deal.

Experience gave Hatfield a sense of timing and perspective useful in this constitutional exercise. But it did not necessarily bring him respect. Just as seniority did not give John Buchanan authority, it did not give Hatfield credibility. "Hatfield?" scoffed one of his fellow premiers. "He was damn near useless. He was goddamned nuts. We thought he had actually lost it. Honest to God, I thought he was an intellectual flake." No one doubted his sincerity, just his strategy. In his determination to get an agreement, Hatfield became something of a parody in the talks. He praised the friends of the accord and bullied its critics. When it came time to build consensus, Hatfield fell in with Devine and Buchanan as the third of Mulroney's marionettes.

If his colleagues treated Hatfield with suspicion, it probably had something to do with his unorthodox political career. Richard Bennett Hatfield and his Conservatives were elected in 1970, ending the decade-long regime of Liberal Louis Robichaud. The new premier was born in 1931 in Woodstock, New Brunswick. He was the son of Heber Harold Hatfield, a lawyer and former member of Parliament. The family ran a potato-chip plant. Hatfield went to Acadia University and Dalhousie Law School. As a student he had studied acting — a training he recommended for all politicians — and promised that he would be premier one day. From the beginning it was clear that Hatfield was an aristocrat among rubes. His entry in the Dalhousie yearbook of 1956 listed his interests as "Italian spaghetti, the sidewalks of New York, salt on the potato chips, appointments made on time, oyster omelettes, kilts in Cincinnati and Arrow shirts at Black's." These passions reflected a taste for the good life, which would become his tragic flaw.

At age thirty, he won a seat in the legislature and he spent nine years in opposition, some of the time selling potato chips — at which he succeeded — and learning French, at which he did not. He won the party leadership on his second try, in 1969, and the next year, his party won the election. He was part of the flush of new faces in the late 1960s — Pierre Trudeau in Ottawa, Robert Bourassa in Quebec, Alex Campbell in Prince Edward Island, Edward Schreyer in Mani-

toba. With a careful mix of political shrewdness and economic reform, Hatfield managed to entrench Conservatism in the province.
He was particularly successful at winning over the Acadians, who
had traditionally voted Liberal. As he broadened linguistic rights,
they came to like this unilingual Protestant from the other side of the
province and they helped re-elect him three more times. By 1986,
however, he was in the deepest trouble of his career. His fondness for
travel and fine things had caught up with him. His leadership was beset by scandal, and his popularity plunged. Among the God-fearing
Christian premiers, this *boulevardier* and *homme du monde* was a gate-
crasher. He was special as much for his eccentricity as his endurance.
"No one really knew what he was about," says a former Ontario official. "He once showed up at a barbecue in a hand-knitted red
sweater with protruding lobster claws. He was running around with
an instant camera, taking pictures and giving them to us. It was
bizarre."

One of the ironies of this peculiar man was that for all his commitment to Meech Lake, for all his alleged shrewdness as a politician, he
was one of the reasons the deal came undone. Six months after Meech
Lake, without having ratified the deal he signed, he went down to the
worst defeat in provincial history. As it turned out, his demise was
the beginning of the end for the accord.

As a group, the premiers constituted a political elite. Americans, who
think themselves the hub of the universe, call the U.S. Senate the
most exclusive club in the world. Canadians, who are loath to say
anything absolute about anything, could call the premiers the most
exclusive club in Canada. After all, it has all the criteria of a club:
standards of membership, rules of conduct, length of tenure, and a
host of privileges, perquisites and prejudices. Some of these are obvious. First, a premier must win election, which automatically qualifies
him for membership, and must stay in office to renew it. However
stringent the requirements of admission, they are not based on
wealth, family, intelligence, religion or race. The people are the directors and the shareholders; they decide who comes and goes. Brian
Peckford was a member for ten years, regardless of what his fellow
premiers thought about him. Thomas Rideout, his successor, was a
member for ten weeks. Newfoundlanders both, they answered to the
same committee of admission.

Second, a premier has to believe in the values of the club — to promote the interest, collectively or individually, of his province. Hence, the province comes first. If the national interest coincides with the provincial interest, so be it. But premiers have always to remember that they must look after their constituencies. The instinct is self-preservation. Even Pierre Trudeau, who disliked the premiers for the narrowness of their vision, still recognized their place in a federal system. "It is their job to try and get more powers, more money, more jurisdiction and what-have-you for their provinces," he said. "All politicians think they can govern better than anyone else; provincial politicians are no exception." In fact, so natural is the role of the premier as spokesman for his province that, when one does speak for the national interest, he is regarded as a freak. Perhaps that is why Clyde Wells's independence in the Meech Lake debate was so unusual. Here was someone defying a premier's traditional role. No wonder they attacked him. Not only had he disagreed with them, he had broken the rules. Here was a traitor, a Judas in their midst.

Third, a premier must play by the rules of the game. Rules define any organization, no less so the club of premiers. The gentlemen's agreement means, for example, that a premier does not discuss in public what a colleague says in private, does not attack him in public and, most of all, does not interfere in another's province during an election. It is clear that a partisanship means far less here than in other forums. Breaking this rule is terribly gauche. One of the reasons David Peterson is not fond of Grant Devine is that Devine has been known to break the rules. When Devine was running for re-election in 1986, he insisted at the annual premiers' conference in Edmonton on mentioning agriculture in the closing communiqué. As one senior official tells it, Ontario agreed to go along. "'I have to say something about it,'" he remembers Devine saying. "Everyone agreed. So we all stood up and saluted the flag." The next year, when the premiers met in Saint John, Peterson was running for re-election. That, however, did not stop Devine from disagreeing with Peterson outside the meeting room. "There he was, attacking us!" says the official. In private session, vigorous debate was acceptable, if not always pleasant. During one session, Devine's abuse was such that Don Getty went over to Peterson and whispered, "Don't bother with Devine. Just forget him."

As a group, the premiers were usually able to overcome differences of region, language and party that might otherwise divide them. Some were friends: Buchanan gave Ghiz a lift to Ottawa on his plane;

Peterson went skiing with Ghiz and Frank McKenna. Some were not: Peterson liked Getty and Ghiz but disliked Peckford; Vander Zalm liked Bourassa and Peckford but didn't trust Peterson; most disliked Devine. Still, what made them work as a group was the need to articulate the provincial view. With the return of co-operative federalism, the provinces had become more powerful, and the premiers, as their representatives, more prominent. Not only had they been meeting each other every summer since 1959, they were meeting more often with the prime minister. Executive federalism, as it became known, had taken root in the 1960s. By the 1980s, it was emerging as a fourth branch of government, both creating Meech Lake and benefiting from it. Pierre Trudeau had been reluctant to convene the premiers, but Brian Mulroney seemed to enjoy their company. He summoned them far more frequently. The premiers were becoming national decision-makers, even national celebrities. With federal-provincial meetings now televised nationally, each premier could look forward to a few minutes to expound on grain subsidies, stumpage fees or oil and gas production. Later, they could make pronouncements to journalists, hungry for the musings, as Eugene Forsey put it, of "The Portentous Vander Zalm" and "The August Devine."

By the time they gathered at Meech Lake, the premiers had become a force in national politics. With growing powers in education and social policy — powers unknown in other western jurisdictions — they were masters in their own house. Their power had been enhanced by a federal government willing to cede authority, as it had to Newfoundland in offshore resources, or to reduce its fiscal presence because of its deficit. In the age of austerity, the federal portion of provincial revenues was diminishing. By the late 1980s, the provinces were learning to accept cuts in the rate of growth in transfer payments from Ottawa. This meant less money than expected for health, post-secondary education and child care. It meant some of the provinces would spend more in those areas of shared jurisdiction, in addition to forestry, mining and agriculture.

Many premiers maintained an international presence, travelling abroad and welcoming foreign leaders at home. With their majority governments, they could command loyalty from their cabinets, their caucuses and their legislatures. (In 1986, only Ontario did not have a majority government.) Hence, the deals they made and the agreements they signed with the prime minister could, and did, become the law of the land. Administrative agreements between levels of government were proliferating. In the absence of an elected Senate, the premiers could claim the right to speak for the regions. It was an authority their predecessors could not have imagined, and it was growing all the time.

So who were they, these first ministers who wanted to rewrite the constitution? Did they reflect Canada? Did they understand Canadians? As representatives of the regions, they argued that they did. The demographic picture suggested otherwise. The premiers who gathered at Meech Lake were all white, male, middle-aged, affluent. When they met in Edmonton to launch the process in 1986, they ranged in age from forty-one (Joe Ghiz) to fifty-five (Richard Hatfield and John Buchanan). All were Christians: one was Protestant (John Buchanan), three were Catholics (Bourassa, Devine, Vander Zalm), three were members of the United Church (Peterson, Peckford and Getty). One was a Unitarian (Pawley), one was Anglican (Ghiz). Four were thought to be millionaires: Bourassa, Peterson, Vander Zalm and Getty. Hatfield had been in politics all his life but was thought to be comfortably off. Ghiz had had a good law practice. Devine ran a successful family farm.

By profession, most were lawyers. Ghiz, Peterson, Bourassa, Hatfield, Buchanan and Pawley all went to law school, though some had not practised. Before entering politics, Peckford had been a schoolteacher, Devine a farmer and lecturer, Vander Zalm a businessman, Getty an investment consultant. Most had been active in politics for several years. Ghiz, who had the least legislative experience, had been an elected member for four years. Hatfield, who had the most experience, had served for twenty-five years. There was probably more diversity in party than in other areas. Five premiers were Conservatives, three were Liberals, one was a New Democrat, and one was a member of the Social Credit party.

Among the premiers, there were no women and no self-professed ethnic Canadians (Ghiz said he did not think of himself as one). In fact, it was more a fraternity than a club. Certainly no one could say the premiers represented a cross-section of the country, though elected bodies seldom do. As a group, the premiers reflected the male, white, Anglo-Saxon ruling class that had governed Canada from its beginning. While more women were being elected to Parliament and appointed to the cabinet, to the Supreme Court and to the office of governor general, they were not to be found at the table. Nor were those of a different race, colour or religion. The Premiers'

Club remained a white gentlemen's club. What made the group's exclusiveness so troubling to so many was that it was no longer talking only about grain futures, fish quotas and tax points. It was writing a constitution that determined rights and privileges in society, and it was doing so largely in private. Their accord left out women, native people, northerners and multicultural Canadians. Had any of the premiers come from those groups, they might have been more sensitive to their concerns.

Of course, no one was talking much about the growing power of the premiers and their provinces in 1986. The constitutional process was just beginning, and the chances of its success were slim. While some Canadians in some provinces saw their premiers as canny advocates of the regional interest, many dismissed them as aldermen, ward-heelers and Kiwanis Club presidents. They were content to let them repair roads, open dams and hire teachers. But the new round of constitutional reform would alert them to the premiers' emerging role in Confederation. By the end of the debate over Meech Lake, Canadians knew their premiers a little better and feared them a little more.

The Ashes of 1982

THE QUEBEC ROUND WAS THE RENEWAL OF A PROCESS THAT HAD BEGUN in 1980. That, in turn, was a renewal of half a century of efforts to bring home the British North America Act. The law of constitutional reform is the law of perpetual motion. Although Canada had amended its constitution in fits and starts, often with long interludes of inactivity, the issue never left the national agenda. Richard French, a former Quebec cabinet minister, calls the constitution "a rolling compromise" to move the country from one stage of political development to the next. Between 1867 and 1982, federal and provincial governments agreed to thirteen constitutional amendments. During those 115 years, the obstacle to bigger changes — such as restructuring the Senate — was that Canada could not agree on a way to patriate the constitution with a workable amending formula. From 1927 on, the dominion government tried several times to bring home the constitution. The stumbling block each time was Ottawa's inability to win the unanimous consent of the provinces, which was considered necessary by convention, if not by law. Talks lurched from failure to failure. The seeds of each round invariably germinated in the ashes of an earlier one.

In 1982, Ottawa and nine provinces finally agreed to patriation. Canada freed the BNA Act from British trusteeship. It would never have to ask Westminster to amend its constitution, an absurdity, if not an embarrassment, for any independent nation. At the same time, a Charter of Rights and Freedoms was entrenched. Canadians now had a code of rights protected by the courts. But the government of Quebec saw itself isolated and betrayed. In April 1982, the Queen came to Canada to proclaim the new constitution, the cheering masses gathered on Parliament Hill, the Snowbirds flew overhead. In Quebec City, flags flew at half-mast and politicians wore black armbands.

The mixed success of constitutional reform in the early 1980s had much to do with the abject failure of the Quebec Round in the 1980s and early 1990s. The Patriation Round began on 20 May 1980, when Quebeckers voted in a provincial referendum to reject sovereignty-association on the promise of "renewed federalism." In September 1980, the federal government unveiled a package that offered patriation, a charter and an amending formula. For the next fourteen months, the proposals were discussed in two federal-provincial conferences, committee hearings and parliamentary debate, scores of amendments, and court challenges in three provinces, which ultimately went to the Supreme Court. Finally, in November 1981, a compromise was reached by all provinces but Quebec. As part of the deal, the Charter had a notwithstanding clause, which allowed governments to override certain rights.

While the federal government celebrated the agreement that fall, many of the leading players were unhappy with it. For them, in fact, the very idea of proceeding without Quebec was a breach of faith. René Lévesque stormed out of the Government Conference Centre, the scene of the treachery. He warned, with an eerie prescience, that the exclusion of Quebec "would have incalculable consequences." Indeed, it would. His key minister and adviser, Claude Morin, fled the room in tears. Both were incredulous over the turn of events. After three days of fruitless negotiations with Ottawa, the other provinces wanted to settle. On the night of November 4, the premiers met and cut a deal. But Lévesque was not there, and he had not been consulted. His response was predictable. Having rejected virtually any compromise, he now lamented Quebec's exclusion. It had a poetic symmetry. Lévesque declared a day of mourning. To express its discontent with the whole exercise, the Parti Québécois government used the notwithstanding clause to exempt every act of the Quebec National Assembly until the return of the Liberals to power in 1985.

More telling were the reactions among francophones over the alienation of their native province. Roger Tassé, for example, the deputy minister of justice under Jean Chrétien, was one of Ottawa's most experienced constitutional hands. Initially, he liked the deal; he thought it was the best he could hope for under the circumstances.

But when he went home the day it was signed, his distraught teen-aged daughter asked him how he could laud an arrangement that left out Quebec. He had doubts but was confident there would be future negotiations. "Every prime minister had tried for fifty years," he says. "My feeling was that we would do this bit here and others would finish the job. The political process would take over." His view was close to the one expressed by Trudeau himself to Serge Joyal, who had chaired the constitutional committee that had shaped the Charter. Trudeau met him; Jim Peterson, his parliamentary secretary; and Jean Chrétien, the minister of justice, the morning after the nine provinces had agreed to a deal. Joyal recalls: "I said it was better than nothing. At least we have it, and there would be future conferences. He agreed that others would have to try and solve it. But Trudeau was not exultant. The large dose of idealism, the 'let's go first class' was gone. It was a glass half full. It was imperfect because Quebec was out."

Tom Axworthy, Trudeau's principal secretary, was a fervent believer in the Charter, which he called "the Ark and the Covenant" of the federal vision. He was crestfallen that it now had a notwithstanding clause that would allow governments to override rights. He would have liked the Charter to go to a national referendum, but his colleagues were opposed. Chrétien told him, "You can talk about a referendum. You didn't have to fight it. I don't want to fight it again." Axworthy worried that the provinces would exempt their legislation from the Charter and undermine its ability to protect minority rights, a *raison d'être* of the Charter. But although he was one of the leading intellectual lights of the Trudeau circle, he could not persuade the cabinet.

If Trudeau was prepared to go along, despite his reservations, it was because he believed that the Parti Québécois would never sign an agreement that could strengthen Confederation. "These compromises are not of my making," he said in accepting the deal. When Mulroney later said that Trudeau's government should have signed a better deal, he assumed that the Parti Québécois would have agreed to one. But most participants, including Claude Morin, suggest otherwise. Marc Lalonde, Trudeau's energy minister, was convinced that Quebec would never sign. He always thought that the Parti Québécois would walk out and the federal government would have to proceed. "I was very happy," he recalls. "I knew all along that there was no way the Quebec government could sign an agreement.

It was like asking them to commit hara-kiri. For Quebec to ratify a federalist document would be to abandon everything they had stood for." Lalonde, like other federal Liberals, thought Lévesque was in an impossible situation. Had he signed, it would have been an admission of defeat that would have split his party. "If I had been a separatist, I wouldn't have agreed with it," says Lalonde. "Why should I? It was only a losing proposition for indépendentistes. The best they could hope for was failure. At least by not agreeing, if they could make it fail, it would postpone things and keep it boiling."

The view that Quebec's position was irreconcilable was shared by others outside the federal camp. Roy McMurtry, Ontario's attorney general and a key player in crafting the compromise, says Quebec was playing coy. He believes that Quebec's agreement to give up its veto and join the other provinces in a common front — the so-called "Gang of Eight" — was simply a ruse by Quebec to appear engaged in a process that it wanted to fail. (On 16 April 1981, all the provinces but Ontario and New Brunswick had agreed to an amending formula that would make all provinces equal. At the time, Lévesque relinquished Quebec's traditional veto.) Ultimately, McMurtry says, Quebec's collaboration was a charade. "Quebec would never have signed," he recalls. "They were saying — and Morin was bullshitting us — that 'if we got the right deal, we'll sign.' They were vague and wanted to keep it that way. Their strategy was transparent: it was to sit back and watch the others fight. They hoped it would never get to the stage where there was a deal on the table they had to accept or reject." Morin argues that Quebec probably would have rejected most deals, but suggests it might have agreed to patriation and a narrow charter of rights with a notwithstanding clause. The question, of course, is whether Ottawa would have agreed to a package with those limitations.

Quebec was free to play the *agent provocateur* at the talks. But McMurtry knew that eventually Quebec would be isolated. The break came early on November 4, the third day of the first ministers' conference, when Lévesque agreed in principle to Trudeau's offer to hold a national referendum on the Charter. In embracing the proposal, Lévesque had isolated himself from the other premiers, some of whom were terrified of a referendum. Although Allan Blakeney of Saskatchewan thought he could fight it and win, most of his colleagues did not relish the prospect of the federal government asking Canadians to approve a Charter of Rights. The polls showed the idea was popular and Ottawa would probably win. "After all these meetings, after all we've been through, we're going to end up with a couple of goddamned referendums, which would be the height of folly," McMurtry told Peter Lougheed, the premier of Alberta. "How do you fight the Charter? It's motherhood!"

When Lougheed realized that Lévesque might be drifting away, things began to move. McMurtry was telling Lougheed that he would have to determine whether the "Gang of Eight" would hang together or try to strike a deal. "At some point you have to decide whether you are separatist or not," McMurtry said. For Lougheed and others, severing the relationship with Lévesque was painful. Theirs had been an unholy, though not an unnatural, alliance. McMurtry says Lévesque never forgave the other premiers or himself: "Until the day he died, he was bitter about what had happened. Not only because it had happened but because he was the author of his misfortune. He inadvertently had provided the ammunition. He was a proud man and he knew it."

So the representatives of the other provinces gathered at the Château Laurier later that night, and cobbled together a deal. Quebec was not at the meeting. No deliberate effort was made to exclude Quebec, they maintained later, a claim Claude Morin accepts in part. But the fact is that the premiers made a deal while Lévesque slept at his hotel across the river in Hull, and the image created was one of skulduggery and deceit. It looked as if English Canada had double-crossed Lévesque. In Quebec, this nocturnal conclave became known as "the Night of the Long Knives." The sense of betrayal it spawned became a reservoir of resentment that would eventually fill Meech Lake.

The revisionist view of the Patriation Round argues there could have been a deal in 1981 had the federal government shown more patience and flexibility. It contends that the process was secretive; that the deal was imposed on Quebec and hence repudiated there; and that Quebec was "out of the constitution" until the Meech Lake Accord brought it in. These assertions gained wide currency in the debate over Meech Lake and coloured its character, particularly in the last months. Brian Mulroney, the principal of the school of revisionism, was particularly fond of reconstituting events. His rewriting of history inflamed passions, created misunderstandings and sowed division. All this had a purpose. To the architects of the Meech Lake Accord, putting a different face on history was convenient and necessary. If the problem — the past — could be made to look worse than it was, then the solution — the present — would look better than it was. To understand Meech Lake, then, it is necessary to understand the interpretations of the events that produced it.

The Process

When the critics said that the Meech Lake Accord had been produced by eleven men locked in a room in the dead of night, its defenders bristled. What, they asked, was so open and democratic about the last round? The settlement that sealed the deal had been put together by three ministers, alone, in what became known as the "Kitchen Compromise." Afterwards, the other provinces had met and negotiated in secret. As David Peterson complained, "Meech Lake was no less glorious than the kitchen deal of Chrétien, McMurtry and [Saskatchewan attorney general Roy] Romanow. That was seen as a neat thing to do. 'Weren't they being cute up in the kitchen?' Why was what we did any less glorious? After all, constitutions are made of men."

But Peterson's lament ignored the fundamental differences in approach between the Patriation Round and the Quebec Round. It is true that the three did meet in the afternoon of 4 November 1981 and retreat to a kitchen on the second floor of the Government Conference Centre, where they negotiated the basics of an agreement. No doubt the Kitchen Compromise gave colour and drama to an arcane issue. The CBC even took its cameras into the pantry as the trio of nation-builders helpfully re-created their talks. Chrétien, McMurtry and Romanow were ambitious politicians (all ran later for their respective party leaderships) who no doubt enjoyed the publicity. But other observers who were there then — and who supported the Meech Lake Accord later — play down the importance of their conclave.

"Most of us laughed about the Kitchen conference because we never had the sense that it was crucial at all," says a former senior member of the federal constitutional team. "We always believed that it was in essence something they were put on earth to do to complete the grand plan, rather than something they had invented themselves. It was destined to happen because it was set up that way." The reality was that they were executing a strategy that was being shaped by their superiors. Brian Peckford, for his part, says that several meetings around the same time as the one in the kitchen were just as important to the agreement. It was Newfoundland, he says, that helped forge a compromise the next day at a breakfast meeting among the premiers. Other veteran constitutionalists, such as Mel Smith of British Columbia, remember Peckford's contribution and also play down the role of the Kitchen Compromise.

While defenders of Meech Lake used the Kitchen Compromise to deflect accusations that their meeting was secretive and isolated, they overlooked the long public debate that shaped the Constitution Act of 1982. The process began in the summer of 1980, when Chrétien held a series of meetings with provincial officials to put together a working proposal to be presented to the first ministers in September. These meetings were widely covered by the national media. They became known as "the Uke and Tuque show," a reference to Romanow, a Ukrainian, and Chrétien, a francophone, who co-chaired the meetings. Over twenty-eight days in July and August, in four cities, provincial and federal officials discussed an agenda of twelve items that had come out of a meeting between Trudeau and the premiers in June. Trudeau eventually rejected the proposals as a provincial shopping list — among other demands, the premiers wanted more power in communications, family law, fisheries and offshore resources — but the summer road show was an exercise in public education.

In September, the government unveiled its draft resolution. After debate at a stormy federal-provincial conference later that month, the resolution was referred to a special joint committee of the House of Commons and the Senate. There, the proposed Charter of Rights was recast. The committee held fifty-six days of televised hearings from November 1980 to February 1981. In session from morning to night, it received briefs or heard testimony from a total of 914 individuals and 294 groups. The hearings became a carnival of participatory democracy, a forum for every major group in society. Of 123 amendments moved, more than half were accepted.

The Charter returned to the House of Commons for debate, where, for months, the constitutional issue had been raised in the daily Question Period and argued in formal debate. Meanwhile, the resolution was moving through the courts in Quebec, Newfoundland and Manitoba, the three provinces that had challenged the legality of the government's package. Ultimately, the case went to the Supreme Court, which heard several days of arguments, deliberated for the summer and delivered a ruling in September. So intense was the interest that Chief Justice Bora Laskin read the judgement on live television, the first time the high court had ever delivered a judgement in that manner. In November 1981, there was a second first ministers' conference (the one of the Kitchen Compromise), where the deal was struck. Even then, the package was not cast in stone. A fortnight later, after lobbying by groups representing aboriginal peoples and women, more changes were made. The package then went back to Parliament for final debate, where it was passed with overwhelming support from all three parties. It was sent on to Britain, where it was debated again and passed by Parliament. By the time the new constitution was proclaimed by the Queen on 17 April 1982, the constitution had been discussed for almost two years — and at such length that the government was accused of neglecting an ailing economy.

A major difference in the openness of the process was that the patriation package was ratified only by Parliament. The Meech Lake Accord, in contrast, had to be ratified by Parliament and the provinces, where it would be debated in each of the legislatures. The Senate and the House of Commons did hold hearings on the accord, but those hearings took place after the accord had been approved by the first ministers in June 1987 — and with the clear understanding that nothing could be changed. Some of the provinces also held public hearings. On the whole, though, the accord was presented as *fait accompli,* a take-it-or-kill-it proposition.

The Promise

The architects of the Meech Lake Accord said that its most important achievement was to accommodate Quebec. Their common complaint was that Trudeau had reneged on his promise of "renewed federalism." Trudeau's promise to Quebec came in a speech on 14 May 1980, at the Paul Sauvé Arena in Montreal, what many call the best of his career. "I know that I can make a most solemn commitment that following a 'No' vote we will immediately take action to renew the constitution and we will not stop until we have done that," he said. "And I make a solemn declaration to all Canadians in the other provinces: we, the Quebec MPs, are laying ourselves on the line, because we are telling Quebeckers to vote 'No' and telling you in the other provinces that we will not agree to your interpreting a 'No' vote as an indication that everything is fine and can remain as it was before. We want change and we are willing to lay our seats in the House on the line to have change." Mulroney charged repeatedly that Trudeau had broken his promise to Quebeckers. On 15 December 1989, he called Trudeau's failure to respond one of "the great disappointments in the history of the province. A few days later, having heard that solemn promise from the prime minister of Canada, Quebeckers voted for change. A year later, Quebec was unceremoniously excluded from the constitutional process."

As Mulroney would have it, Quebec got nothing out of patriation. Only Meech Lake could "repair the constitutional debacle of 1981." This was a matter of interpretation. Many would argue there had been a renewal of federalism in 1981. The constitution was brought home, eliminating the last vestige of British colonialism. A charter of rights was proclaimed, which would limit the powers of government and enhance the basic liberties of all Canadians, including Quebeckers and almost one million francophones outside Quebec. Five amending formulas were approved, improving the prospects of future reform. There was a commitment to define aboriginal rights and to reduce regional disparities. Quebec and other provinces gained greater authority over natural resources and external trade. They were also able to opt out of constitutional amendments that transferred powers to the federal government, in some cases, with compensation. Moreover, they won a veto over federal institutions, which ensured Quebec three judges on the Supreme Court. It was untrue to say that the constitution had nothing for Quebec. If anything, it gave the province more powers while reserving its right to seek more in the future as the price of accepting the constitution, which is what Quebec did at Meech Lake.

At the same time as he was talking of broken promises, Mulroney was attacking Quebec's rejection. "Above all, we must never forget that, in 1982, Quebec was left alone, isolated and humiliated," he said on 2 June 1989. "How could we, for a single moment, accept Quebec being excluded from national life? It was the worse injustice ever inflicted on Quebeckers." To drive home the point, he argued often that Ottawa would never have left out Ontario. "To me it is absolutely inconceivable that in 1981–82 there could have been a constitution without Ontario," he said on 26 December 1979. "If Queen's Park and the people of Ontario had said, 'We don't want this constitution,' do you think the Queen would have come over here and there would have been a big party in front of Parliament Hill with everybody in striped pants celebrating a constitution without the industrial heartland of Ontario? The answer is clearly no." The subtext here was that this wrong was perpetrated by the English on the French but would never have been perpetrated by the English on the English.

On both counts, his argument is puzzling. It is conceivable that a federal government would have been freer to move ahead without Ontario, particularly because Ontario was not threatening to leave Canada. Had Pierre Trudeau had his way, he would have proceeded without *any* of the provinces. Moreover, the implicit suggestion of an English conspiracy is curious. The fact is that the "injustice" was undertaken by a Liberal government with overwhelming representation in Quebec. The prime minister was a Quebecker who had been elected with large majorities from his native province since 1968. A third of his cabinet was from Quebec, including senior ministers in finance, health and justice. Moreover, the Liberals had elected seventy-four of seventy-five MPs from Quebec, seventy-one of whom supported the package. A good many provincial Liberals supported it, too. If this was humiliation, it was at the hands of les Québécois.

In arguing that Quebec was "excluded" and "isolated" in the 1982 deal, Mulroney and others subtlely sowed the impression that the new constitution did not apply in Quebec at all. There is no doubt that, politically and symbolically, the government of Quebec was isolated, even if it was by choice. There is also no doubt that a political endorsement, through the provincial legislature, was absent. The Parti Québécois rejected the deal and refused to participate in subsequent constitutional talks other than as an observer. On the other hand, opinion polls in 1982 showed the patriation package, particularly the Charter, was popular in Quebec. Furthermore, Quebec was legally bound by the document; the rights and privileges of the Charter applied in Quebec as everywhere else. Quebec was never "out of" the constitution, however useful the myth. It was a canard profitably exploited by the Parti Québécois. Furthermore, any claim for exempting itself from the deal disappeared when the Supreme Court ruled later that Quebec had no legal or conventional veto over the package.

The Substance

While Mulroney said he opposed the deal in 1982, he reserved special contempt for the notwithstanding clause in the Charter of Rights.

The "non obstante" clause, as it was called, allows federal and provincial governments to pass laws even if they contravene the Charter. The clause was proposed during private discussions at the first ministers' meeting in November 1981, and eventually became the basis of the Kitchen Compromise. It was inserted to satisfy the western premiers, who were suspicious of the Charter, and not to appease Quebec. (However, Claude Morin said Quebec was happy to have it, and pleased to see others do its bidding here.) Trudeau opposed the notwithstanding clause. He said so privately and publicly, but relented to get a deal. When asked to assess the package a few days later, he called it "an abject failure."

In the last months of the debate over Meech Lake, Mulroney turned against the notwithstanding clause with unbridled hostility. It was now noxious and vile, a scourge wrapped in an abomination. "It isn't worth the paper it's written on," he said of the Charter with a notwithstanding clause. His interpretation raised new questions about the accord: Did the notwithstanding clause make the Charter impotent? If so, did Mulroney oppose it in 1981? Did he try to remove it at Meech Lake? And did he condemn Quebec for using it in 1988?

The notwithstanding clause was actually around long before the Charter of Rights. It was in the Canadian Bill of Rights of 1960, which John Diefenbaker called one of his proudest accomplishments but which, in fact, offered little legal protection to individuals. It was also included in the bills of rights in some of the provinces, including Quebec. It can be invoked to override only fundamental legal and equality rights — sections 7 to 15 of the charter — and must be renewed every five years. The clause does not apply to other rights in the Charter on language or sexual equality. In practice, it has been used rarely outside Quebec, where the Parti Québécois did pass a blanket exemption for all its laws in 1982. The Liberals repealed that exemption in 1986 but used the clause in 1988 to pass Bill 178, its law banning English on outdoor signs. Lawyers questioned the impact of the Charter in its first eight years, but the notwithstanding clause did not prevent the Supreme Court from making important rulings on abortion, pornography, prostitution and labour rights. The Charter was widely seen as an instrument of social change. The notwithstanding clause may have circumscribed the power of the Charter, but it did not emasculate it.

If Mulroney opposed the nothwithstanding clause in 1981 or later, there is no evidence of it. All his public and private statements suggest that he supported it and the patriation package. In *Where I Stand,* a collection of his speeches published in 1983, Mulroney does not attack the agreement or the notwithstanding clause. Rather, he questions whether Lévesque was ever serious about signing a deal: "Why should we be surprised because Mr. Lévesque has refused to agree with a concrete gesture that would prove Canadian federalism is, in effect, flexible and can work?" In the same book, he also asks whether Quebec had any right to block a deal once it had given up on unanimity and ceded its veto. Jeffrey Simpson, columnist for the *Globe and Mail,* writes that Mulroney told him in January 1981 that Trudeau had no choice but to patriate in the face of a separatist government in Quebec. Peter Blaikie, former president of the Conservative party, says Mulroney was indulging in "staggering" revisionism. The suspicion here is that Mulroney's anger was manufactured after Meech Lake to generate support for the accord.

During the negotiations at Meech Lake, Mulroney never raised the notwithstanding clause he found so heinous. If he was prepared to do something as radical as abolishing the Senate, why not the notwithstanding clause? Similarly, Mulroney was restrained in his condemnation of Quebec for overriding minority-language rights in December 1988. He said that it had "always been my personal view that a notwithstanding clause is incompatible with a Charter of Rights" but was slow to attack Bourassa for using it or to repudiate his secretary of state, Lucien Bouchard, for supporting it. Pressed by John Turner to condemn the clause, he replied that it was "disappointing" and "unsatisfactory" that Quebec had chosen to use it. Hardly fighting words. It soon became apparent that, while he attacked the clause, he rarely did so in Quebec.

Mulroney used the events of 1982 as much to sell the virtues of the Meech Lake Accord as to score political points. During the Liberal leadership race in 1990, the prime minister tried to paint Jean Chrétien as the architect of Quebec's humiliation. Again, Mulroney was playing with history. Chrétien was a key player, but one of many; his pre-eminence is doubtful. One senior federal official says Chrétien's whole role, not just in the Kitchen Compromise, was overstated. Others, such as Roger Tassé, the deputy minister of justice, or bureaucrat Michael Kirby, were more important. "Chrétien was a figurehead," he says. "He was probably the most senior centurion in battle, but not the key strategist." Still, it made political sense in Quebec for Mulroney to portray the next Liberal leader as the culprit in this act of treachery. If it was Chrétien and the Liberals who had sold out Quebec in 1982, the Tories argued, it was Mulroney and the Conservatives who had tried to restore its dignity at Meech Lake.

After patriation, there was little interest on the part of the federal government or the provinces in reopening constitutional talks. The issue had played itself out. The goodwill had been exhausted. The economy was slipping into recession. The two antagonists — Pierre Trudeau and René Lévesque — retreated to their lairs, looked menacingly at each other and waited to see who would leave politics first. It was clear that, as long as either remained, there would be no progress. Quebec withdrew. In November 1981, Quebec announced it would not participate in any more constitutional meetings. In December 1982, the Supreme Court ruled unanimously that, in law, Quebec did not have a constitutional veto, even if it claimed one in convention. Lévesque asked Trudeau to restore the veto or give Quebec full compensation on opting out and an exemption on language rights in Section 23. Trudeau said he would support an attempt to restore the veto and rewrite Section 23 if Quebec would support the constitution. But he added that Parliament could not act on this alone; all the provinces would have to agree. With the economy in recession, none of them was in a mood to talk.

The only formal activity on the constitution in the early years after patriation was annual federal–provincial conferences on aboriginal rights. An amendment to the constitution in 1983, the first since patriation, established three more constitutional conferences to define the meaning of aboriginal rights. When these ended in 1987, the month before Meech Lake, nothing had been resolved. Quebec had attended the conferences only as an observer, not as a participant, and its effective absence hurt the prospects of an agreement. The effort ended in failure. Participants described the process as acrimonious, tortuous and, above all, frustrating.

The constitutional process showed signs of renewal after Trudeau left office in June 1984 and Brian Mulroney was elected in September. Mulroney, conscious of the need to appeal to the disaffected nationalist vote, struck a conciliatory note during the election campaign. In a speech at Sept Iles, Quebec, on 6 August, he raised the possibility of accommodating Quebec. He said Québécois would not be satisfied with "mere words" after having been left out in 1982, but he offered a few anyway. He committed his government "to convince the Que-

bec National Assembly to give its consent to the new Canadian constitution with honour and enthusiasm." (For some reason, the phrase
"honour and enthusiasm" was dropped from the English text.)
Moreover, he talked about co-operative federalism and generosity
and a new beginning. "We are on the threshold of a true national renewal," he said. "Let us replace the bias of confrontation with the
bias of agreement. Let us open avenues to solutions instead of putting
up obstacles. Let us listen in order to understand, rather than condemn without hearing."

The speech was crucial. It had been written largely by Lucien
Bouchard — the nationalist, future ambassador and cabinet minister
who would play a critical role in the last days of Meech Lake — with
help from Senator Arthur Tremblay. Here, Mulroney was extending
an olive branch. The man who had once accused Joe Clark of playing
"footsie" with the separatists, who was suspicious of the Parti
Québécois ("I'm not prepared to sit down with René Lévesque and
give him one plugged nickel until he tells us what he will offer Canada"), was now prepared to do both. At Sept Iles and beyond, Mulroney was making common cause with old-line nationalists and
members of the Parti Québécois, building an electoral alliance that
would produce big Tory majorities in the province in 1984 and 1988.

Lévesque, too, was talking of a new beginning. That fall, he persuaded his party to abandon its pledge to run on sovereignty in the
next election, a policy that would cost him seven cabinet ministers. In
October, he announced that he would seek a rapprochement with
Ottawa to explore new constitutional discussions. "*Le beau risque,*"
he called it — this taking a chance on federalism. He met with Mulroney in early December, and both of them sounded the right note.
But while Mulroney talked about renewing negotiations, he preferred to wait until a federalist government came to power in
Quebec, led by Robert Bourassa. Certainly the bureaucracy was
counselling caution. There did not seem any purpose in opening negotiations with a lame-duck government, particularly one breaking
with its past at the eleventh hour. "The advice coming from the public service was not to engage before an election," recalls a senior public official. "One reason was the extent of their [the Parti
Québécois's] demands. The second was that a failure could revive the
PQ, which was on its backside. There was always some question as to
whether a failure for them would be better than a success." Even
then, the federal government was already worried about the impact

of a failure of constitutional talks. The fear was that a collapse would help the Parti Québécois. In the end, it was the negotiations with a Liberal government that ended in failure, making the Parti Québécois a big beneficiary.

A success for the Parti Québécois in 1985 would be the acceptance of the conditions it declared in May of that year. Taking Mulroney's commitment to accommodate Quebec at his word, the province made twenty-two demands. Most important, it insisted the constitution recognize Quebec's distinctiveness and "the existence of a people of Quebec." This, Quebec said, would be the heart of any compromise. Once the federal government and the provinces had agreed to that, Quebec would be ready to talk. The province also wanted the exclusive right to determine its official language and to legislate on any matter within its jurisdiction. At the same time, it promised to guarantee the English minority the right to health and social services, as well as cultural and educational institutions. It wanted its own provincial charter to take precedence over the Canadian Charter (with the exception of democratic rights), and wanted a veto on changes to federal institutions and the establishment of new provinces. In addition, it wanted compensation for opting out, or refusing to accept a constitutional amendment that might transfer provincial power to the federal government.

The Parti Québécois also wanted a limitation on the federal spending power, so provinces opting out of programs would be compensated. In addition, it sought the abolition of the old powers of disallowance and reservation, which permitted the federal goverment to suspend provincial laws. Predictably, the Parti Québécois also demanded more powers in other areas of federal jurisdiction: manpower and training, economic development, immigration, communications, family law and international relations. It wanted the entrenchment of three judges from Quebec on the Supreme Court and the exclusive right to appoint judges to the Quebec Court of Appeal and Superior Court.

All told, these proposals were more moderate than those the Parti Québécois had made in the the past. The differences, though, were shades of grey. Granting Quebec everything it wanted would have sanctioned the emergence of a sovereign state with exclusive powers and privileges within Canada. It would have given Quebec de facto independence. Opting out of the Charter alone would have destroyed the document as a uniform standard of values and rights for all Canadians. However, the PQ platform was useful to Bourassa and the Liberals, who were then preparing to take power. During the debate over Meech Lake, Bourassa often pointed to his predecessor's shopping list and declared that his were the most moderate demands ever made by a premier of Quebec. That, probably, was true. Although five of the PQ's demands — the recognition of the distinct society, the limits on federal spending power, the return of the veto, the increasing powers over immigration, the three judges on the Supreme Court — did become part of the Meech Lake Accord, Bourassa could still say he had asked for less. That Bourassa was supposed to be a federalist and that Lévesque was supposed to be an *indépendentiste* were lost in the translation.

All this, of course, was academic. Lévesque could talk of "*le beau risque*" and Mulroney could call for national conciliation, but nothing was going to happen in 1984. Mulroney happily accepted the slender yellow document — presented to him personally by Louis Bernard, Quebec's top civil servant — and put it on the shelf. Arthur Tremblay recalls that the elements of the PQ proposal were to be implemented in stages, and he thinks there was "a possibility there." But, in reality, the government had no plans to proceed. Constitutional reform at that time and with those players was impossible. A month after unveiling these proposals, Lévesque followed Trudeau into retirement. His successor, Pierre Marc Johnson, became leader and premier in October and quickly called an election. On 2 December, Robert Bourassa returned to power. Now the die was cast and the stars were aligned. Once again, Canada would embark on its search for country and constitution.

From Mont Gabriel
to Meech Lake

THE CONSTITUTIONAL CHANGES OF 1987 WERE CONCEIVED ON THE SIDE
of a mountain, not on the shores of a lake. The year before the premiers and the prime minister gathered at Meech Lake, their sherpas
met at a conference at Mont Gabriel. While the distance between the
mountain and the lake is short, this journey would be long. On the
way, the constitutional train stopped in Edmonton, Ottawa, Quebec
City, Toronto and all the provincial capitals. At every stop, emissaries from Quebec introduced their proposals, measured the response,
returned home, consulted Ottawa and resumed the journey. Provinces got on and got off. By the time the train pulled into Meech
Lake, the fundamentals of the accord were in place.

A conference on the future of Quebec and Canada was proposed by
Peter Leslie, the director of the Institute of Intergovernmental Relations of Queen's University, and co-sponsored by l'Ecole nationale
d'administration publique of Quebec. The idea was to convene representatives of business, labour and academe. There had not been a major conference on the constitution for years because there was little to
discuss after 1982. By early 1986, with the arrival of new governments in Quebec and Ottawa, the situation had changed. The conference, called "Rebuilding the Relationship: Quebec and Its Confederation Partners," was held at Mont Gabriel, a ski resort in the
Laurentian Mountains, north of Montreal, from 9 to 11 May. Most
of those who attended were scholars, politicians and bureaucrats.
Only a few representatives of business came. "It was difficult for
businessmen to convince themselves the constitution was something
they should become involved in," Leslie recalls. "I think that was one
of the difficulties of the whole process. No one could convince themselves it was serious until it became a crisis."

People arrived on a Friday, clad in sports shirts and cotton sweaters. The Quebec spring was in full bloom. From the imposing lodge perched on the hill, they could gaze at the grassy, sculpted slopes. There were few distractions. The ski season was over and the pleasures of Montreal were far away. The isolation encouraged thoughtful, vigorous discussion.

The conference drew the constitutional *cognoscenti*. In fact, it was by virtue of the sixty-five participants that Mont Gabriel launched the Quebec Round. Peter Meekison and Oryssia Lennie came from Alberta, Jean-Claude Rivest and Diane Wilhelmy from Quebec, Gary Posen and Douglas Carr from Ontario, Don Dennison and Barry Toole from New Brunswick, Stuart Whitley from Manitoba, Andrew Noseworthy from Newfoundland, Brian Barrington-Foote from Saskatchewan. The federal government sent Louise Bertrand and Claude Lémelin, and Secretary of State Benoît Bouchard. There were also several influential journalists (as participants) and scholars: Paul-André Comeau of *Le Devoir,* Graham Fraser of the *Globe and Mail,* Alan Cairns of the University of British Columbia, Andrée Lajoie of the University of Montreal, John Meisel and John Whyte of Queen's. Senator Arthur Tremblay and Gordon Robertson, the former clerk of the Privy Council, were also there. "For us, it was a good forum," recalls Gil Rémillard, Quebec's minister of intergovernmental affairs. "We didn't want a popular forum. We just wanted to see if there were grounds to open talks."

There is a pattern to these events. Papers are delivered and dissected. New minds present themselves like debutantes at the seasonal ball, a kind of intellectual coming-out. Discussion spills into the restaurant and the bar, where food and drink enhance the search for the arcane in the abstract. Masons have conventions, clergymen have conclaves, philosophers have colloquies, professors have conferences. However, anyone who thought this meeting in the mountains would be purely an intellectual exercise — removed from the here and now — was set straight when Gil Rémillard began delivering a speech that would establish Canada's constitutional agenda for the next four years.

Rémillard is tall and lanky, with hollow cheeks and wiry black hair. That day at Mont Gabriel, he was among friends. He had once made a profession of attending conferences and arguing the nuances of the British North America Act. He had then opposed the inclusion of the notwithstanding clause, which he would later, as a politician, defend. (An accomplished equestrian, Rémillard named one of his horses "Non Obstante.") In 1985, he had left the Ivory Tower to run for the provincial Liberals. As the story goes, he was talked into politics by Leon Dion, the noted political scientist at Laval University, as the two men strolled together one evening in Sillery. Finance Minister Gérard Levesque was on his porch. Dion mentioned their discussion to him, and Rémillard soon found himself a candidate. He won, and Bourassa appointed him minister of intergovernmental affairs, a plum position in a new government looking for a new relationship with Canada.

Rémillard was known as bright, imaginative and impulsive. "Rémillard was a loose cannon in all this," said one senior Ontario adviser. "No one knew what he would say next, no one knew how to control him. I saw many occasions when Bourassa took out the horsewhip and brought him into line. He is an academic, not a politician, and he does not talk about the art of the possible." Like Lowell Murray in Ottawa, Roland Penner in Manitoba and Ian Scott in Ontario, Rémillard was his government's constitutional spokesman. Although he was restrained most of the time, he would sometimes roam the deck and fire a broadside. In a memorable address at a Liberal party convention in early 1990, Rémillard warned that Quebec would not "turn the other cheek" or endure "another humiliation" if Meech Lake failed. Strong words, almost demagogic, inhaled by a cheering audience. A far cry from the measured language of the classroom and the courtroom.

His speech at Mont Gabriel had been billed as a major addresss on the constitution. The conference organizers were instructed to schedule the address for Friday afternoon rather than Saturday evening, as had been originally planned. If not, the minister would give the speech another time. Leslie moved the speech and alerted the media.

What was immediately striking about Rémillard's remarks was the tone. It was conciliatory and moderate. Gone was the familiar rhetoric of the Parti Québécois. There was no hand-wringing or fear-mongering or breast-beating. The strongest words Rémillard used to describe the events of November 1981 were "the injustice" it represented and "the isolation" it caused. Later, Brian Mulroney's reading of constitutional history was less forgiving. Rémillard's restraint reflected a genuine desire to break with the past. In his speech, for example, he went out of his way to emphasize the positive aspects of

patriation, such as the Charter of Rights. "It is, on the whole, a document which we, as Quebeckers and Canadians, can be proud of," he
said. "Its greatest merit no doubt lies in gradually giving us a new
outlook on the respect of human rights." He added that there was no
reason to continue using the notwithstanding clause, which is why
his government had repealed the blanket exemption imposed by the
Parti Québécois. "We want to be fair to Quebeckers, who are also
full-fledged Canadians," he said. *Voilà.* In one stroke, Rémillard had
acknowledged that Quebeckers were Canadians — something his
predecessors had been loath to do — and had praised the reviled
Charter. Such generosity of spirit had not been seen from a provincial
minister from *la belle province* in ten years. The audience leaned forward and listened attentively.

Rémillard then got to the heart of the matter: Quebec's conditions
for accepting the constitution. First, Quebec would have to be recognized as a distinct society. This was a "prerequisite" for any talks if
Quebec's support were to be enlisted. From that day at Mont Gabriel
until the end, the notion of the "distinct society" dominated the debate. Of all the conditions, it was the most controversial and the most
ambiguous. It was the *pièce de résistance* of the constitutional repast,
the sine qua non of the Quebec Round. "We must be assured that the
Canadian constitution will explicitly recognize the unique character
of Quebec society and guarantee us the means necessary to ensure its
full development within the framework of Canadian federalism,"
said Rémillard. Curiously, he did not say what such recognition
meant or where in the constitution the clause would go. The assumption was that it would be placed in the preamble, where it would be
largely symbolic, rather than in the main body, where it would carry
more weight. In their election platform, the Liberals had suggested
putting it in the preamble. At Mont Gabriel, Rémillard was not
specific.

Second, Quebec wanted power over immigration. If Quebec were
to be recognized as distinct, controlling immigration would help preserve its culture. It wanted "sole power to plan immigration," which
it already exercised, in part, under an agreement signed with Ottawa
in 1978. As well, Quebec sought a limitation on the federal spending
power, which would allow it to act alone in its areas of jurisdiction
without interference from the federal government. "You are no
doubt aware that this power allows Ottawa to spend sums of money

in any area it wishes whether it falls under federal jurisdiction or not," Rémillard said. "This situation has become intolerable." He called this a Sword of Damocles hanging over the province's spending. He wanted the federal government to remove itself from areas outside its jurisdiction, and to give Quebec the money it would have spent on those programs. (This was called "opting out.") Rémillard maintained that this provision would "contribute greatly to the functioning of the present federal system." Others thought it would lead to its dismemberment.

Quebec's fourth condition was a veto over constitutional amendments. It wanted financial compensation if it rejected amendments that transferred powers to the federal government. It also wanted to block changes to federal institutions, such as the Senate and the Supreme Court, which were listed in Section 42 of the BNA Act. "We demand a right of veto able to protect us adequately against any constitutional amendment which goes against Quebec's interests," said Rémillard.

Lastly, Quebec wanted a say in appointing judges to the Supreme Court, because the court, too, could alter the constitution by virtue of its power to interpret it. Rémillard did not suggest a selection mechanism. At the same time, Quebec wanted to clarify the status of the three judges from Quebec. If, in fact, Quebec's representation on the Supreme Court was not already enshrined in the constitution but, rather, was a creation of statute — a subject of debate among the experts — Quebec wanted it entrenched. A constitutional guarantee would ensure that those three judges would come from Quebec. It would make changing the high court subject to the constitutional amending formula, which required unanimity and therefore gave Quebec a veto.

These five conditions became the basis of the talks. Rémillard also raised the protection of francophones outside Quebec. This concern, he said, would be "especially important" in the talks but would not be a sixth condition. The minister argued that francophones should have a right to manage minority-language school boards, and he suggested that the "where numbers warrant" clause on minority-language education should be reopened. The idea was to broaden and deepen rights. "At the same time," Rémillard said, "Quebec would ensure the rights of anglophones in Quebec." There was no reason to doubt Rémillard. He represented a new government, and his speech was generous. The promise contrasted sharply with the actions of a government that later opposed the extension of francophone rights in Alberta and limited anglophone rights in Quebec.

At Mont Gabriel, all that was still far away. Rémillard was practising the politics of conciliation. Canada and Quebec could live with each other if Quebec could re-enter Confederation with pride. "Quebec's future is within Canada," he concluded. "We believe in Canadian federalism because, within the federal system, Quebec can be faithful to its history and unique identity while enjoying favourable conditions for its full economic, social and cultural development."

There it was, then. Canada had always asked what Quebec wanted. Now it knew. A fifteen-page speech, five conditions. Little detail, because detail meant trouble. Just principles, because principles were flexible. Finally, though, Quebec had declared itself. It offered its vision in a tidy package and delivered it with open arms. Rémillard sat down to enthusiastic applause.

The speech electrified the audience. The participants responded like archaeologists unearthing an ancient artifact. The consensus was that the list was short, the content reasonable, the spirit conciliatory. Having heard Quebec's position, the public servants could return home and advise their premiers to open negotiations. "There was a sense that there was nothing in the speech that was so impossible that we would have recommended against discussions because there was no hope," remembers one civil servant. "It was in the ballpark. It wasn't the twenty-two demands of the Parti Québécois." Graham Fraser recalls the mood of anticipation that weekend: "You could see the old pros rolling up their sleeves and preparing to go at it again," he remembers. Veterans observed that these proposals were less than Quebec had held out for in 1971. In fact, what was striking about the list was what was missing — such as control over communications, manpower training and family law, all of which had been Quebec's traditional demands.

The real question, though, was whether the provinces would limit the proposed round of constitutional talks to these areas. Would eleven governments agree to deal with only five conditions, or would there be more? Wouldn't Alberta or British Columbia, both of which had long-standing grievances, insist on putting something else on the table? Suddenly the list would be longer, the complexity greater.

Rémillard had talked strategy in his speech, not tactics. But it was clear that Quebec wanted the next round to be its round. Other provinces would have to defer, and voice their demands later. More important, this was Quebec's bottom line. These were minimum demands, and there was not much flexibity beyond them. Within the principles, there would be room for adjustment, but there would be no retreat from the basic points. Quebec had made that clear from the beginning. Although it subsequently narrowed its demands on spending power and the Supreme Court, it never abandoned its fundamental assertion: these were the pillars of an agreement. Pull one down, and the whole house collapses.

Rémillard called them "conditions" but they were really demands. However polite, moderate and restrained his remarks, they remained demands. The question was how far to go with them. Rémillard had fixed his position and staked his claim. A retreat would be considered a defeat. There was no room in the future for compromise — say, three of five conditions — because Quebec argued that its position already represented a compromise. Later, Bourassa maintained that, in fact, he was asking for very little, and this was the least he could accept. "I am coming with the most moderate proposals of any Quebec premier," he would say repeatedly. In the months before the accord died, Canadians heard that claim often. It began to sound like a Gregorian chant. But Bourassa was not wrong. From his point of view — which became the orthodoxy in Quebec — these were moderate proposals. To walk away with less, he warned, would make him "the laughingstock of Quebec." Indeed, the five conditions were less than Quebec had asked for in 1985, in 1980, in 1978, even in 1971. One winter's afternoon in 1990, when the consensus was coming apart, Bourassa slumped onto his beige leather couch, his eyes red and his face drawn. "I came with proposals to be sure they would be accepted," he recalled with frustration. "I thought if they had been offered before, they would be acceptable. The prime minister was also anxious to solve the question. I said, if this is the case, I will go. I will try."

The proposals, it was true, had been suggested before by the federal government. The Supreme Court and the veto had been raised in 1971, immigration in 1978, the distinct society in 1980. Limits on federal spending power were discussed at different times. The argument that they were tried and tested before was a powerful one for Bourassa. He used it often to show that the elements of the Meech

Lake Accord had come from the mainstream of constitutional thinking, as if to say that it was innocuous because it was familiar. But the
concessions Bourassa was seeking had never been offered by the
federal government all at once, and when they had been presented individually, they were not identical to Bourassa's five conditions.
Moreover, what Ottawa had discussed was part of a larger negotiation. As Pierre Trudeau argued later, "Over a period of ten years we
were trying to negotiate. We would offer one thing. If it would not
work, we would try something else. We would take the first one
back and put something else on the table, always trying to trade to
get a patriation of the Canadian Constitution."

The position Rémillard presented at Mont Gabriel, whatever its
historic roots, came from the party platform called "Mastering Our
Future." The document, which was issued in February 1985, defended the importance of guarding Quebec's jurisdiction, while recognizing the need for balance. "We must keep in mind that at times
Quebec must wage a vigorous defence of its interests within the federal system, and assert the autonomy of the National Assembly in the
face of the over-zealous intrusions by the central government," it
said. "Yet we must rise above simply defensive reactions, and reject
the idea that Canada is nothing more than a fruit to be squeezed dry."
This platform, unlike others, was not discarded after the Liberals
took office. One of its architects, Ghislain Fortin, let slip later that he
had never thought anything would come of it. "I was of the view that
it was too much for English Canada," he said. "I always thought it
was something to get past the 1985 election."

The document explains the logic of Quebec's proposals. In the
context of the subsequent debate, for example, it is significant that
the Liberals were originally prepared to place the distinct-society
clause in the preamble of the constitution. Later, at Meech Lake,
Quebec insisted on putting it in the main body. That prompted discussion of whether it conferred new legislative powers on Quebec, a
sticking point in the debate until the end. In addition, the party platform contained elements that would be included in the Mont Gabriel
proposals on immigration, the Supreme Court and spending power.
It also denounced the Parti Québécois for giving up Quebec's veto on
16 April 1981, when it joined all the other provinces but Ontario and
New Brunswick in a common front opposing Ottawa's patriation
package. (As part of this "April Accord," Quebec was given the right
to opt out of constitutional amendments that transferred provincial

powers to the federal government by keeping those powers with full financial compensation.) The Liberals said that renouncing the veto was "a dramatic setback for Quebec, which is now left with very limited means to prevent centralizing measures which might occur in the future. Quebec thus became a province like all the others, with no explicit recognition of the distinct nature of its society." To set things right, they asked for a veto over changes to federal institutions.

At Mont Gabriel, Quebec was presenting a firm, minimalist position. At Meech Lake, Quebec got everything it wanted and more. When the accord collapsed three years later, it got nothing at all.

What convinced Bourassa and Rémillard to launch this cautious exercise was their reading of the national mood. They had wanted to know if Canada was ready for another round of constitutional talks. Mont Gabriel helped them take the country's psychological temperature, and they decided to proceed. Both knew the importance of timing. In politics, as in comedy, sports and sex, timing is everything. Bad timing here would doom the initiative and leave scars. "Better to have tried and failed than not to have tried at all" was good advice for explorers and athletes, but not for nation-builders. If Canada was going to reopen this vexing issue, everyone had to be sure it would succeed. Failure at this juncture, with its deadly symbolism, could mean the end of the country itself.

Bourassa knew the dangers. "There was a risk for me," he observed in 1990. "My choice was to miss what appeared to be an occasion to solve the question. A lot of people told me not to touch that. It's too risky. But I said Canada will be a country with an unfulfilled destiny, with a major partner not being part of the constitution. This is not healthy." Some disagreed, arguing that it was unnecessary to reopen the question. In a private lunch in early 1987, three months before Meech Lake, Pierre Trudeau reminded Bourassa that he had been elected on an economic, not a political platform, and advised him to ignore the constitutional issue. Bourassa rejected his reasoning; in fact, he could have reminded Trudeau that the former prime minister had not been elected with a mandate to change the constitution in 1980. If the prime minister had gone ahead, so could the premier. A few days after Meech Lake, Bourassa allowed that he did not have to proceed in 1986 and was surprised when an agreement came together. "We could have waited until next year; we could have waited until after the next federal election," he said. "We were under no pressure. I was serene, but when I saw that it was falling to us piece by piece, I said to myself, 'Bien voilà, there it is.'"

On the face of it, the timing was favourable in 1986. There were new governments in Ottawa and Quebec, as well as the new circle of premiers. Moreover, there was a climate of national reconciliation. Mulroney had worked hard to restore "a little civility" to federal-provincial relations, largely by accommodating the provinces. It was not difficult to find compromises between levels of government when the senior partner was suddenly willing to be generous to the junior partners. For Quebec, the federal government had found a seat at international conferences; for Newfoundland, a new agreement on the management of offshore oil; for Alberta, an end to the National Energy Program. The Liberals had been unwilling to make all those concessions. Moreover, instead of Pierre Trudeau — tough, ornery and aloof — here was Brian Mulroney — flexible, conciliatory and charming. "This list [of powers] is far from exhaustive, but it is a start," Mulroney had told the premiers at his first meeting with them on Valentine's Day, 1985. No wonder they were enchanted. For them, Mulroney was a fellow Conservative who believed in free enterprise and opposed economic interventionism, who talked their language. And when he did, it was not to insult and humiliate them.

A year later, Bourassa could read the mood as well as anyone could. The new people and the new attitude were critical. So was a lack of interest among Canadians. Trudeau said that was reason not to proceed. No one was interested. Nationalism was at a low ebb. Business, not politics, was the new passion in Quebec. People were more interested in making money. As one businessman told the conference at Mont Gabriel: "Just when exhaustion [caused by the Patriation Round] is giving way to stability and enthusiasm, you invite me to come and participate in reopening the dossier on our collective insecurity. I'm not interested. Recalling the two solitudes is outdated. The presumed isolation of Quebec is an abstraction. I don't want a new constitutional debate, and especially not a new election or a new referendum on the subject. Our job now is to contribute to material well-being." At the same time, participants warned that nationalism was dormant, not dead. A union leader predicted that if any attempt was made to remove Quebec's control over the language of education, or to attack Bill 101, there would be "a new mobilization of opinion on national questions." Eventually, that is what happened. The feeling was that, for most Quebeckers, nationalism was a positive force, even if it was invisible in 1986.

But Bourassa saw the lack of interest in the constitution as reason to go ahead. From his point of view, the timing was perfect. If not now, asked Bourassa, when? If not me, who? Amid this surging confidence, it was easy to ignore the dangers of failure. The impulse in Quebec was to propose a deal now, in a climate of tranquillity, before another constitutional crisis made a settlement impossible. Inevitably, there would be a resurgence of nationalism. The greatest irony of the meeting at Mont Gabriel was the consensus on the fear of failure. It was as if the participants foresaw the issue unravelling. "The constitution is a genie in a corked bottle," Peter Leslie wrote in the conference report. "Before uncorking it, one must be sure the genie will not grow to unpredictable proportions, or become unmanageable." The advice of the conference: limit the agenda to the five conditions. (Quebec did.) Do not let the other provinces use the talks to air grievances or push claims that would broaden the agenda and endanger the agreement. (They did, and it collapsed.) "Great damage would be done, in terms of Quebec public opinion, if talks began and then failed," said the conference report. "Thus a preliminary set of informal discussions must take place behind closed doors, and the outcome of these discussions should determine whether prospects for agreement are good enough to move the talks into a public phase."

In retrospect, the report reads like one of those unread strategy papers historians find in government files decades later. What makes it relevant today is that it captures much of the irony that runs through this story. In 1986, constitutional reform seemed like the right thing to do, even if no one was asking for it, and pushing ahead carried grave risks. "Although Quebeckers had grown tired of constitutional reform for now, and constitutional issues seemed remote and outdated to the youth of Quebec, a new wave of Quebec nationalism is bound to occur sooner or later," warned the report. "This makes it essential to resolve outstanding constitutional differences before a new crisis arrives." When Rémillard spoke at Mont Gabriel, he could not have known that the differences he wanted to resolve, the spirit of compromise he tried to forge, could not prevent that constitutional crisis. In fact, it helped to precipitate it.

Rémillard did not remain at the conference, but the reviews of his speech were encouraging. Quebec decided to continue its cautious, confidential exploration. Three weeks later, in early June, Bourassa met Mulroney and both agreed to go the next step. On 4 July, Mulroney announced a formal initiative by the federal government to accommodate Quebec. It would be led by Senator Lowell Murray, who had been appointed minister of federal-provincial relations four days earlier. On 21 July, the prime minister wrote to the premiers, urging them to co-operate with efforts to open talks. The letter was not made public and was not announced by the Prime Minister's Office. Murray recalls that it warned the premiers to avoid "paralyzing linkages" (tying progress on their issues to progress on Quebec's issues), which might undo the whole exercise. Coughing and lurching, the constitutional train was finally leaving the station.

In Quebec, Rémillard and his officials were beginning to make contact with their counterparts in other provinces. A team of four visited the provincial capitals to brief officials on their proposals. They were André Tremblay, a law professor at the University of Montreal; Jean-Claude Rivest, a former member of the National Assembly and Bourassa's constitutional adviser; and Diane Wilhelmy and Michel Boivin, senior officials in the Ministry of Canadian Intergovernmental Affairs. Wilhelmy, in particular, was well known to her provincial colleagues. Bright and passionate, slender and dark-haired, she was called "Madame Meech" for her energy and devotion. "It wasn't easy being a federalist on the Grande Allée, and she was," said one admirer in the Prime Minister's Office.

The point of these early discussions was to see whether the premiers were ready to put aside their own constitutional agendas when they met at the annual Premiers' Conference in August. Quebec said flatly that it would not proceed with constitutional talks unless the new round was to be the Quebec Round. Rémillard discussed this with Murray in July, and Murray then went to see James Horsman, Alberta's minister of intergovernmental affairs, whose province was hosting the meeting in Edmonton. Horsman agreed, and later so did Richard Hatfield, who began to work the phones. When Rémillard and his officials travelled to the provinces in late spring and early summer, it was to feel them out, propose ideas, raise questions. Nothing was final. All the while, Bourassa was lying low. In the early stages, he did not want to be personally associated with a shaky initiative.

By and large, nothing much happens at these premiers' conferences. Since the first one, held in 1959, they have become primarily an opportunity for the premiers to fraternize. There is a dinner, a social event, a group photograph and, always, a little "fed-bashing." Running down Ottawa is customary fare. Because the premiers seldom do anything important at these meetings, they use them to complain about high interest rates, falling transfer payments or the latest encroachment on their jurisdictions. In federal-provincial relations, this kind of lament is always in season. Even when things are relatively good, as they were in 1986, the premiers find something to complain about.

The 27th Annual Premiers' Conference, held on 10 and 11 August, was not much different. On the surface, perhaps, it was a little less hostile; this was, after all, the Age of Reconciliation. Out of the neglect of the *ancien régime* had come a new civility. Brian Mulroney had opened his arms and invited his fellow first ministers to come and reason together. The premiers were receptive to his entreaties, but they still grumbled about regional alienation and the dominance from the centre.

All the more surprising, then, that the premiers suddenly agreed at Edmonton to put aside their constitutional agendas and deal only with Quebec's. Such a meeting of minds was unexpected. One premier said the debate lasted three hours, another said it took fifteen minutes. Joe Ghiz cannot recall any discussion at all. Nonetheless, over lunch at Government House and in talks afterwards, they agreed that the next round of talks would be Quebec's. In other words, they would address Bourassa's five conditions in isolation, outside the traditional web of concessions and compromises. There would be no trading of wheat for the Supreme Court, of the fishery for the distinct society, of property rights for immigration quotas. Here was a promise to restrict the agenda to Quebec's five demands, and, out of this, a mandate to launch the Quebec Round.

They wrote all this down, the premiers did, in a typewritten communiqué on white bond paper. It had the elegance of a laundry list. "The premiers unanimously agreed their top constitutional priority is to embark immediately upon a federal-provincial process, using Quebec's five proposals as a basis of discussion, to bring about Quebec's full and active participation in the Canadian federation," it said. "There was a consensus among the premiers that then they will pursue further constitutional discussion on matters raised by some provinces, which will include, amongst other items, Senate reform, fisheries, property rights, etc."

They called this statement, somewhat grandiosely, "The Edmonton Declaration." It would not be one of the great manifestos or proclamations of modern history, but on the road to Meech Lake it was a landmark. David Peterson called the agreement "a great day for Canada." His enthusiasm seemed misplaced. After all, he was talking about a statement two sentences long that ended in "et cetera." It was a communiqué on the constitution from a conference that was supposed to discuss the economy. It had an enigmatic, Delphic wording, which one participant interpreted as "Quebec's agenda if necessary, but not necessarily Quebec's agenda." (In fact, one of the points of debate among the premiers was the meaning of the word "then.") But what mattered most was the message it sent. The premiers were saying, as one adviser put it, "Quebec is the problem. Fix it, and then we'll look at everyone else's problems. It is an historic opportunity. Don't blow it!"

The premiers had no doubt they had done the right thing. "The tone was very upbeat, very strongly Canada-oriented, not provincially oriented," says Brian Peckford. "It was unusual. We felt we were breaking new ground. We were trying to do something correct. The feeling overtook us all." Some premiers, such as Howard Pawley, went along to get along. He was lukewarm and scoffed at Don Getty's stewardship. "Getty took pretty seriously the honour of chairing the premiers' conference," Pawley says with a guffaw. "I don't think he should have." Others saw the commitment as a recognition that, unless Quebec accepted the constitution, there would be no progress on other issues. "We all knew we weren't going anywhere [on the constitution] until Quebec signed," recalls Richard Hatfield. "That was a big factor. There was some tension, some worry, some wringing of hands by some premiers. We did, in fact, reach an agreement very quickly, but I knew it wasn't based on soul-wrenching conviction. It was practical."

British Columbia was the most skeptical. While Vander Zalm accepted the decision, his chief constitutional adviser, Mel Smith, was fuming. He resented the fact that he and others had been left out of the discussion and that the declaration had been sprung on the premiers. "There was one copy pulled out of someone's pocket at lunch," he recalls. "This thing was read to them, and they said, 'Oh, that sounds like a good idea.'" Smith says that Alberta and Quebec wrote the communiqué and persuaded the rest to accept it. He thought that it was a foolish concession because it meant the provinces had surrendered their bargaining power. As long as governments would not consider their own requests until they had dealt with Quebec's, what power did they have? "It was ridiculous, absolutely ridiculous," he says today. "In any negotiation, you have to give and take. I think the rest of the provinces tied their hands behind their back."

If that was the advice from Smith, why did Vander Zalm agree? The premier had been in office a few days. He wanted to show his colleagues that he did not have horns, hooves and a tail. But he did not have the experience or confidence to dissent at his first meeting of first ministers. He looked perplexed, perhaps because during the talks two of his ministers joined two others who had already quit his cabinet. Smith explains Vander Zalm's situation: "Here he was, in a group of ten premiers who were all more seasoned, and they all said, 'Yes, yes, let's do this.' So, who would he be, even if he had been briefed, to stand up after less than a week in office and say, 'No, I'm not going to sign this.'" Yet, had Vander Zalm or any of the others done that, the Quebec Round might have been stillborn.

Smith's analysis, coupled with the premiers' effusive statements at the time, suggest that the provinces gave up something in Edmonton, that they acted selflessly, even altruistically, in the interests of the country. Brian Peckford, who had never been shy about his designs on the fishery, says others were telling him, "Look, Peckford, we understand your problem. It will be addressed at some point. But for the good of the country . . . " Peckford agreed to step aside and return to his demands later. It was the same with Hatfield on property rights, and Getty on Senate reform. There would be no talk of other agendas in the Quebec Round. This was the spirit of Edmonton, a spirit the premiers remember fondly. Of course, that is not the way it turned out. The promise of Edmonton was pure and bright, but it grew to mean less and less as the accord was shaped to fit the Procrustean bed of constitutional politics.

Having made preliminary visits to the provinces before gathering in Edmonton, the Quebec officials now embarked on a second, more intensive round of talks. The team had perfected its presentation and refined the five conditions. At each stop — some provinces they visited several times — they gave the same presentation. "We were one group with five cassettes," recalls Jean-Claude Rivest. "Diane [Wilhelmy] started with the distinct society. André [Tremblay] did the amending formula, Diane with immigration, then Tremblay with Supreme Court. We mixed up spending power." These detailed proposals — building on the conditions unveiled at Mont Gabriel —

were never presented in writing to the provinces, and never made public. Quebec still wanted to know what the other provinces could accept, and the early soundings suggested problems. The demands were too long, too short, too vague, too specific. It was evident early that this process would take a long time. The fun would be in the fixing.

Sensing a natural ally in Ontario, Quebec made Toronto one of its first stops in early October 1986. The meetings at Queen's Park that autumn were particularly probing. As the country's wealthiest province, Ontario wanted to play a leading role in this round. It put together a constitutional team that included Ian Scott, the attorney general; Patrick Monaghan, Scott's policy adviser; Gary Posen, the deputy-minister of intergovernmental affairs; Peter Hogg, a leading constitutional expert; Ian McGilp, a constitutional lawyer and Scott's former law partner; Don Stephenson, the premier's constitutional adviser, and Andréw Szende, a senior official in intergovernmental affairs. When Rémillard and company came calling in October, the Ontarians listened attentively and asked questions. Scott was rigorous to the point of rudeness, and confessed feeling a little guilty later. Rémillard, for his part, says he enjoyed this seminar in federal-provincial relations. "The proposals were in rough form," said one of the Ontario officials. "They hadn't thought of the implications of what they were doing."

On immigration, for example, Quebec wanted powers like those of the federal government. Ontario wanted to know how it would reconcile its demands with the mobility clause, which guarantees a person the right to move anywhere in Canada. The question was whether that clause took precedence over Quebec's desire to legislate immigration. If an immigrant lands in Ontario, they asked, are you going to say he or she cannot later move to Quebec? Quebec had thought about people moving to the province from other countries, but not about immigrants to Ontario moving to Quebec from Ontario. On spending power, Quebec had wanted stringent limits on Ottawa's participation in past and present shared-cost programs, including restrictions on direct grants to individuals. Ontario said no; that was far too broad. On the Supreme Court, Quebec proposed alternating French and English chief justices. That had been the tradition, but entrenching it was something else. On the distinct society, Quebec now wanted the clause in the body of the constitution. If the multicultural character of Canada was an interpretive provision in the main body of the text, it asked, why should Quebec's distinctiveness not be there too? At the same time, Quebec denied that the distinct-society clause gave it new powers. Ontario suggested that if it did not mean that much, put it in the preamble. But if it is something else, Ontario asked, what is it? (This recollection of inserting distinct society in the preamble does not jibe with the recollections of other provincial officials, who said it migrated to the main body later in 1986, when the Parti Québécois made an issue of it.)

The tone of this discussion with Ontario was exploratory. Quebec did not so much argue its case as describe it. "Here are the proposals. Study them. Tell us if they are realistic." One of the Ontarians recalls that Rémillard was really saying, "I don't expect an elaborate exposition from us or an elaborate criticism from you. I simply want to know, from your point of view, whether this is so fundamentally unreachable that we should call this thing off. The worst that can happen to us is if we get into this thing and it fails. It would be disastrous. If it won't work, let's decide this right now." The proposals were more detailed than the general ones presented at Mont Gabriel. After hearing them, Scott was pessimistic. He thought unanimous agreement would take years. He saw this meeting as the first of a series, like the search for consensus in the 1960s and 1970s.

What was most intriguing about these talks was Quebec's obsession with secrecy. When Rémillard and his officials met their counterparts in Toronto, or Halifax or Edmonton, they never presented written proposals. They left no paper. All they had was a working document for reference. "No one's name is on it," one official recalls Rémillard saying. "It's just a piece of paper. We'll show it to you. You can see it, but you can't keep it." When an Ontario official asked to photocopy it, Rémillard refused. A secretary was allowed to take notes, which included the proposals. These were then typed and circulated and sent for legal analysis. A bit underhanded, one official concedes sheepishly, but that was all Quebec would allow. Rémillard said he did not want to negotiate in public. Whatever became public would become the bottom line. Quebec was accommodating in private talks but worried it would have less latitude if its proposals got out. The Parti Québécois would make them an absolute minimum, limiting the government's ability to negotiate. Hence, Quebec could not risk leaving anything that might find its way into the newspapers. If a working document leaked, it would have no letterhead and no signature. The government could then deny any knowledge of it.

All this seemed like a shrewd bargaining ploy. The question here, as it was at Meech Lake, was whether a constitution could be negotiated like a collective agreement. For those who were suspicious of Quebec's true motives, the absence of a written text was not reassuring. At the meeting between Ontario and Quebec, one of the Ontarians confessed: "Really, I was trying to find the secret agenda. I didn't accept that this was all there was. I had a sense that there was something else we weren't hearing about, that we would get into this process on the basis of five conditions, and Quebec would say there are now more. Lévesque had done that historically. I was waiting for the other shoe to drop." That suspicion might not have arisen if the process had not been secretive, but the fact was that only Quebec knew exactly what it was saying to the other provinces, even though the officials insisted the presentation never changed. "We could have made a video," says Rivest. "It was the same show." Still, that modus operandi put Quebec in the driver's seat. To learn what other provinces were thinking, they had to call each other. Quebec would not divulge any of its conversations.

At each stop on the Quebeckers' journey, the response to the five conditions was a little different. Every province wanted to know the impact on them, and their responses usually reflected the positions of the premiers. Nova Scotia, New Brunswick and Prince Edward Island were agreeable. Manitoba was still not enamoured of the idea of constitutional talks, but went along. Alberta continued to worry about the future of Senate reform.

If Quebec was received skeptically by Alberta, it was greeted coolly by British Columbia. "When Rémillard came around with his points, he didn't get a very good reception here," remembers Mel Smith. "In the initial stages, Quebec's five points were for the special advantage of Quebec. Quebec must have this immigration power, Quebec must have three judges on the court. Quebec this, Quebec that." As had Alberta, Smith argued that the patriation package had embraced the concept of the equality of provinces. In other words, it was not enough to talk just about Quebec. What it got, Smith argued, everyone must get. Early in the game, British Columbia was planting a seed that would flower at Meech Lake. "I thought any package from Quebec was not salable unless the rights set out were also available to the other provinces," Smith said. "If Quebec wants more powers over immigration, the other provinces should have them. If Quebec wants three judges on the Supreme Court, there ought to be a role for the other provinces."

Other provinces had raised this point on one issue or another, though perhaps not as directly as had British Columbia. They all knew that it was no longer enough — if it ever had been — to deal solely with Quebec's agenda. They did not necessarily want to discuss new areas, though they were not opposed to that. Rather, they wanted to address Quebec's conditions in light of how they would affect the other provinces. At the least, they wanted to reinterpret the Edmonton Declaration. At the most, they were in wholesale retreat. But there was no doubt, only a few weeks into the talks, that the provinces were staking their claims to new power and influence. By invoking the equality of the provinces, the premiers meant to get a little something, if only a little something, for themselves. It was as innocuous as the greedy, bawdy innkeeper in *Les Misérables,* who sings: "Here a little cut, here a little slice." Whether they wanted it or whether they went along with it, the other provinces would profit from the reconciliation of Quebec.

If "equality of the provinces" was a rallying cry, it was also a justification for the devolution of more power. Alan Cairns, who was at Mont Gabriel, says this process defines the accord. "Overall, the Meech Lake constitutional outcome is best characterized as a provincializing round," he writes. "The role of the Quebec government was to set the terms for the enhancement of the powers of all the provinces. This outcome was rationalized in terms of the principle of the equality of the provinces. This principle, however, was elaborated and strengthened in the very process of bargaining which produced Meech Lake."

How the Quebec Round became the Provincial Round is one of the curiosities of the Meech Lake Accord. No premier came out and cried, "We want more!" Some denied they ever wanted new powers. It would be easy to suspect a conspiracy among the provinces to enrich themselves but there is no evidence of that. It just seemed to happen, via a *deus ex machina.* Despite what the premiers said in Edmonton, it was always assumed that Quebec would have to address their interests when it addressed its own. If Quebec asked for another power, the provinces had to know its effect on them. If the impact was substantial, they argued they should have to have it, too. So accepted was this, so naturally did it flow from the discussion, that there seemed nothing unusual in it.

The talks, then, continued into November, December, January. The Quebeckers, now in teams of two, returned to the provincial capitals with revised proposals. The message the provinces gave them was to clarify and define their conditions. That Quebec was still proceeding was considered good; it meant the willingness to compromise was there, even though the compromising was being done in private, and Quebec would get little credit for it later. When the premiers and the prime minister met in Vancouver in November for their annual conference on the economy, Bourassa wanted a statement issued in support of the process. The other premiers shrugged and agreed. "Privately, there was a hell of a lot of drafting over what to say about the constitutional process," recalls Lowell Murray. "There was a lot of scrambling." Quebec wanted to reaffirm the Edmonton Declaration, with the prime minister now adding his support. A short statement — though still longer than the grandiloquent Edmonton Declaration — was issued on 21 November 1986. It said that the premiers were satisfied with the process and the "important progress towards a better understanding" of Quebec's proposals that had been achieved since Edmonton. It said the talks should continue, and the contacts should be "intensified and expanded in order to evaluate more fully the chances of success in eventual formal negotiations." It reasserted the premiers' hope that they would reach an agreement to bring in Quebec, and then would talk about Senate reform, the fishery and property rights.

No call to arms, but enough to satisfy Quebec. If no one paid much attention, it was not hard to see why. As a progress report, the statement seemed to reflect as much movement as the annual retreat of the Athabasca Glacier. Making progress towards "a better understanding" and evaluating the chances of "eventual formal negotiations" suggested nothing was happening. It is possible this statement genuinely reflected the state of negotiations in November. More probably, it was a subtle attempt to confirm the usefulness of the effort while trying not to arouse too much interest in it. Everyone knew that the whole exercise, this Quebec Round, was not terribly popular in some parts of the country, particularly the West. Of course, that assumed people knew and cared. Canadians were talking about free trade and softwood lumber that November. The constitution was far from the public mind and the premiers and the prime minister were content to keep it that way.

The Vancouver meeting formally brought Brian Mulroney into the process. Because he had not attended the meeting in Edmonton, which launched the Quebec Round, the negotiations might have

looked like solely a provincial exercise. Of course, he had been following every step closely. The constitutional question was high on
Mulroney's agenda in 1986. National reconciliation and a free-trade
agreement with the United States were the pillars of his program. At
mid-term, his government slowed by scandal and falling popularity,
he badly wanted a deal with Quebec.

The constitution question had never been a passion for Martin
Brian Mulroney. Still, as a Quebecker, born in Baie Comeau in 1939,
he knew the issue was always there. For anyone who had grown up
on the north shore of the St. Lawrence River, attended Laval University and lived in Montreal, the constitutional question was a part of
life. The reconciliation of the races and the place of Quebec were top-
ics of everyday conversation, as much as the weather or the Montreal
Canadiens. "When I attended law school, much of every working
day was spent discussing the constitution," Mulroney remembers. It
was at Laval that Mulroney was identified with the constitution,
however marginally. In the early 1960s, he and his classmates —
among them Lucien Bouchard, Pierre de Bané, André Ouellet,
Clément Richard, all future politicians in Quebec and Ottawa — organized a conference called "The Canadian Experiment: Success or
Failure" at which Mulroney chaired a panel discussion.

Mulroney was one of six children, the son of an electrician. He
studied at St. Francis Xavier University in Nova Scotia, and spent a
year at Dalhousie Law Schoool. (Clyde Wells was there at the same
time.) After Laval he went to Montreal, where he joined the law firm
of Howard, Cate, Ogilvy in 1964. He practised law, particularly
labour law, and in 1974 was appointed to the Cliche Royal Commission, which investigated violence in Quebec's construction industry.
The commission gave him exposure and helped launch his unsuccess-
ful bid for the party leadership in 1976. He came second on the first
ballot, then his support evaporated. It is said that he took his defeat
badly. He returned to Montreal and became president of the Iron Ore
Company of Canada.

Politics had been a passion for him since he was a child. At age
twelve, he told friends that he wanted to be prime minister and spent
the rest of his life pursuing it. He made his debut as a Tory as elected
whip of the campus Conservatives at St. Francis Xavier in 1955. He
later headed Youth for Diefenbaker, worked for former minister of
agriculture Alvin Hamilton, and served on numerous party committees and fundraising campaigns. He refused to run for office until

1983, after he won the leadership. In fact, when the first ministers gathered at Meech Lake, he had the least legislative experience of anyone at the table.

It was during this period — before and during his leadership campaign — that Mulroney began to articulate a view of constitutional reform. In the early 1980s, if his speeches are any guide, he was a federalist in the Trudeau mold. He stood for a strong federal government; he would not deal with René Lévesque or the separatists. In *Where I Stand,* he asserts that the federal government must ensure the equality of services and opportunities, preserve the security and integrity of the nation, and foster the enjoyment of freedoms. The provinces could handle other matters. He wrote: "The dominant feature of our ongoing constitutional negotiation reflects . . . the philosophy of the late Samuel Gompers, one of America's first labour leaders. When asked what he wanted, he said, 'More, more, always more.' There is only so much to go around; there is only so much authority that can be diluted or transferred before the strength of the nation begins to ebb away." Mulroney thus put distance between himself and Joe Clark's community of communities, or Robert Stanfield's deux nations. "In any discussion of constitutional reform, I start from the premise of an indivisible Canada," he said. "The word is clear. It means the same in English as it does in French. I do not believe in the theory of two nations, five nations, or ten nations."

Despite such ringing statements, no one ever accused Mulroney of being ideological or intellectual. During the leadership race in 1983, he wrote the nine points of his constitutional position "on the back of a Quebecair barf bag" somewhere between Trois-Rivières and Rivière-du-Loup. His position on this and other matters was not fixed. Above all he was a pragmatist — a negotiator, a fixer, a broker, a mediator. He used the language of the gambler before he was in politics to describe constitutional bargaining, and he used it after he became prime minister in his approach to nation-building.

By the election campaign in 1984, Mulroney had already reversed himself; after saying he would not give René Lévesque "a plugged nickel," he was prepared to open negotiations with him. When John Turner said that he would await a new government, an irate Mulroney chastised him for his "nerve" in rejecting talks with "the duly elected, legitimate government of Quebec." Of course, everyone knew that Mulroney would rather negotiate with his old friend, Robert Bourassa. But he was quick to see an electoral advantage in appealing to the Parti Québécois vote. No one could ever say that Brian Mulroney did not recognize opportunity. In the end, on the constitution, he would do what was necessary to get a deal.

Behind Mulroney, co-ordinating and choreographing the constitutional *pas de dix,* was a team of seasoned federal officials. Lowell Murray, the soft-spoken, self-effacing Nova Scotian, was the lead minister. Appointed to the Senate in 1979 by Joe Clark, with whom he shared some mannerisms, Murray was astute and assiduous. Allan Gregg, the Tory pollster, called him the smartest man in the government. Born in Nova Scotia, Murray was educated at St. Francis Xavier and Queen's universities, and spent a career in the front and back rooms of Canadian politics. He worked as a chief of staff to former minister of justice Davie Fulton and executive assistant to Robert Stanfield, when the latter was opposition leader. He had also been a deputy-minister to Richard Hatfield in New Brunswick. The constant in his career was a loyalty to the Conservative party, and the Senate was his reward. Fluently bilingual, he knew Quebec and felt its isolation keenly. Hatfield remembers running into Murray outside the Government Conference Centre that day in November 1981 when Quebec was left out. "He was absolutely outraged with me," Hatfield recalls. "He said, 'The day will come when you regret this.' It was said with something close to hatred." Although Murray had been a university classmate of Mulroney's and an usher at his wedding, their relationship cooled after Murray refused to support Mulroney for the leadership in 1976. But, in 1986, with the party in government, that no longer mattered. When Mulroney was looking for a minister to spearhead the constitutional talks that spring, he looked to Murray. Here was someone who understood Quebec, who had credibility elsewhere and who did not sit in the House of Commons, where he would be exposed to Question Period. More than anything else, Murray understood Mulroney. "Mulroney's prerogatives here [on the constitution] are more primus than anywhere else," he said in 1989. "The advantage I bring is that I know where he stands as an individual. We've been friends for thirty years. I don't have to run every week to see what he might think about something. I know it in my head, in my gut, where he will come down on most things."

The other major federal player was Norman Spector, secretary to the cabinet for federal-provincial relations and deputy-clerk of the

Privy Council. Spector, like Murray, had been recruited for this task.
A Montrealer by birth, Spector had studied at McGill and Syracuse
and had completed a doctorate in communications at Columbia. He
lectured at the University of Ottawa, and worked for the governments of Ontario and British Columbia, serving in the last four years
before his appointment to Ottawa as deputy-minister to Bill Bennett.
A large, hawk-eyed presence with a balding dome, Spector was described as sharp, acerbic and able. Most important, Spector was
known and trusted in the provinces; he was not a part of the Ottawa
establishment. His appointment fit nicely with Ottawa's larger strategy in 1985 and 1986 to court the premiers. In hiring Spector, Ottawa
was hiring one of the provinces' own. He was different from Michael
Kirby, who had orchestrated the previous round of constitutional negotiations and had gained notoriety for his famous memo proposing
to divide the provinces. That notwithstanding, Professor Ron Watts
of Queen's says Kirby's style was more collegial. "Spector plays it
much closer to the chest," he says. "It's much harder with Spector to
know exactly. He keeps the strategy to himself. There isn't the personal warmth there. He is a little bit more aloof. He may not be a
good diplomat but he is a superb choreographer."

The other key members of the federal team included Bernard Roy,
the prime minister's chief of staff, who dealt with Bourassa and
Rémillard when they did not want to bother Mulroney; Frank
Iacobucci, the deputy-minister of justice; and later, Roger Tassé,
Iacobucci's predecessor, who had left the government for private
practice. Senator Arthur Tremblay, a constitutional expert, was also
consulted. Murray chaired an advisory cabinet committee, which included John Crosbie, Ray Hnatyshyn, Jake Epp, Jean Charest and
Marcel Masse. As Murray explains it, the challenge for Ottawa in the
early stages was simply to keep the talks going. Once the premiers
had committed themselves to the process, their involvement had to
be nurtured. "We were exploring very discreetly to see if the PM,
with any prospect of success, could call a first ministers' conference to
crunch the issue," he says. "I had no idea. We knew we would have
to close the book at some place if Quebec's demands ran up against a
brick wall." A little before Christmas, Murray met Roland Penner of
Manitoba and Ian Scott of Ontario on consecutive days in Ottawa.
They had concerns, but not enough to kill the process; Murray was
impressed that they were suggesting solutions. The same was true for
Alberta, Saskatchewan and Nova Scotia. Officials from those prov-

inces told Murray that the constitution would not sell wheat or fish, but they knew it was important to Mulroney and agreed to go along.

Meanwhile, Rémillard was drawing his own conclusions. He was running into stormy weather in British Columbia, but nothing strong enough to blow the talks off course. Most of the questions were on the distinct society, or, more specifically, linguistic duality. A common question was the impact on individual provinces. Typically, the premiers would ask: "What obligation does this impose on me, the premier of Nova Scotia or Saskatchewan? Does it mean that I have to do more than I want to do or than I already have to do under the Charter?" Other reactions were immediately clear. Alternating English and French chief justices on the Supreme Court was unacceptable. The veto for Quebec alone was a problem. Would it be a veto over everything, or just some items?

Murray was hearing the same things Rémillard was, and he began to think a deal was possible. There was still no paper on the table. "The officials were scribbling away, but neither Rémillard nor I was operating in that context. We didn't want leaks or bottom lines. All that would have done is constrict the negotiations." For Murray, it was imperative to keep this away from the technical. He did not want to discuss a legal text until the political issues had been resolved. Whenever a province asked for a full ministerial meeting, he demurred. They wanted to get everyone into a room and go at it, the traditional way of negotiation, and Murray balked. He did not want this to become a fight among lawyers. Just before Christmas, he and Spector visited Mulroney at 24 Sussex Drive. Their report was positive. "We knew it was worth pursuing. It was far from dead. What persuaded me was the political will was there."

This kind of private, isolated negotiation was different from that during the last round. The decision had been taken early not to replicate the way it was done in 1980. That round had largely been shaped by officials, particularly in the summer of 1980. When the premiers stepped in, it fell apart. That would not happen this time. Of course, there would be a price: private talks helped seal the deal but made it hard to sell. Roland Penner, whose government signed the accord, said the extent of Manitoba's involvement was his meeting with Rémillard and his officials, his meeting with Rémillard alone, and one ministerial meeting with the promise of more. "The process was dictated more by the imperative of electoral politics than by any vision of Canada's constitutional life to meet the needs of the last part of the

twentieth century," he said in 1989. "Don't tell me about public discussions. The difficulty with Meech Lake was that there were none."

By the spring of 1987, Murray's deadline was approaching. A decision had to be made to call these informal bilateral talks a failure or to
summon the premiers to a meeting to go the next step. To evaluate
the progress of the negotiations, the federal government called a two-
day meeting of federal-provincial officials in Ottawa on 5 and 6
March. After months of intergovernmental talks, all eleven governments would, for the first time, discuss the five conditions at the
same time, in the same place. There was still no working text. Murray wanted officials to talk about principles, much the same way the
first ministers would talk about principles at Meech Lake, leaving the
legal wording for later.

There had been some progress. Quebec had agreed to entrench existing agreements on immigration, had narrowed its demands on limiting federal spending power and had consented to extend more
power to all provinces in choosing justices to the Supreme Court. It
had already modified its demand for a veto; after Edmonton, it had
talked about approving most amendments to the constitution with
the formula of seven provinces making up 75 percent of the population rather than the existing formula of seven with 50 percent of the
population. (The revised formula would give a veto to Quebec and
Ontario, each of which had more than 25 percent of the population,
and to the western provinces and eastern provinces combined. Quebec would be recognized in perpetuity as having 25 percent even if it
dropped below that.) But British Columbia was still uncomfortable
about the whole process. "I felt frustrated," said Mel Smith. "I
thought we'd sold the store at Edmonton." The province accepted
Quebec's suggestions on spending power, immigration and the Supreme Court, but it opposed the distinct society and the notion of duality. Murray was exasperated. "Even on the conceptual level, I had
trouble with them," he remembers. "They were trying to wrap up
linguistic duality into multiculturalism. You wondered how we were
going to get these people on the same wavelength as other governments." After the officials' meeting, however, Smith was promoted
to deputy provincial secretary. With him gone, federal officials found
British Columbia more accommodating.

The meeting in early March went badly. Afterwards, an Ontario
adviser thought the initiative was dead. "If it stays like this," he

thought, "it is going nowhere." The impasse led many to think that informal talks would continue indefinitely. But, less than a fortnight later, Mulroney decided to convene the first ministers. He was willing to take the next step, whatever the progress of the private negotiations. The invitation to lunch came as a surprise but was worded so casually as to seem unimportant. "In my view, ministers and officials have progressed as far as they can without a further review of the issue by First Ministers," he telexed the premiers on 17 March 1987. "I have concluded that, as another step in our informal process, First Ministers should take stock of the progress already made and consider next steps. I therefore invite you to a private meeting of First Ministers on Thursday, April 30, 1987, at Willson House, Meech Lake. Our discussions would begin over lunch, starting at 12:30 p.m., and continue into the afternoon."

A luncheon by the lake. A stock-taking. A chat. A review. Another step in the informal process. In the middle of March, after a long season of negotiations, it was as simple as that. It could have been an invitation to the annual meeting of the Philately Society of Oak Bay. Who could have suspected anything serious would happen? One couldn't blame those premiers who dismissed the telex from the prime minister. After all, this was a private discussion among friends at a lakeside lodge, not a full-dress federal-provincial conference.

Thus ended nine months of private talks between Quebec and the provinces, between Quebec and Ottawa, and among the provinces themselves. From the time the premiers left Edmonton in August and arrived at Meech Lake in April, the five proposals had been explained, expanded, recast, reduced. Even then, after this exhaustive exercise in honing and refining, most premiers were not optimistic about reaching agreement. If anything, their doubts showed that changing a constitution was difficult in Canada, even under the best of circumstances. Here were historically moderate demands, limited in number, that had been proposed in whole or in part before. Here were a federalist Quebec, an accommodating federal government and nine provinces that accepted Quebec's agenda. Here was a favourable political climate, an abiding goodwill and a rare chemistry among the first ministers. Despite all this, the agreement at Meech Lake was still largely a surprise.

Canada's constitutional past suggested the process would be fitful, so it was not terribly surprising that the accord nearly came apart five weeks later at Langevin, just as the Victoria Charter had come apart in 1971. The premiers argued that the climate and players at Meech Lake were different, but history implied that their declarations of a new era were premature. The inevitable was already taking shape. When the accord began disintegrating three years later, throwing the country into a crisis of self-doubt, the constitutional universe of Canada was simply unfolding much as it always had.

Daylight at Langevin

THE FIRST MINISTERS LEFT MEECH LAKE THAT LAST DAY OF APRIL, IN-
toxicated by their success. They had reached unanimous agreement
on fundamental constitutional reform more quickly and more easily
than anyone had expected. No wonder euphoria greeted the accord
the first week of May. Public opinion was favourable. The federal
government supported the deal, the provinces supported it, the Liberals and Conservatives supported it. So did most of the provincial
opposition parties. The chorus of approval was resounding.

John Turner and Ed Broadbent offered endorsements quickly, too
quickly it seemed, to those who thought both leaders were trying too
hard to curry favour in Quebec. Even orthodox federalists cheered
Meech Lake. Senator Eugene Forsey, most notably, quickly offered
Mulroney his congratulations. The blessing of a former Liberal senator, particularly one who championed the Trudeau vision, pleased
the prime minister, who proudly showed Forsey's letter to Howard
Pawley. In those early days, there was hardly a prominent politician
in the land who opposed the accord.

That soon changed. Within a fortnight, critics in all three parties
began to speak up. Tony Penikett, the government leader of the Yukon, railed over the exclusion of the North. Donald Johnston and
Charles Caccia of the Liberals, Pat Nowlan of Conservatives and Ian
Waddell of the New Democrats protested in and out of caucus. Historians Ramsay Cook, Michael Bliss and Jack Granatstein brought
their sense of the country's past to the accord and declared it a tearing
of the national fabric. The opposition Conservatives in Ontario, and
Liberals in New Brunswick, Nova Scotia and Newfoundland attacked the accord. The Parti Québécois called it a sell-out. Franco-

phones outside Quebec, and representatives of women, native people, northerners and ethnic Canadians expressed their anger. Finally, in the most dramatic intervention of this period, Pierre Trudeau broke three years of silence and excoriated the accord in a searing polemic in the country's newspapers. He called Mulroney "a weakling" and said Canada was destined to be governed by "snivellers" and "eunuchs."

Still, this opposition to the Meech Lake Accord was relatively undeveloped in the early days. "Intellectually, there was a tremendous amount of criticism," says Michael Bliss. "It had no political significance then, but you knew you were right to question the accord. It was an unsound document." The general public saw the constitution as an elitist issue, best left to the first ministers and a phalanx of scholars and lawyers. It was said that no more than two hundred people in Canada knew much about the constitution, and it was probably true. Certainly the first ministers understood that and played on it. A quick and easy resolution of this issue was in their interest. While none would admit it, each understood Pierre Trudeau's advice at the closing session of the Patriation Round in 1981. "We better take this and run before anyone changes his mind," he warned. Perhaps they sensed the lesson they would learn later: the more that Canadians knew about the accord, the more they would doubt the claims of its architects.

By 2 June, when the first ministers gathered in Ottawa to sign the deal, the premiers were unmoved by the ripples of opposition. The North was too small to matter. The Johnstons, Waddells and Nowlans were cranky malcontents. The Parti Québécois would never sign any constitution. Traditional federalists would always resent limits on federal power. Women and native people were mere interest groups. Trudeau was irretrievably Trudeau, beyond fear or favour. Still, some of the premiers were feeling the heat. In Ontario, Trudeau Liberals, provincial Tories, women and multicultural groups were asking David Peterson to ensure the distinct society would not overrule the Charter of Rights. In Manitoba, New Democrats were urging Howard Pawley to ensure that the spending-power condition would not prevent the federal government from launching new programs.

It was always assumed that there would be a meeting after Meech Lake to approve the legal text of the document. The accord itself was a statement of principles, not a constitutional amendment. The challenge was to draft a text that would become part of the constitution.

After Meech Lake, this next stage seemed like a formality — "a piece of cake," as Professor Peter Hogg saw it. But the legal drafting was absolutely critical. What was written in it would endure for years. It would be etched in stone. The words and phrases would inspire citizens, influence lawmakers and guide judges in interpreting the law. This was not just a matter of dotting "i's" and crossing "t's." The product of ten hours of haggling and philosophizing and compromising among the premiers had to be cast in legal language. The ambiguities had to be clarified, or at least appear to be clarified, and most of the drafting had to be done by provincial officials who had not been at the table at Meech Lake. "The difficulty later was that no one had sat in the room, listening to all the compromises that went into the words which represented the principles," says an Ontario official. "We had to translate them into constitutional language. Later on, every government wanted to refight the battle that the premier had fought in the room. If eleven people were going to agree on five words at Meech Lake, they probably started with twenty-five words. There was a hell of a lot of compromise. Now you ask someone else to turn those five words into beautiful sculpture. We could only try to shape the clay in a way we thought our guy really wanted."

Predictably, the meetings held to draft a text were sometimes acrimonious. Manitoba was particularly insistent on strengthening the spending power. One of its legal advisers, Bryan Schwartz, a brilliant, rumpled wunderkind who taught law at the University of Manitoba, clashed often with other provincial officials. He was troubled by their quiescence. When he asked one of his counterparts about her premier's position, she replied: "What am I supposed to do, tell [the premier] he fucked up at Meech Lake?" The last meeting in Ottawa, ostensibly to finalize the draft, began on a Friday afternoon, broke late at night, reconvened the next day and went until midafternoon. "It was all a matter of getting the right words," says the Ontario official. "If you had six different views, you would reconcile five and not the sixth. When you got the last, you might lose others." The minions did lose the others, lots of others. But their labours did produce a text with the contentious parts in brackets. Now, in the early days of June, it would be up to the first ministers to resolve the remaining problems.

The first ministers were to meet in Ottawa, approve the text and sign the accord in a nationally televised ceremony at the Government Conference Centre. The meeting was initially scheduled for eleven o'clock in the morning. The premiers were to approve the legal text before gathering across the street. They expected to be out by early afternoon. They did not emerge until dawn the next day, nineteen hours later. The only concession federal officials made to the storm signals before the meeting — suggestions that it might take longer than they thought — was to advance the session an hour so it began at ten o'clock.

This time the venue was not a lakeside retreat but a downtown office building. The meeting was held at the Langevin Block, an eclectic mix of architectural styles on Wellington Street. To the north, the building faces the green, gentle slope of Parliament Hill, to the south the Sparks Street Mall. It dominates the block between Metcalfe Street and Confederation Square. The building — on the nameplate it is called a "block" — accommodates the Prime Minister's Office and the Privy Council Office. Built in the late nineteenth century, it was named after Hector Louis Langevin, a journalist who represented Quebec at the Confederation Conference in Charlottetown in 1864. Langevin, a Father of Confederation, served as minister of public works in Sir John A. Macdonald's cabinet. He was later implicated in the Pacific Scandal and left Ottawa in disgrace. Why the glorious pile retained his name is not known. Critics who saw only ill in this historic meeting would mutter that the building now commemorated not only an ignominious Canadian but an inglorious event. Be that as it may, in this theatre of the absurd, the meeting at Langevin would be first among sequels.

There was never any doubt that the second session would be held in Ottawa; the rustic intimacy of Willson House could not hold the legion of advisers the premiers would bring with them this time. Not everyone made it to the Langevin Block. Some remained across the street, in the Conference Centre. Others camped out in provincial offices which had sprung up in the capital like foreign embassies. They were in touch by facsimile machine and cellular telephone. Meanwhile, top advisers took up positions on the fourth floor, down the hall from the boardroom where the premiers would meet. Delegations commandeered offices usually used by the Privy Council. For the next nineteen hours, this was where delegations would caucus with their premiers during recesses in the talks.

Room 414 North is cavernous and rectangular, with high-set windows facing north. The walls are an institutional brown chosen from the School of Brutalism. Sparsely furnished, it has a clock on one wall that looks like a special at Canadian Tire. The room is usually used for smaller gatherings of ministers or officials. As they did at Meech Lake, the premiers sat in order of precedence. The oval, maple table was littered with paper, water glasses and microphones for translation, which was provided by interpreters in a glass booth. (Translation was rarely used. Bourassa usually spoke in English, except when dealing with more complex questions with Mulroney.) Again, Norman Spector, the head of federal-provincial relations, and Oryssia Lennie, an assistant deputy-minister from Alberta, were the only two officials present. Again, no formal minutes were kept.

The tone would be different here. It was time to make decisions. Precision would concentrate the mind. The legal text would tolerate less vagueness. Huey Long, the white-suited demagogue of the American South, advised revealing as little as possible in making important decisions. Glance rather than stare, stare rather than wink, wink rather than nod, nod rather than whisper, whisper rather than speak, speak rather than write. No doubt many wanted to frame the constitution that way. Ambiguity meant flexibility. It allowed the drafters to avoid fixed positions. Making hard decisions meant a flaring of tempers, a clash of wills and, ideally, a meeting of minds.

Mulroney opened the meeting with a few remarks. "Gentlemen, thank you all for coming," he began. "It's been an extremely difficult time but we've made much progress at Meech Lake. As you know, since then, a lot of people have been criticizing us. One is the former prime minister, Pierre Trudeau. He still thinks he is governing this country." Before him were newspaper clippings and sheets of paper. Mulroney then began to quote from the newspapers. *Le Devoir* says this, *The Gazette* says that. Quebec is exuberant, he said. Canadians like Meech Lake. So do the opposition parties. Mulroney seemed worried that support among the premiers might have been eroded by the recent attacks. For a quarter hour, perhaps longer, he read, shuffled, grimaced, gesticulated. The glasses came on and off, the forefinger slashed the air.

"No one seems to know this," said Joe Ghiz later, his voice dropping with a touch of the theatrical. "But there was another man in the room that day. We talked about him quite a bit. He was there. He was there in spirit. He was Pierre Trudeau." Ghiz said the prime minister could not let go of the former prime minister. It was as if he were exorcising a ghost. As Ghiz says, "He went up one side of him and down the other!" Mulroney rejected Trudeau's arguments and

attacked his credibility. It was clear that Mulroney, who had once admired Trudeau, had been stung by his frontal attack the week before.
Ghiz was uneasy. "It was beginning to grate on me," he said later.
"Who cares?" Others also wondered about the point of it all. Trudeau had not changed their minds. Still, Mulroney continued the
shadowboxing until Richard Hatfield interrupted. "Look," Hatfield
said, "will you forget about him!"

If Mulroney had been concerned that Trudeau had persuaded the
premiers to change their minds, he need not have worried. In the
course of the discussion, John Buchanan vowed, "I won't be called a
snivelling eunuch!" Buchanan remembered the animosity of the past,
as did Peckford and Bourassa. They detested Trudeau and could
hardly be swayed by him. "Trudeau's attack had no effect on me,"
recalls Hatfield. "I understood it. It was based more on personality
than principle." If it left Ghiz and Hatfield unmoved, it probably
stiffened the resolve of Getty, Devine and Vander Zalm. The subject
had come up at the annual meeting of the western premiers in May.
Whatever Trudeau's objections, the West would not waver.

When the first ministers finally got down to business, they moved
quickly through most items on the agenda. The sections on immigration, the Supreme Court and the Senate were approved in about two
hours. The wording here was not a problem. Some changes — such
as ensuring the Charter of Rights applied to the immigration sections
— had been made at the officials' meetings. On most matters, there
was little change between the principles enunciated at Meech Lake
and the legal amendments written at Langevin. The meeting was
really about the distinct society and the spending power. "We didn't
discuss five items at Langevin, we discussed two," Ghiz said. "For
nineteen hours, we went over and over them." The two became an
issue because Ontario and Manitoba wanted changes. Peterson argued for a tougher clause on the distinct society. He worried that it
might be used to override minority rights. Pawley pushed for
tougher limits on the right of provinces to opt out of federal programs. He argued that the guarantees of the federal government's
right to spend were not strong enough. The other premiers, for the
most part, saw no great difficulty with either. The prime minister
acted as mediator more than advocate.

No one knew what to do about the distinct society. Most of the
premiers thought that it posed no threat to the Charter of Rights.
Even if it did, Getty, Vander Zalm and Devine probably did not care,

since they had no great respect for the charter as a vehicle of social change. Peterson, on the other hand, was under pressure from groups who were worried that the Charter was being undermined. He was facing an election within months and did not want to alienate his constituency. To clarify or not to clarify? "I think it had to be ambiguous," recalls one of Peterson's officials. "The court would balance it."

As he went into the boardroom, Peterson was advised by his delegation to consult more regularly than he had at Meech Lake, where the premiers were closeted for most of the session. "With each proposal, stop, and come out and let's discuss it," he was told. "Don't wait five hours and come out with five different things that we have one hour to discuss." This way Ontario could argue its points more effectively. Peterson was under pressure from Ian Scott, his attorney general, who was the first to corner him whenever he came out. Scott was most concerned about the Charter. If it could not be protected, and he was not sure it could, he thought the deal would collapse. Each time Peterson emerged, Scott and others ensured he was asking the right questions. Peterson was up to the task. He was trained as a lawyer — though he had never practised law — and he understood the arguments. Unlike some of his colleagues, he could carry this alone. In the end, he would have to.

The other premiers were also in and out of the room often. A battery of officials was next door, sitting in an adjoining room, around another large oval table. The rest were in offices down the hall. The premiers came and went, their officials dutifully rushing to greet them for news from the front. Some premiers relied on their bureaucrats, some did not. At one point Richard Hatfield walked out and threw the latest draft at his officials. "There," he told them. "Amuse yourselves!" For some premiers, Langevin became an endurance test. "We were out to the bathroom a lot," remembers Peckford with some pride. "I went to the bathroom the least. The officials would ask me: 'What do you have for a bladder?'"

At about two o'clock in the morning, Bourassa complained that he was tired of hearing Peterson refer to the arguments of his experts. Let them speak for themselves, he suggested. "Bourassa raised himself up to a height he had never raised himself to before," Hatfield remembers. "He said, 'Who are these people? Bring them in here!'" A few minutes later, four advisers from Ontario entered the sanctum sanctorum. In addition to Ian Scott, there was Patrick Monaghan, his policy adviser; Ian McGilp, a constitutional lawyer; and Peter Hogg, one of the country's leading constitutional experts. In making his argument, Scott chose a hypothetical case: the restriction of the linguistic rights of the English minority in Quebec. In the event of a court challenge, he asked, which would take precedence: the collective rights of Quebec, through the distinct society, or the individual rights of the anglophones, under the Charter? Bourassa questioned the example. "And what is the interest of an elected Ontario politician in the language dispute in Quebec?" he asked. His tone was polite and restrained, but, as one of the Ontarians put it, the subtext was, "Who do you think we are, a bunch of animals? Why would you accuse us of oppressive legislation?" Scott was taken aback; he told colleagues later that, if this view were right, there was more of a problem than he thought. It had not occurred to him that Ontario could not raise the rights of a linguistic minority in constitutional talks. A moment later, Hatfield interjected: "It's none of our business."

Frank Iacobucci, the deputy-minister of justice, and Roger Tassé, the former deputy-minister of justice, were in the room when the Ontario quartet appeared. Iacobucci, in particular, contradicted Scott's position, and so did Tassé. Then Hogg added that he, too, did not share Scott's concerns. Some suggest that the document might have been different had Hogg objected more strongly. In the eyes of the other premiers, he was more credible than Scott because they considered Scott more a politician than a lawyer. Although he knew constitutional law, the attorney general was discredited as an advocate; he wanted stronger wording. The premiers, though, thought his example poorly chosen. "They were defensive for Bourassa," said an Ontario official. "It would have better received if he could have referred to an English province." Of course, because the distinct society would apply in only Quebec, there was no other example. Months later, Quebec officials bristled over the incident. Bourassa, for his part, was not upset. He remained cool, antiseptic and restrained, as he did throughout the session.

Peterson, plagued by doubt and steeled by Scott, continued to push for a clause guaranteeing the supremacy of the Charter. He got only Section 16, what Hogg calls "a cautionary provision," which safeguarded aboriginal and multicultural rights. Some premiers were so sensitive about making reference to aboriginal rights by name that they insisted this section refer to other sections of the constitution only by number. Be that as it was, the idea was to show ethnic communities that recognizing Quebec's distinct society was not inconsistent with the protection of other groups. Critics later called the section inadequate. Peterson knew that, but needed it for political purposes; he had to show his constituencies he was safeguarding their interests. As one Saskatchewan official told Grant Devine, Peterson had to look after "his ethnics in Toronto."

The premiers called on independent legal advice more than once that night, which made federal officials uneasy. The meeting was like a trial to the officials; they did not want questions asked to which they did not know the answers. If the experts cast doubt on the meaning of the distinct society, if they argued that it would mean special legislative powers for Quebec, the consensus would dissolve. The premiers, almost all of whom were against any idea of special status — a contradiction of the "equality of the provinces" they held so dear — would then reverse their support. It was a risk Mulroney thought worth taking. And so another battery of talent was ushered in. There was Hogg, making his first visit; Frank Iacobucci and Roger Tassé, and André Tremblay, a professor of law at University of Montreal. The experts' diversity of opinion enhanced their credibility. Tremblay was one of Bourassa's leading advisers and had been involved since Mont Gabriel. Tassé was a former deputy-minister of justice and a confidant of Jean Chrétien; Hogg was an esteemed scholar retained by Ontario; Iacobucci represented the federal government.

One senior official later described this mid-evening meeting as "the big bang," a turning point in persuading most of the premiers in the debate over the distinct society. All the experts agreed that the distinct society would not confer any new authority on Quebec. Hogg argued that it could mean an advance for the province "on the margins" but would not mean "a radical accretion of power." The advice was important; the skeptical premiers were won over. But that did not make Ontario happy, and it kept asking for changes. It eventually succeeded in adding a protective clause in Section 1 that said that nothing in the distinct-society clause "derogates from the powers, rights or privileges" of Parliament or the provinces. That meant that the recognition of the distinct society would not take powers away from either the central government or the provinces. It would not take away anything from Parliament, the argument went, nor would it give Quebec new powers, because they could come only from Parliament.

That wording was not enough for Peterson and Scott. They still worried that Quebec could use the distinct-society clause to add new authority to areas shared by both governments, such as communications, foreign poicy or banking. While the first ministers were talking, Peterson and Scott dispatched Ian McGilp and Patrick Monaghan to meet André Tremblay and Diane Wilhelmy to talk about strengthening the clause. The Quebeckers did not think the distinct society clause conferred new power. Said McGilp: "If that's so, let's say so." He and Monaghan suggested using the word "alter" instead of "derogate from." They pushed the wording so hard that the two Ontarians became known as the "Alter Boys." Tremblay and Wilhelmy accepted the wording and took it back to Rémillard and Bourassa. Within minutes, an answer came back: there would be no change. Quebec would preserve the ambiguity of the distinct society.

The distinct society was not the only issue the first ministers debated. At the same time, they wrangled over the translation into legal language of the provision on spending power. At Meech Lake, they had agreed that a province would get compensation "in a future national shared cost program in an area of exclusive provincial jurisdiction if that province undertakes its own initiative on programs compatible with national objectives." But Howard Pawley — and the federal New Democratic Party — were uncomfortable with that wording. In a conversation with Mulroney after Meech Lake, Ed Broadbent proposed adding the definite article "the" before "national objectives." Mulroney agreed. The clarification was Broadbent's contribution to nation-building.

But the wording still displeased Pawley. He complained that it was too vague; it did not say who established either the program or the objectives. There had been talk in some quarters about changing "compatible" to "equivalent," and "objectives" to "standards." Both would strengthen the power of the federal government. Pawley did not suggest those changes per se, at the table, but his lingering doubts reflected the classic clash between clarity and ambiguity in this exercise. Pawley, like Peterson on the distinct society, wanted to leave no doubt about what the clause meant. Bourassa and other premiers saw safety — they called it manoeuvrability — in ambiguity.

In the weeks after Meech Lake, Pawley spoke to Broadbent often and told him he was worried that the wording was too loose. "You should be on guard," he warned Broadbent the day before he left for Ottawa. "There is a good chance I will walk out." Broadbent, whose party was supporting the accord, implored Pawley not to sabotage the deal. The two were friends who disagreed profoundly. "You know if Manitoba walks out and blows this thing up, it isn't just Manitoba that is going to be blamed for this," Pawley recalls Broadbent saying. "I'm going to be carrying that yoke around my neck because you're the only NDP premier in the country."

Meanwhile, Pawley's two legal advisers were unable to agree. Whenever he left the boardroom, Pawley had to referee loud, long arguments between Bryan Schwartz and Stuart Whitley, a senior official in the Department of Justice. Pawley recalls the frustration. "The most exasperating thing was having the two of them argue. They were taking diametrically different views. There was no grey between them." Ginny Devine remembers poor Pawley, standing between Schwartz and Whitley, both of whom were giving him different interpretations in both of his ears. To make matters worse, Roland Penner had returned to Winnipeg. He had promised his wife he would baby-sit that evening. Unable to find an understudy, the attorney general had suddenly decamped. The premier was displeased. "Penner just checked out," remembers Pawley. "He didn't tell anyone he was leaving. Let's just say there was some *annoyance* within the Manitoba group." The departure compounded Pawley's problems. Uneasy with the agreement, isolated from his party and confused by conflicting advice, he now lost his closest confidant. As Pawley ruminated, the other premiers were chiding and badgering him to come on side. Often when Pawley and Peterson left the room to confer with their delegations, Devine and Hatfield would follow them out a few minutes later to tell them to hurry up.

Watching impatiently was Bill Vander Zalm. He became increasingly unhappy as the session dragged on through the afternoon. "This was settled a month ago!" he kept saying, berating Peterson and Pawley for delaying the process. He interrupted virtually every hour, threatening to leave for the airport. "Gotta get back to B.C.," he muttered repeatedly, the phrase like a religious mantra. Vander Zalm did have a 6:15 p.m. flight to Vancouver. He had labour problems at home and a cabinet meeting the next day. "You guys are wasting our time," he fumed. "I expected the signing ceremony to be at 12:30 and it's six o'clock and we're still sitting here." Mulroney, fearing that the talks would collapse if Vander Zalm left, tried to as-

suage the impetuous premier. Joe Ghiz remembers their exchange:
"The only reason that Vander Zalm stayed is that the PM kept assuring him that he would fly him back. . . . 'Don't worry, Bill,' says the PM. 'I gotta go,' says Bill. Mulroney says: 'Bill, please, Bill, I'll get you home. Don't worry, Bill.' Then the PM turns to Spector: 'Norman, Norman, we have the plane for Bill, don't we?' Spector nods. Mulroney says: 'Bill, it's okay.'" Vander Zalm twice got up to leave. Then Hatfield, the bon vivant whose peregrinations were well known, grinned and asked: "Perhaps you'd give me a jet? There's a marvellous party going on in New York this evening." Vander Zalm yielded to Mulroney's entreaties, and Spector found him a plane.

By early morning, the experts had been heard, and the points had been made. There was a stalemate. The spirit of Meech Lake was gone. Pawley and Peterson were refusing to relent and so was Bourassa. At one point Bourassa stood up, brought his hand down on a copy of the accord and declared: "It will be Meech Lake, nothing more, nothing less." Other premiers tried to console him. The air was getting stale. Vander Zalm was smoking his pipe, Peckford was drawing on a cigar, and Spector and Peterson were sharing a package of menthol cigarettes. Two dozen doughnuts were brought in and demolished. Tempers were short. When Don Getty began lecturing Joe Ghiz on the history of the National Energy Policy, Ghiz reminded him that he had gone to "a place called Harvard," where he did a degree in law and wrote a thesis on mineral rights. The premiers were exhausted and testy, but the decision was made to keep talking. Mulroney recalled later: "People were getting pretty tired, but by then I had made it quite clear that we were going to go on until we either got an agreement or we didn't."

Some of the premiers now regret staying as long as they did. Ghiz thinks he should have walked out at two o'clock in the morning and come back the next morning. "I should have said, 'I'm tired. We've been going since 10:00 a.m. I'm going to bed. I'll see you tomorrow morning.' I didn't do that and it weakened the document." Ghiz argues that the accord would have had more public legitimacy if the premiers had avoided that all-night session: "Meech Lake would have been stronger even if it had stayed exactly the way it was, if we had left and gone to bed and come back the next morning. If everything had remained the same, we would have avoided the perceptual problem of staying there all night, the sun coming up and giving interviews on the steps of Langevin. That was absolutely nuts." Pawley, one of the two hold-outs, says he was close to walking out at about two o'clock. He still wanted tougher wording on spending power and he wasn't getting anywhere. Moreover, he had an agreement with Peterson that the two would go together. Neither would leave the other alone.

It was not surprising that Pawley and Peterson would hold out for changes on the distinct-society and the spending-power clauses. Both drew their support in part from minority groups. Pawley was a New Democrat, and Peterson a Liberal, and the two were compatible. In Ontario, Peterson had co-opted the agenda of the provincial NDP in his own power-sharing accord. To dislodge the ruling Tories in Ontario, he had moved to the left. His record on the environment, pay equity, women's rights, labour law and the extension of French-language services was arguably more liberal than Pawley's. Pawley, for his part, would take allies wherever he could find them. Since 1982, he had been the only New Democrat among the premiers. Peterson's willingness to challenge Mulroney made him a kindred spirit to Pawley.

In the last hours of the session at Langevin, both premiers decided they had another role in this constitutional exercise: to protect the interests of the central government. Peterson, representing a province that had always identified most strongly with the centre, was worried that Ottawa was prepared to cede too much power. Pawley, as a social democrat, was concerned the federal government would lose its ability to implement a national day-care program or an industrial strategy. During the negotiations, both questioned Mulroney's role. "We're fighting your battle," they said. "You should speak up." Or, their other refrain: "Surely this concerns *you*, Prime Minister. You are the prime minister." Both began to see themselves as the unlikely champions of centralism, though, in the end, they abandoned their efforts. Here was one of the ironies of this exercise in nation-building: the *provinces* making the case against the devolution of powers.

The other premiers were also getting impatient. Hatfield, for one, had had enough. "We basically had an agreement, but Pawley and Peterson were fussing," he recalls. "I was told the two of them were down in an office that Ontario had usurped. It had to do with women's rights and the distinct society. I went down there and listened. I said, 'What you're saying is bullshit. If you're not prepared to go along with this, go in and say so.'"

Now, in the hollow of the night, Peterson was preparing to walk out. It was around three o'clock, and the accord was coming apart. There had been little progress on spending power or the distinct society. In the climactic moment of the session, Peterson announced that he could not agree. He looked at Bourassa across the table and said, "I'm sorry, Robert. I just can't go along with the wording." Bourassa looked down and said: "There's no reason to say you're sorry." Peterson, who had become friends with Bourassa, apologized again, reiterating that he could not accept it as it was. A distraught Bourassa tried to console Peterson. His eyes moist, he whispered: "You're not the problem, David. I know who the problem is. It's that bastard Trudeau."

An eerie silence descended. Mulroney called a recess.

The premiers, like prizefighters wearying in the last round, retreated to their corners. Mulroney went downstairs to his third-floor office where he was joined by Norman Spector, Bernard Roy and Roger Tassé. He wanted to give it one more try. When the premiers returned, he would put the question: Would there be a deal or not? The talks were now in their seventeenth hour; what more could be gained by prolonging this trial? "We were very low at the time," remembers Tassé. "We thought it was game over. Ontario wasn't moving." Neither was Quebec. "I knew when it went past four o'clock there would be a solution," Bourassa said later. "If we had postponed at twelve, I would have asked: what would happen tomorrow?" The premier was sitting like a sphinx. As one Ontario official put it, "Bourassa knew he had it. He didn't really have to agree to anything. He knew he was going to get everything he wanted. It was just a question of waiting. His advisers were urging him not to agree, and I'm not sure they were wrong."

This last recess, like the others, found the delegations from Manitoba and Ontario huddling. Pawley conferred with Ginny Devine; Schwartz; Whitley; Cliff Scotton, his chief of staff; and Jim Eldridge and George Ford, two senior public servants. Penner was long gone. Pawley recognized that he was in a position of maximum authority. He was worried about being seen as obstinate, and, worse, as a bigot from Manitoba. He recalls his predicament: "We were two of eleven. Undoubtedly the pressure was great, not just within the room, but because of Broadbent's position and because of the perception of Manitoba. I was always seen as the odd man out; we were always quarrelling. I didn't want to be seen as an obstructionist premier from an obstructionist province. I wanted to be co-operative."

Wanting to be co-operative meant, in the end, accepting the deal. Such was the psychology of the group. Pawley said later the pressure in the room was unbearable. Outside, his people were still divided. "It was four o'clock in the morning," he remembers. "We should have recessed. Our two leading advisers didn't interpret one goddamn thing alike." Pawley, then, had all the burdens he had before — party, province and conscience. He had the fear of isolation. What was worse, he was getting mixed signals — a constitutional cacophony — from those who knew the most. The other premiers were hectoring him. "I gave Pawley a hard time," Peckford concedes. "I just couldn't make too much sense out of some of his arguments, and I told him so." To many of them, Pawley was too "left wing" on the environment, the economy, women's issues. The more they saw him, the more they disliked him. And now, after hours of talks, he had the temerity to hold up a new constitution.

Pawley listened carefully to Joe Ghiz, who urged him to accept the deal because Bourassa would reject anything less. Ghiz had helped strengthen the wording on the spending-power clause by ensuring that all social programs were "established by the government of Canada." At this hour, though, that advance did not dampen Ghiz's pessimism. "She's dead," he said of the accord. But Pawley was cracking. After consulting Peterson, he decided to go ahead. It was now a political decision more than a legal one. Pawley concluded there was nothing more he could do to change the deal. "I will take responsibility for whatever I sign," he told his advisers.

Meanwhile, the Ontario delegation was holding a meeting of its own. Because there were no assigned offices, they invoked squatters' rights all over the fourth floor. Anyone within earshot could hear their conversations. At one point, Frank Iacobucci and Ian Scott, who were old friends, got into a shouting match over a critical agreement on wording Ontario had reached with Quebec. Scott was furious a deal had been struck, only to be vetoed by the federal officials. "They were screaming at each other," recalled one premier who was within earshot. "Ah, Jesus. They were roaring. People were standing and shouting like the country was going to come apart. I couldn't believe what I heard. Afterwards, they were saying it was the greatest thing since sliced bread."

As Ontario officials tell it, it was during a final meeting in the stair-well that they learned, through Bryan Schwartz, that Pawley was giving up. The Manitobans, for their part, say they decided to quit when Ontario did, an interpretation of events that irks the Ontarians. "Suddenly, we were alone," recalled one of the province's senior ad-visers. "We were just disconsolate. To be alone in that setting was terrible. I must say the premier kept up the fight and did extraordi-narily well. What ticks me off is the revisionist Manitoba theory that *they* were alone and *we* had given up. It is not true. They had caved." If this was true, Peterson now faced the critical decision alone. If he could not change the accord, should he kill it? Should he risk the vilification?

Peterson was reminded that, for Quebec, Canada was Ontario. Pawley might worry about racism in Manitoba, but Quebeckers were unmoved; the franco-Manitoban community, in their eyes, was already gone. The province didn't count for much. Ontario — Or-ange, Protestant Ontario — was different. To stand against Quebec now would be devastating. The headlines the next day would read: "Ontario Rejects Quebec" or "Peterson Deserts Bourassa." That would be the historical verdict, and it would haunt Canada for a gen-eration. The political questions for Peterson, late at night, had come down to these, as posed by one of his people: "Are you prepared to say no to this? To say that the Charter is so important that you will scuttle the deal? Is this such a high principle for you that you are pre-pared to take that stand and understand what the historical judgement will be?" Peterson understood the questions. He asked the adviser what he would do. The reply came slowly, haltingly: "I don't think that it is worth it. I'm prepared to take the risks and the shit that goes with it. It would be disastrous to walk out tonight. We would be back where we were in the 1960s."

The premier was facing the most agonizing decision of his political life. Joe Ghiz tried to calm his fears and urged him to accept the deal. Still, Peterson was not sure what to do. An associate describes the de-cision facing Peterson after hours of wearying debate: "It is now four in the morning. This is it, Premier. There is no more compromise. Everything has been tried. There have been nineteen drafts. You've tried your argument on everyone, the same one for the last four hours. No one is wilting. You're wilting. What are you prepared to do?"

Peterson canvassed his delegation, and said, "We are going to make or break the deal. This will be it." Then he returned to the boardroom. Even then, it was still not clear to some of his advisers what he would do.

When the premiers reconvened just before five o'clock, Mulroney called a final vote. He went around the table, asking each premier in turn. Shrewdly, he ignored the usual order of precedence. He knew who was for, and who was against. The question was whether Pawley and Peterson had changed their minds. He began with Bourassa, who accepted the document. Getty, Devine, Buchanan, Peckford, Hatfield, Ghiz agreed. Vander Zalm, confident that he would see British Columbia today, was enthusiastic. "Bang, bang, bang, he went down the row," remembers Tassé. "A lot of yeses." Mulroney then turned to Manitoba. Pawley said that he wasn't happy, but he would take the deal back to Manitoba and hold public hearings as required under provincial law. He said that his agreement was conditional, but agree he did. (Pawley thinks Mulroney turned to Peterson first, but the consensus is Pawley was asked first.) "I'm signing this," he said. "But you should know my reservations. If those public hearings give me additional concerns, I'll be back at the table. They will not be a rubber stamp."

Then Mulroney turned to his right, where Peterson was sitting. "Well, David, do we have a deal?" There was a long silence, perhaps a minute or more. Peterson then spoke for about five minutes, expressing his reservations about the deal but accepting that it accommodated Quebec. He tossed his pencil in the air and said: "I'm in, Prime Minister." He slumped in his chair, red tie askew, white shirt a canvas of creases, looking dazed and distraught. Unlike the consensus at Meech Lake, this one caused no euphoria. No rush to congratulations, no standing ovation, no search for autographs. After almost twenty hours, there was a numbing fatigue and, for some, nagging self-doubt.

Outside, the army of reporters and technicians had been camping on the grassy knoll of Parliament Hill all night. Eagerly they watched for a sign, a movement, an arrival or a departure of an official. Those snippets of information were manna for journalists, even though many were long past their deadlines. They watched the building at sunup, its broad shapes emerging like the image on an instant photograph. From the broad chimneys, they almost expected to see the first wisps of white smoke, signalling a decision after almost a day of deliberation. In the Vatican, the smoke would signal a new Pope; in Ottawa, it would announce something only slightly less exalted: an amended constitution. At 5:30 a.m., the prime minister made his way downstairs, where he congratulated some of the officials. The premiers, who had been asked to wait for him to leave first, had also assembled. Seeing Joe Ghiz by the door, Mulroney shook his hand and said: "You're quite a Canadian, Joe Ghiz." Ghiz smiled tightly and said, "You're a quite a Canadian yourself, Prime Minister." Then Mulroney appeared on the sidewalk, announced the deal, and got into his car. His rumpled colleagues followed him, offering the same sentiments but forgoing long exchanges with reporters. It was simply too late — or perhaps too early. In a few hours, they would gather across the street to consecrate their new Covenant of Confederation.

In the early hours of 3 June, as the light began to dispel the darkness, the weary nation-builders confronted the dawn. Joe Ghiz walked down the deserted street to his hotel and ran into a street cleaner. "Do we have a deal?" he asked the premier. "We do," said Ghiz, touched that the man knew and cared. "That's great," said the cleaner.

Ian Scott was too agitated to go to bed. He roamed the streets of Ottawa, trying to make his way to Dow's Lake, an eyeglass of water a brisk walk from Parliament Hill. In his daze, he wandered for two hours. From Meech Lake to Dow's Lake; the constitutional tableau passed before him. He contemplated rights and freedoms and the Charter. He was known as a liberal and a civil libertarian, and he was plagued by self-doubt. Had he protected his constituencies? Had he done the right thing?

His colleague, Gary Posen, was doing some soul-searching of his own. Posen knew better than most the difficulty of writing constitutions in Canada. He had spent much of his professional life in sessions like this one. Until now, they had known only failure. Some of his provincial counterparts felt personally responsible for the outcome at Langevin. One associate considered offering his resignation if his premier rejected the deal. "What credibility would I have," he asked, "if in the end the premier walked?" No wonder the public servants were as relieved as the politicians when the deal was done.

Posen did not remain for the signing ceremony. His father was to have an operation that day in Toronto. Posen returned to his hotel and fell into a taxi. He had a migraine headache; the anxiety of nineteen hours had drained him. As the taxi made its way to the airport, he began to shake. A few minutes later, as the capital faded behind him, his convulsions stopped. The headache went, the tension lifted, and the phantoms took flight.

CHAPTER
6

The Essential Accord

THE INITIAL ENTHUSIASM FOR THE MEECH LAKE ACCORD CAME FROM A country less interested in the content of its new constitution than in the peace it seemed to represent. Few Canadians knew or understood what was in the accord and few cared. Canadians simply liked the idea of an agreement. The national reaction was like that of an adolescent more infatuated with the idea of love than with its supposed object. It is not hard to see how goodwill could overwhelm good sense. Confrontation is unpleasant. The critics were called nay-sayers, defeatists and dinosaurs. They were said to be on the wrong side of history. Inevitably, though, the hard questions came up. They triggered a deluge of doubts about the accord that marked the beginning of its undoing.

What did it say, then, this agreement that generated such mixed emotions? The accord finalized on 3 June had three parts: a political accord, which confirmed the agreement reached by the first ministers and committed them to ratifying it; a motion for a resolution, which was to be approved by Parliament and the provincial legislatures; and a schedule to the resolution, or the text of the amendments in seventeen clauses. Simply put, the accord was a series of amendments to the Constitution Act of 1867 and the Constitution Act of 1982. These amendments, offered as a package, were to be passed by Parliament and the ten provincial legislatures within three years of the date that the first government ratified it. When Quebec approved the accord on 23 June 1987, the formal deadline became 23 June 1990.

The three provinces that held up the accord and ultimately killed it were reflecting growing public skepticism on many levels. One level of doubt was that the accord created two countries, one English and one French, and marked the end of a bilingual, bicultural nation. Another was the accord's ambiguity, the sense that it promised too much and defined too little. A third was the accord did not provide solutions to problems it created. A fourth was the perception of a loss of federal power to the provinces. A fifth was the belief that the accord conferred special status on Quebec. Collectively, these reservations were the reason that the more Canadians learned of the accord, the more they began to question it. An examination of its basic elements helps explain why the early enthusiasm waned so quickly.

The Distinct Society

This idea was at the heart of the accord. Recognition as a distinct society was Quebec's foremost demand, set out in section 2 of Clause 1. The first two of the section's four subsections define the country. The accord said the constitution must be interpreted in a manner consistent with "a) the recognition that the existence of French-speaking Canadians, centred in Quebec but also present elsewhere in Canada, and English-speaking Canadians, concentrated outside Quebec but also present in Quebec, constitutes a fundamental characteristic of Canada; and b) the recognition that Quebec constitutes within Canada a distinct society." The next two subsections offer instructions to legislators. They say the role of Parliament and of the provincial legislatures is "to preserve the fundamental characteristic," while the role of the legislature and government of Quebec is "to preserve and promote the distinct identity of Quebec." Hence, the accord asked different things of different entities. Parliament and the provinces, through their legislatures, were instructed to preserve the French fact. But, in Quebec, both the government and the legislature were told to preserve *and* promote it. The difference between legislature and governments is that a government can promote a policy through cabinet order, whereas a legislature has to seek statutory approval by a formal vote.

Recognizing Quebec as a distinct society was not a new idea. The British North America Act, in recognizing Quebec civil law and special language rights, already acknowledged the province's distinctiveness. In past constitutional talks, it was suggested that Quebec be called the *foyer,* or hearth, of French-speaking Canada. In the accord, the distinct-society clause was said to recognize a sociological, political and historical reality in a province that has its own language, culture and legal system. To the framers of Meech Lake, enshrining Quebec's distinctiveness in the constitution was strictly symbolic.

"The distinct society is nothing more than political window-dressing," said Don Getty. Brian Mulroney claimed it was "nothing to worry about." During the long debate, they and others argued repeatedly that the distinct-society clause granted no new legislative powers to Quebec; it just recognized the status quo.

To Quebec, the clause meant much more. Bourassa argued that enshrining Quebec as a distinct society was not merely symbolic because the constitution would have been read in that way. "It cannot be stressed too strongly that the entire constitution, including the Charter, will be interpreted and applied in light of the section proclaiming our distinctiveness as a society," Bourassa told the National Assembly in 1987. "As a result, in the exercise of our legislative jurisdictions, we will be able to consolidate what has already been achieved and to gain new ground." That new ground would extend not only to language, but to "culture, and our political, legal and economic institutions."

Here, then, was the first problem with the clause: its ambiguity. The clause meant one thing in English Canada and another in French Canada. It was left undefined because, as Bourassa put it, "We wanted to avoid reducing the National Assembly's role in promoting Quebec's uniqueness." Gil Rémillard was more specific in his interpretation. He talked about Quebec's new authority in international relations, banking, communications. Did it mean that the Caisse populaire, the province's home-grown financial institution, could be expanded? Did it mean that Quebec could broaden its foreign activities? Did it mean that Quebec could introduce content regulations in broadcasting, even set up a Quebec broadcasting regulatory agency? Many, if not most, experts said it conferred no new powers. Others said it might. But neither side could be certain, and the uncertainty was troublesome. If the clause meant as much as Bourassa thought, it would bring Quebec new powers. But if it meant as little as Getty thought, Quebec would feel cheated. It was not hard to imagine the response of a government, using its newly acquired distinctiveness to justify a new law, only to have it struck down by the Supreme Court. The Quebec nationalists would inevitably feel duped again, as they thought they had been misled in 1980 by Trudeau's promise of "renewed federalism." Then there was the peculiar view of the Parti Québécois. Jacques Parizeau promised to use the clause for all it was worth, and if it was worth nothing, to use it to illustrate Quebec's weakness in Canada. For the Péquistes, it was a no-lose proposition.

Peter Hogg, who supported the accord, argued that the clause neither conferred nor denied power. He said it would be relevant only when the rest of the constitution was unclear. He called it "an affirmation of sociological fact with little legal significance." A key part of the distinct-society clause was the non-derogation stipulation, which said that nothing about the distinct society "derogates from the powers, rights or privileges of Parliament," or the federal government or the provinces, including rights on language. The purpose here was to ensure that the interpretation of the distinct-society clause did not detract from, or take away, rights. But it said nothing about *broadening* the rights of either level of government. In addition, another section of the accord (Clause 16) said that nothing in the distinct-society clause affected the rights of aboriginal people and multicultural groups. Both this clause and the non-derogation clause were inserted at the meeting at the Langevin Block. No one could foretell their impact.

The other problem with the distinct-society clause was the notion of duality, the idea that it created two Canadas — one of them English where nine provinces could, conceivably, preserve the status quo of English dominance and French subservience; the other French, where the government and the legislature of Quebec could promote — and not just preserve — French as the predominant language and culture. The fear was that the accord would allow francophones outside Quebec, and anglophones in Quebec, to wither and die. In other words, the distinct society would be a return to "deux nations," a theory of the 1960s. This was Trudeau's chief complaint: that the accord undermined the vision of a bilingual Canada. Not long after Meech Lake, Alberta and Saskatchewan moved to curtail francophone language rights. Bourassa refused to criticize the government of Saskatchewan, and actually argued against extension of rights in Alberta to francophones, ostensibly to avoid a precedent there that could be used against Quebec at home. In 1988, Quebec itself limited English language rights with its sign language law.

The Senate

To the surprise of the provinces, the accord gave all of them a role in choosing senators. The first of the two clauses on the Senate said that, in the event of a vacancy, the government of the province represented by the senator "may . . . submit to the Queen's Privy Council for Canada the names of persons who may be summoned to the Senate." The second clause said that until the Senate was reformed, the person summoned to the chamber "shall be chosen from among persons whose names have been submitted . . . by the government of the province" where the vacancy arose and had to be acceptable to the cabinet.

A province would submit a list of names when one of its senators (each province had an allotted number, like seats in the House of Commons) died or retired. The federal government, which used to pick senators on its own, would choose one. If it didn't like any of the proposed candidates, it could reject them and ask for another list. But the accord did not specify the length of the list or provide a way of breaking a deadlock. Nor was there any mention in the accord of appointments from the Yukon or the Northwest Territories. Two potential problems arose: What if the list was too short? What if the two parties could never agree?

The appointment clause was offered as an interim measure in anticipation of Senate reform. But the critics feared that it would not be temporary at all. They thought this arrangement could become permanent, particularly because Senate reform, under the accord, required unanimity of the federal government and the provinces. Meanwhile, the balance of federalism would shift. As Peter Hogg wrote, "The Senate might gradually evolve into a 'house of the provinces' with its members feeling themselves primarily beholden to their province of origin rather than to any federal political party. This would probably change the character of the institution, making it more assertive in representing provincial or regional interests."

The appointment clause was seen, then, as taking power away from the federal government. But it disturbed critics less than the accord's amending formula, which required unanimity among all the provinces and the federal government for changing federal institutions, including the Senate. Before Meech Lake, such changes needed the approval of Parliament and seven provinces with half the population. The Meech Lake Accord, therefore, would have made Senate reform harder than ever. There was also another obstacle to reform. A "Triple E Senate" (elected, effective and with equal representation for all the provinces) would take dead aim at executive federalism and the power of the premiers. After all, if senators were to speak for their regions, who would need the premiers? An elected Senate would represent the provinces, undermining the role of the first ministers as national decision-makers. Senators would be elected by region but sit in a national chamber, accountable to a national party, charged with taking national decisions. It was doubtful all the premiers would support an institution that diminished their role and strengthened the legitimacy of the central government.

In the absence of reform, the Meech Lake Accord would have legitimized an unelected and unrepresentative body. (In the 104-seat chamber, Ontario and Quebec each has twenty-four seats; Nova Scotia and New Brunswick ten seats each; Newfoundland, Manitoba, Saskatchewan, Alberta and British Columbia six seats each; Prince Edward Island, four seats; the Yukon and Northwest Territories, one seat each.) The Senate would still retain its right to veto all legislation coming from the House of Commons, except constitutional amendments, which it could delay for 180 days. "Under Meech Lake, the appointed Senate will prevail over the elected House of Commons, thereby entrenching the most undemocratic power of any living democracy," argued constitutional lawyer Timothy Danson. He and other critics feared what Hogg predicted: the emergence of a regional body of activist senators, armed with a veto over matters of federal jurisdiction. Bryan Schwartz foresaw those senators jettisoning their traditional role, refusing to rubber-stamp legislation. He heard them saying, "Okay, we're not elected. But we were appointed almost the same way as the Supreme Court of Canada, and it exercises real power. We may show the House of Commons a lot of respect, but we're not going to be like those toy puppies you see in car windows — in the back seat nodding, nodding. We're going to be watchdogs now."

As Meech Lake was negotiated, that kind of Senate seemed like a distinct possibility. Stan Waters, who was the first elected senator in 1989, claimed a democratic legitimacy. If all provinces had held their own elections and forced the premiers to submit the names of the winners, the Senate would have changed in complexion. Although the senators would have been elected, each province would have had the same number of senators, which would mean some provinces, such as British Columbia, would have remained underrepresented. Meanwhile, the powers of the Senate would be the same. It was a recipe for constitutional deadlock.

Immigration

The accord defined new roles for both levels of government in managing immigration. Under the Constitution Act of 1867, those powers are shared, although the federal government retains primacy. In recent years, Quebec has sought and obtained a greater say in immigration. It is worried by its low birth rate and by the fact that it receives only 15 to 17 percent of Canada's immigrants although it comprises 26 percent of the country's population. It has signed agreements with the federal government, most notably the Cullen-Couture Agreement of 1978, giving it a voice in selecting immigrants to Quebec. Six other provinces have agreements, but none is entrenched in the constitution. The immigration amendments looked insignificant but they were not. To Jean-Claude Rivest, Quebec's constitutional adviser, "immigration was our most important gain in the accord, bigger than the distinct society."

Five sections in the accord spelled out the method of writing and implementing immigration agreements. The first clause (95A) said Ottawa must negotiate an agreement with the provinces on immigration "appropriate to the needs and circumstances of that province." The second clause (95B) said that the agreement must not contradict federal legislation that established "national standards and objectives" on immigration or general classes of immigrants or level of immigration. Although the point of these provisions was to put the control and level of immigration in the constitution — beyond the reach of legislative whim — this section preserved the right of the federal government to set the rules. Hogg argued that, in the event of a disagreement, a federal law setting standards and objectives would have primacy over a provincial immigration agreement. He said "the phrase 'national standards and objectives' thus marks a crucial boundary line. It is not exhaustively defined, and is obviously far from clear." The important thing, he noted, was that Parliament was able to act in the national interest if alterations in immigration were required by economics, changing values or international obligations.

The Charter remained paramount, particularly in relation to mobility rights, the right of any person to move anywhere in Canada, regardless of where he or she had settled originally. Accordingly, a person who had come to Quebec under the conditions of Quebec's agreement did not have to stay there. Interestingly, the framers of the accord made the supremacy of the Charter explicit here, which they did not do with the distinct-society clause. They also used such words as "national objectives" and "standards" here, even though they rejected these terms in defining the federal spending power.

Under Meech Lake, the Cullen-Couture Agreement would have been entrenched. The accord also guaranteed Quebec an annual share of immigrants equal to its population, which Quebec could exceed by

5 percent. It also declared that Ottawa would transfer its responsibility for immigrant settlement to Quebec and pay it "reasonable compensation" for assuming these new responsibilities.

The regime envisioned by Meech Lake raised a number of questions: was the federal government giving up its supremacy, since any agreement it negotiated was now to be written into the constitution, where it could be changed only under the amending formula? How could one guarantee Quebec's share of immigrants proportionate to its population? If immigrants did not want to go to Quebec, could other provinces take its share? Did all other provinces have a right to 5 percent more than their share, as did Quebec? If they did, how was that possible?

At root, the immigration provisions seemed to foster a lessening of federal power. The withdrawal of federal services for receiving and integrating immigrants would have impeded the development of a national purpose, the ability to tell immigrants that Canada is more than a collection of provinces. Moreover, it would have represented a fragmentation of national policy. Quebec would have its own immigration policy, and so would those other provinces. Eventually, there would have been a patchwork of provincial immigration policies that would have seen provinces competing with each other for the wealthiest, best-educated immigrants.

The Supreme Court

Since 1982, the high court has become an instrument to assert individual rights and right collective wrongs. As a result, it has come under greater scrutiny. There has been more interest in who sits on the court, how they are chosen, the powers they wield. Meech Lake addressed some of those questions. It entrenched the size and composition of the court, guaranteeing a presence for Quebec. Most important, it gave the provinces a role in choosing justices.

Although the accord was seen by many as an assault on the federal government, it did strengthen the court, a federal institution, by recognizing it in the constitution. "The net effect [of the accord] actually is to confirm and guarantee the authority of a central institution," wrote Bryan Schwartz. The high court would now be beyond the reach of federal power. Previously, the federal government could change the court simply by passing a law; it now had to seek a constitutional amendment, which would have, under the accord, required unanimous consent. While it was unlikely that Parliament would ever abolish the court, it was possible without the accord. "It is inappropriate that the court, which serves as the guardian of the constitution, should be unprotected by the constitution," said Peter Hogg.

The accord made the Supreme Court the court of last appeal. It fixed the number of judges at nine — a chief justice and eight associates — and entrenched the statutory requirement of appointing three judges from Quebec, reflecting its distinct legal heritage. At the same time, it guaranteed that the tenure and salaries of judges would be set by Parliament, not the executive. While the legal community welcomed this judicial independence, it worried about fixing the number of judges. The Canadian Bar Association, for example, argued that the court, already labouring under a heavy caseload, would be unable to add more members, as it had done three times before. Some experts feared that a federal government might pack the court to support its policies, as Franklin Roosevelt tried to do to the Supreme Court of the United States in 1938. Freezing the number would make that less likely, as would allowing the provinces to nominate judges.

Entrenching the court and affirming its size and jurisdiction simply confirmed the status quo. On the other hand, involving the provinces broke new ground. Under Meech Lake, if a vacancy came open on the court, provinces would have submitted a list of candidates and the federal government would have chosen one. The only requirement was that candidates had to have been members of the bar for at least ten years. Because they are not provinces, the Northwest Territories and the Yukon could not have proposed names.

The selection system now works this way: upon the death or retirement of one of the three justices from Ontario, for example, the federal government chooses a successor, usually in consultation with the provincial attorney general. The same method is used for replacing any of the three judges from Quebec. The other three judges come from the regions, and the government tries to ensure a balance. Under Meech Lake, the government would have given up that flexibility. If it had rejected all the candidates, it could have asked for others. The provinces, for their part, could have drawn up a new list, which Ottawa could have also rejected. There would then have been a deadlock with no means to break it.

In giving the provinces power over appointments — which Quebec had sought only for itself — the framers of the accord settled on an inconclusive mechanism. The accord said the provinces "may" submit names but the federal government "shall" appoint one of them. A recalcitrant premier could have stalled the business of the court by refusing to present nominees. A separatist government in Quebec, for example, could have submitted the names of three separatist judges or nominated none at all, a tactic the Parti Québécois might have used twice when there were vacancies in Quebec between 1976 and 1985. If the federal government rejected the nominees, the court would have had to sit without full membership, all the while hearing cases under Quebec's Civil Law. Would the court then have been constitutionally constituted? Even if it could legitimately operate at less than full strength, its effectiveness would have been in doubt. Peter Russell of the University of Toronto was unfazed by the possibility. He argued that the court often sits with seven judges. "Delay in filling vacancies is a lesser evil than appointing judges who lack the respect of both levels of government," he wrote.

A deadlock would be less of a problem in appointing judges from outside Quebec. If the federal government did not like the names submitted by Nova Scotia, for example, it could choose one from Newfoundland. Some suggested the arrangement would have created healthy competition among provinces to produce the best candidate. By tradition, one judge has come from the four Atlantic provinces and two from the four western provinces. Up to now, the idea has not necessarily been to represent the region. A judge is not expected to rule with his or her native province in mind, or to favour those who come from there. Involving the provinces in the selection process, however, raised the prospect of weakening that principle, if only because some provinces could have been tempted to use their new powers of nomination to put forward unreconstructed advocates of their interests.

Spending Power

Only one clause of the accord (Section 106A) dealt with the federal spending power. It said: "The Government of Canada shall provide reasonable compensation to the government of a province that chooses not to participate in a national shared-cost program that is established by the Government of Canada . . . in an area of exclusive provincial jursidiction, if the province carries on a program or initiative that is compatible with the national objectives." The effect of the spending provisions of the accord would have been to entrench the spending power of the federal government but with new limits. When Ottawa established a program in an area of exclusive provincial jurisdiction, or an area under the direct control of the province, that province could have refused to participate. A province that opted out could then set up its own program, as long as it was "compatible with the national objectives." In return, it would have received money from the federal government to run the program.

The federal government implements shared-cost programs — in health care, post-secondary education and social welfare — to guarantee the same level of basic services throughout the country. Before Meech Lake, provinces could opt out of these programs and establish their own, but they were unlikely to do so because they got nothing in return from the federal government. The provinces always resented funding a program they had not designed or conceived, arguing that programs were forced upon them. Under Meech Lake, the right to opt out would have been enshrined in the constitution. The objection, though, was that by respecting provincial autonomy, the accord would inhibit new national programs. The fear was that social services would become a crazy quilt, a patchwork of different standards in different regions. Pierre Trudeau said, "[Fair compensation] will enable the provinces to finish off the balkanization of languages and cultures with the balkanization of social services. After all, what provincial politician will not insist on distribution in his own way . . . and to the advantage of his constituents, the money he'll be getting painlessly from the federal treasury?" Provinces could reject a federal program, claim the money and spend it on something else. Conceivably, there would be no new federal programs in education, the environment or technology.

Programs are hard to launch as it is; there have been no new shared-cost programs since 1969. "Some provincialists suffer from the delusion that the federal government will happily ante up money for the provinces to spend as they choose," wrote Schwartz. "On the contrary, if the federal government cannot express and effect a sense of national community and purpose through shared-cost programs, it will cease to provide them."

Ontario attorney general Ian Scott, on the other hand, argued that provinces would create programs compatible with national objectives. He said that opting out would allow provinces to tailor programs to local needs. While even the accord's supporters acknowledged that the language was vague, they thought both sides would co-operate in defining terms. But that assumption was dubious. The reality of Meech Lake was that the language of this section, like that of so many others, was ambiguous. The provinces could take the money and run. (Some had always planned to. As David Peterson put it, "There is no question that Quebec came in at Meech Lake and wanted to use social program money for roads. But at the end of the day, that is not what they got.") The accord did not say who would decide whether the provincial plan met national objectives; it did not say whether the national objectives meant standards; it did not say what was meant by "compatible" and "reasonable compensation." Without such definition, the accord gave the provinces carte blanche. The criteria were broad and nebulous.

Some in the provincial camp argued that the provinces gave up too much because the accord recognized the right of the federal government to spend in areas of provincial jurisdiction. The provinces could no longer have challenged the government on the grounds that it was establishing a new program on their turf, which they could before. Under the spending-power clause, they could object only if their compensation was not adequate, or it was denied them on the grounds that it was not compatible with national objectives.

The Amending Formula

Quebec alone had asked for a veto over constitutional change, but Meech Lake gave all provinces one. In amending the constitution, the framers actually made it harder to amend. Thus, if the accord was a weak document, casting it in stone would make it worse. The accord proposed that any changes to federal institutions — the House of Commons, the Senate, the Supreme Court, the extension of existing provinces and the establishment of new ones — would require the unanimous consent of Parliament and every provincial legislature. Introducing proportional representation to the House of Commons, making the Yukon or Northwest Territories a province, creating an elected Senate — all would have had to be approved by both levels of government. Under the old rules, amendments of this type needed the consent only of seven provinces with more than half the country's population. The new rule, though, would have entrenched what had always been the biggest impediment to constitutional reform: the need for unanimity.

Historically, achieving unanimity had frustrated change. Because the two levels of government failed to agree on the content of a new constitution, it took fifty-four years to bring home the British North

America Act. Indeed, there was no movement on the issue until Pierre Trudeau threatened to move unilaterally in 1980. Even then, the constitution was patriated and the Charter of Rights proclaimed without Quebec's consent. It was not unreasonable to suggest that the amending formula would have created a constitutional straitjacket that would bind the flaws in the accord. The fear was that it would kill reform for a generation.

The hardest area of reform to achieve would have been the Senate. Although Meech Lake ensured it would be discussed at annual constitutional conferences, finding consensus would have been more difficult than before; that was why Getty's insistence on unanimity was so surprising. By requiring unanimity, the accord would have entrenched a process that provided no means of breaking a deadlock on the appointment of Supreme Court judges and that froze the number of judges. For Getty and others in favour of Senate reform, their goal was now harder to achieve, not easier, and the existing system was now more entrenched, not less. Similarly, the unanimity requirement would have dashed the hopes of the territories that they might one day become provinces. After all, existing provinces were unlikely to dilute their power by adding to the total number of provinces.

The supporters of unanimity argued that its problems were overstated. After all, the provinces and the federal government agreed unanimously in 1940 to establish an unemployment-insurance program, and to set up old-age pensions in 1951 and 1964. Hogg admitted that the amending formula "is even more rigid and difficult" than before, but Meech Lake "itself demonstrates that unanimity is not unattainable." Besides, it could be argued that since the creation of new provinces necessitated new fiscal arrangements, the existing provinces should have a say. As Grant Devine put it, "I thought if you were a new province coming in, you would kinda like everyone giving you a hug anyway."

However, unanimity would not be required in all cases. The general amending formula of Clause 38 — seven provinces with half the population — would have remained intact under Meech Lake. Under Section 41 of the 1982 act, unanimity is required for changes in five areas, including the composition of the Supreme Court of Canada and the office of the governor general. The accord would have required unanimity for other parts of Section 42 on federal institutions, but the Senate and the creation of new provinces were the only ones that really mattered. Gordon Robertson, the former clerk of the

Privy Council, thought Senate reform would not go ahead anyway without all the provinces, whether unanimity was required or not.

The second change to the amending formula would have allowed provinces to opt out of a constitutional amendment that transferred provincial jurisdiction to the federal government. For this, the provinces would have gotten compensation. In the Patriation Round, such compensation was limited to cases involving education or culture. Opting out, of course, would not have extended to federal institutions; a province could not opt out of the Senate or the Supreme Court. But it might have invited a checkerboard Canada, with different programs in different provinces, some better than others. Critics thought it would have led to the fragmentation of Canada, the rise of provincial power, and the weakening of the national will.

First Ministers' Conferences

This point was not one of Quebec's five conditions. It was one of those items, like the selection of senators, that was added to the accord to placate Alberta and Newfoundland. The clause provided for conferences to be convened "at least once each year to discuss the state of the Canadian economy" and the constitution. In particular, these conferences would have discussed Senate reform, or "the role and functions of the Senate, its powers, the method of selecting Senators and representation in the Senate." They would also have discussed "roles and responsibilities in relation to the fisheries." The accord said only that constitutional conferences had to be held every year and that those two items, the Senate and the fishery, had to be discussed at every meeting, ad infinitum. As is the case for other provisions in the accord, its impact could have been more far-reaching than imagined. Peter Russell, a supporter of the accord, called it "a ridiculous idea." Bryan Schwartz ranked these conferences with Senate appointments "as the most gratuitous threat to constitutional sanity in Canada."

In effect, federal-provincial conferences would have been entrenched as a virtual branch of government with the legislature, the judiciary and the executive. All this in addition to executive federalism, or the collaboration of the prime minister and the premiers. In 1964, the federal government negotiated the Auto Pact with the United States and informed the provinces as a courtesy. In 1985, the provinces demanded — without success — a seat at the free-trade talks and veto over the agreement. Pierre Trudeau met the premiers fourteen times in sixteen years; Brian Mulroney had met them twenty-one times in six years. Between 1984 and 1990, there were regular annual first ministers' meetings on the economy, in addition to ones mandated by the constitution on aboriginal rights, which ended in 1987.

This kind of power-sharing symbolizes the changing face of Canadian federalism which produced Meech Lake. But, while the role of premiers in national decision-making has evolved over the past two decades, it is more a creature of convention than law. The prime minister could summon the premiers to discuss national issues but he did not have to. The idea that the provinces could call federal-provincial conferences was raised by John Robarts, the premier of Ontario, when he was planning his Confederation of Tomorrow Conference in 1967. The invitation implied that the federal government and the provinces were equals. Lester Pearson, who had always been identified with co-operative federalism, rejected the idea and refused to attend the conference. "This is an extremely dangerous line of argument for the federal government and nothing should be done that appears to suggest any acquiescence to it," he wrote then. Trudeau was not terribly fond of the premiers and would not meet them unless it was absolutely necessary, as it was in 1980 and 1981 to find agreement on patriation. He seldom convened conferences.

But, by 1987, three years after Trudeau left office, constitution making had devolved into the hands of eleven persons, who, because of the rigidity of the party system in parliamentary democracy, wielded extraordinary power. A prime minister or a premier with a majority government could almost always deliver Parliament or the provincial legislature. It is no surprise, then, that these conferences have become forums to resolve intergovernmental disputes over the constitution and fiscal arrangements. "[The first ministers] are able to make commitments to each other of executive or legislative action which they are in a position to carry out," says Hogg. "No American president or state governor possesses comparable powers."

Enshrining these conferences in the constitution was criticized on the grounds that they might come to serve as platforms from which the provinces could attack the federal government. Given the history of federal-provincial relations, such conferences could have easily turned into a forum to play out constitutional struggles. Under Meech Lake, ten provinces would have had a place to press their demands on one prime minister — demands any prime minister, particularly a weak one, would have found hard to refuse year after year. Jockeying for power has long characterized intergovernmental negotiations. In 1976, the premiers asked for eleven items in the constitutional talks, including a say in immigration, more control over resource taxation, concurrent jursidiction in culture, more power in communications, as well as limits on the federal spending power. In 1978, the premiers added five more demands, including the abolition of the federal power of reservation and disallowance, and provincial jurisdiction over fisheries. In 1980, the provinces wanted many of these powers in addition to more control over offshore resources, communications, and a new Senate or a thirty-member Council of the Premiers.

Many of the powers sought in earlier rounds were yielded in 1982 and 1987. In future rounds contemplated by the accord, the provinces would surely ask for more. As a result of intergovernmental conferences, Canadians would have seen more of the John Buchanans, the David Petersons and the Grant Devines. The ten premiers threatened to become national decision-makers, a directorate of eleven, endowed with authority to make critical decisions in private.

Looking at its individual elements, it is easy to see why the accord gave cause for concern. The relationship between the distinct society and the Charter, the idea of duality, the impact on federal spending, the prospect of a patchwork of immigration policies, the establishment of annual first ministers' conferences — all seemed to suggest a transfer of power from the centre to the regions. That Canada in 1987 was already the most decentralized federation in the world was evident in fiscal, economic and foreign policy. It seemed to become even more decentralized all the time. The provinces, for example, were spending far more of public revenues, largely because the federal government was allowing them to. Pierre Trudeau, the supposed implacable centralist, had actually enhanced the power of the provinces by giving them a greater share of the public purse. The federal government was becoming a cash register, responsible for collecting taxes and then handing over money to the provinces to spend. In the end, the premiers, not Ottawa, would get the credit.

The provinces not only spent more money, they had erected a welter of trade barriers to protect and promote their regional economies. Quebec, for example, discriminated in favour of provincial compa-

nies in its stock-ownership plan. Other provinces favoured local sup-
pliers with government purchasing or hiring policies. The pursuit of
advantage among the provinces served to thwart the creation of a national will. It even affected international affairs, which was once virtually an exclusive federal jurisdiction. In recent years many of the
provinces have created foreign presences for themselves. As they promoted their interests around the world, they challenged the federal
monopoly on foreign policy. No longer content to let Ottawa express their concerns, they stated their own. Collectively, the provinces ran over seventy-five offices abroad, almost as many as the government of Canada. They created a parallel foreign service and in the
future, it was likely they would ask for even more powers in that
realm.

Indeed, it is the seeming inevitability of "province-building" that
alarmed opponents of the Meech Lake Accord. As the debate took
hold, the problem for many was not so much Quebec's five conditions as the weakening of the central government. That, of course,
and the host of other grievances — the need for unanimity on institutional reform, the exclusion of the North, the failure to address aboriginal Canadians or the multicultural character of Canada. Those
questions, negotiated in secrecy and written in ambiguity, fuelled the
debate over the accord until the end. The dissent it generated was
enough to split the Liberal Party of Canada, make Pierre Trudeau
break his silence, and bring to power three governments opposed to
the accord. The collective anxiety precipitated a national soul-
searching, and, eventually, a national crisis. Only a few months after
the accord was sealed amid such euphoria, the miracle of Meech Lake
had become a mirage.

CHAPTER
7

Liberal Agonistes

THE MEECH LAKE ACCORD WAS A POLITICAL DEAL BETWEEN THE PRE-
miers and the prime minister, presented to the country as a *fait accompli*. Because this train of events left little role for the opposition, it is
easy to conclude that the Liberal Party of Canada was a bit player, out
of season and out of favour. But the Liberals are a part of this story
from the beginning to the end. In office, they set the stage for Meech
Lake; in opposition, they became its first casualty. Meech Lake took
hold of the Liberal party like a slow-growing cancer, infecting its or-
gans, sapping its strength, blurring its vision. It ravaged the party,
exposing its intellectual weakness, alienating its foot soldiers and philosophers alike. For four years — from a regional-policy conference
at Ste.-Hyacinthe in 1986 to a leadership convention in Calgary in
1990 — it brought only turmoil. Coups and cabals. Secret letters and
broken promises. Lost opportunities and dashed hopes. Fratricide
and regicide. A leader crossed and a leader crowned. Ultimately, its
effect would be the most poisonous in politics: the denial of power.

All this seemed improbable in November 1985, when John Napier
Turner was trying to bind up the wounds of a party he had led to defeat in the election the previous year. Buoyed by the momentum
from a regional-policy conference in Halifax, where he had received
one of the great ovations of his leadership, he decided the party
should have a new position on Quebec and the constitution. To this
end, he assembled a team to draft a platform. It included Serge Joyal,
the former secretary of state and co-chairman of the Special Joint
Committee on the Constitution in 1980–81; Michel Robert, a prominent constitutional lawyer and a future party president; Raymond
Garneau, a former Quebec cabinet minister and the party's finance

critic; Eric Maldoff, a Montreal lawyer and former head of an English-language rights group, Alliance Quebec; and Michèle Tremblay, a journalist who had joined Turner's staff as an adviser on Quebec. Tremblay co-ordinated the effort and did most of the drafting. The committee's mandate was to come up with a position that the party, and the province, could accept.

The committee forged ahead quietly that spring. It was so independent that Stuart Langford, Turner's chief of staff, did not even know about it. The committee was completing its work in May, around the time Gil Rémillard was presenting Quebec's conditions at Mont Gabriel. Before unveiling the platform, Garneau met with Jean-Claude Rivest, Bourassa's chief constitutional adviser. Rivest liked what he saw. He told the Liberals if the federal government had made the same offer, Quebec would have to accept it. (His response suggested that Quebec was prepared to accept less at Meech Lake than it actually got.) The platform, then, had passed its first test: winning Quebec's approval. Now it had to win support from the caucus and the party.

Turner unveiled the platform in an interview on 11 June with *Le Devoir,* Quebec's prestigious daily newspaper which was essential reading for the elites. The platform had five main parts. It proposed a preamble to the constitution that would recognize "the distinct character of Quebec, the principal homeland of francophones in Canada; and the linguistic duality and multicultural character of Canada." To ensure cultural security, it confirmed Quebec's power to select immigrants. It also proposed amending Section 23 of the constitution to allow minority language groups to control their educational institutions, while withdrawing the restriction of providing education only "where numbers warrant." It promised to restore to Quebec the veto over federal legislative and judicial institutions that affected its cultural security. It offered compensation to the provinces for transferring powers to the federal government. Lastly, it promised to repeal the notwithstanding clause.

The accompanying story in *Le Devoir* declared that Turner had broken with the constitutional past of his party — the vision of Trudeau and Chrétien — because he wanted to give Quebec what it had been refused in 1981. His platform was seen as a new beginning after the years of Liberal centralism. That weekend, a resolution comprising these elements of the platform was unanimously adopted by a general meeting of the Quebec wing of the Liberal party held at

Ste.-Hyacinthe. Turner's interview was timed to coincide with the meeting.

When Turner returned to Ottawa, he found that many Liberals, particularly those from English Canada, were incensed by the party's new position. They saw it as a reversal of Liberal policy. "The interview was a bombshell," recalls Charles Caccia, a former minister in the Trudeau cabinet. "All of a sudden we hear a position on federalism which took us all by surprise. There was no effort to find out what we might be thinking." Opposition came not only from Caccia, but from Sergio Marchi and John Nunziata of Toronto, and David Berger and Donald Johnston of Montreal. Eventually, all became opponents of the accord, and of Turner himself. Of all the critics in caucus, Johnston was the most outspoken and impassioned. He had been urged to enter politics by Pierre Trudeau, for whom he had acted as lawyer. After winning a seat in Parliament in 1978, he held a string of senior economic portfolios. In 1984, he ran unsuccessfully for the leadership, refusing to throw his support behind either Chrétien or Turner on the last ballot. Johnston was sharp, intelligent, ornery. A keeper of the flame, he watched for any wavering from Trudeau federalism and opposed it vigorously. On economic and social policy, he was a maverick; now he was prepared to be the same on the constitution. His dissent cost him his position as critic in the shadow cabinet, then drove him from the caucus itself. It soured his relationship with Turner and alienated him from fellow Quebeckers. No matter: Johnston decided early what he would do and never retreated. Meech Lake became a crucible for him, the cause of his life, as free trade was for John Turner.

Johnston was angry about the substance and the process. He was miffed that no one had consulted him, although Michèle Tremblay insists all Quebec MPs had access to the drafts. After all, Johnston said, Trudeau had always sought his opinion on Quebec policy, acknowledging his role as a spokesman for the 800,000 anglophones in Quebec. More important, Johnston worried about what the new platform represented. "It was really a statement of special status, a pandering to the Quebec nationalists," he said in 1989. "It was farther than the party had ever gone in the creation of two Canadas. I was concerned with the whole way the debate was going. Turner said he was relying on his Quebec advisers. He seemed psychologically to have written off the English community in Quebec." Turner was getting advice from Quebeckers and did not apologize for it. He believed it was Quebec's turn. But he denies any effort to exclude English Liberals like Johnston, whose position he already knew. "I knew where he was coming from," says Turner, "and whose ideas he was reflecting — Trudeau's."

Why was the party raising the question at all? Johnston asked. His riding, St. Henri–Westmount, was almost equal parts French and English. No one had raised the issue in 1986. "I never got one letter on it, one phone call, one question," he said. "And here I'm told everyone is wringing their hands, lying awake at night, saying, 'Isn't this terrible?' It was total nonsense. There was no issue. The fact that Quebec didn't sign was just a curiosity." That August, Johnston went public with his reservations in an article in the *Globe and Mail*. His intervention did not endear him to his former cabinet colleagues from Quebec, who had already concluded that he was beyond persuasion. "He has no influence in today's Quebec," says Serge Joyal. "He wrote in the *Globe,* not *La Presse.* That says something. The debate was in Quebec, not in Toronto." Other Liberals said Johnston didn't play by the rules. "I thought we were taking his views into account, and then, all of a sudden, he goes outside the debating society to shoot at issues with larger artillery," remembers Robert Kaplan. "To appeal for public support for his position, while all the rest of us were trying to find something to agree on, made it hard for us to continue our work."

Johnston's reluctance to reopen the question may have been shared by his caucus colleagues, but it was too late to stop the preparation of a party position. In September, when the caucus met in special session before Parliament resumed, the constitution had become even more divisive. The meeting was stormy. "The shit hit the fan," says Tremblay. "As a Quebecker, sitting in that hall, I felt hostility, even racism. It was absolutely unbelievable." At the end, Turner gave what Tremblay calls "the speech of his life," which was conciliatory and inspiring.

In an attempt to find common ground, Turner formed a second committee. Chaired by Kaplan, the former solicitor general, and Lucie Pépin, an MP from Montreal, it held a series of weekly discussions to broaden the platform. The discussions now included Johnston, who commended the effort to accommodate differences of opinion. As part of the process, Kaplan and others visited Trudeau in Montreal. The former prime minister listened politely and then challenged the need to raise the issue. His view was rejected. Turner also met Trudeau, a meeting arranged by Joyal, and that, too, was fruit-less. Kaplan understood Trudeau's argument for lying low but thought it impossible. "An opposition can't function like that," he says. "We can't watch the government initiative and reply, 'Take it back and save it for ten years.' The provinces, Quebec and Mulroney had made it their priority, and we were being urged by these wise elders not to do anything. Trudeau would have liked to have run the show that way, but unfortunately it wasn't ours to run." The party believed it had to respond formally to Quebec's isolation and to its five proposals unveiled in May 1986. A revised resolution, reflecting a broader consensus, was presented at its national-policy convention in November.

Resolution Eight embodied most of what had been adopted at Ste.-Hyacinthe. In the preamble to the constitution, the party would rec-ognize: "i) the commitment of Canadians to maintain and reinforce across Canada the linguistic dualilty of the Canadian federation; ii) the distinctive character of Quebec as the principal but not the ex-clusive source of the French language and culture in Canada." In the same clause, it would also recognize multiculturalism, the value of re-gional identities in shaping Canadian society, the contribution of ab-original peoples and the advantages of developing the economic union of Canada, elements added to the platform to broaden the con-sensus. At the same time, the new resolution dropped the word "*foyer*," or homeland, which had been in the Ste.-Hyacinthe resolu-tion. It reminded Donald Johnston of South Africa.

Like the earlier resolution, this one proposed Senate reform, guar-anteeing Quebec a minimum number of seats and requiring a double majority of both English and French senators for passing laws on lan-guage or culture. On immigration, the party promised to entrench the Cullen-Couture Agreement. On language, it would recognize the right of language minorities to control and manage their schools and would withdraw the "where numbers warrant" stipulation. It, too, would withdraw the notwithstanding clause. Where the resolution also differed from the earlier one, reflecting the internal review, was on the amending formula (it wanted a return to the Victoria Charter) and on spending power (it promised only to convene a federal-provincial conference to discuss Ottawa's spending power in areas of provincial jurisdiction and federal commitments on regional equality and entitlement programs). Lastly, the party urged Ontario to be-come officially bilingual.

While hard-core dissidents, such as Charles Caccia, could not support the resolution, Johnston could live with it. To show that he was not using the constitutional question to attack Turner, Johnston met him before the convention to offer his support. They had a cordial chat, during which Johnston expressed concern about Turner's vagueness on some issues, including free trade. Turner assured him their views were alike on many issues (Johnston supported free trade), and Johnston thought that after Turner was confirmed, he would be freer to take stronger positions against the Herb Grays and the Lloyd Axworthys, who opposed free trade. At Turner's request, Johnston prepared memoranda for Turner on some of Johnston's pet issues — fiscal reform, education, research and development, a guaranteed annual income. He delivered them and never heard a word from Turner.

Because the real issue at that convention in Ottawa was John Turner's leadership — 75 percent of the delegates gave him a vote of confidence — the constitutional question attracted little attention. The modified resolution passed overwhelmingly with little debate, though a spirited attack on it was mounted by a lone provincial legislator from Manitoba, Sharon Carstairs. Still, it reflected a shift in the party's position from the Trudeau vision, a shift that became more pronounced when the accord was announced five months later.

If John Turner was taking the Liberal Party into new constitutional territory, it was not a complete surprise. Although he had served Trudeau as justice minister and finance minister, he never seemed at home in his philosophical camp. Turner was more comfortable with the co-operative federalism of Lester Pearson, whom he had served and admired. He had always been more sympathetic, however muted his feeling, to the nationalist impulse in Quebec and to the cause of provincial rights in general. Perhaps it was telling that while Pierre Trudeau was savaging Maurice Duplessis and his autocratic regime in *Cité Libre,* Turner was attending hockey games with the premier. "I recognized there had to be some equilibrium between collective and individual rights," Turner observes today on the ideological differences between Trudeau and himself. "Mr. Trudeau was stronger on individual rights. He didn't emotionally understand as fully the urge in Quebec for an understanding that there was a collective psychology. It was there. It was not an accident that *Le Devoir* took my position in an editorial during the leadership fight in 1968. But I didn't define it as 'special status.' I was not for 'two nations.'"

If his position was not "special status" or "two nations," it lay in between. Turner had hinted at special recognition for Quebec before. In a speech in 1967, he said: "I have said that this province represents the majority of French-speaking people in our country. For that reason, Quebec should play, within the Canadian framework, a different role, and this role should be played in a fashion different from that of the other provinces." Trudeau loyalists never believed that Turner was enamoured of their approach to Quebec. He did guide the Official Languages Act through the House of Commons and he did conduct constitutional negotiations with the provinces, but he never embraced the Trudeau vision. Says Marc Lalonde: "I remember in the late 1960s and early 1970s Turner tended to be a special-status guy. You know, 'Let Quebec be French and the rest of the country English.' It came out in discussion in cabinet and elsewhere. It was not too surprising that he could come to live with Meech Lake." Tom Axworthy, Trudeau's former principal secretary, is more definite. "Turner has been entirely consistent in his approach," he says. "He hasn't changed his mind. The differences were either subtle or submerged, but they were there." Michèle Tremblay, for her part, recalls that when Turner hired her he said he recognized the distinct society in 1968 ("It's nothing new for me," he said) and noted that he had long disagreed with Trudeau on the constitutional question. To her, and to others, Turner was always more generous and open to Quebec, more in tune with its moods and rhythms.

Turner himself had renewed doubts about his commitment to Trudeau Liberalism when he returned to politics in 1984. At the press conference announcing his candidacy on 16 March 1984, Turner cast doubt on a parliamentary resolution backing minority language rights in Manitoba, a controversy that had been raging all winter. While Pierre Trudeau was appealing for tolerance and Brian Mulroney, the newly elected Conservative leader, was battling his provincial cousins, Turner was equivocating. He talked in vague terms of provincial rights and of respecting jurisdiction. Later, as he did more than once during his leadership campaign, Turner recanted. But the damage was done. Turner had distanced himself from the party on minority rights.

No wonder that Trudeau, as he prepared to retire in 1984, was thought to believe that Mulroney was closer to his position than Turner. As one story had it, Trudeau had told Mulroney to "keep up the good work on language rights." Many of Trudeau's associates thought that he doubted Turner's commitment to federalism and was more comfortable with Mulroney. After all, it was Mulroney who had fought for the "Non" side during the referendum and intervened in Manitoba. Turner, for his part, had said little in political exile. In fact, before resigning as leader in 1990, he revealed that he had privately opposed the patriation package because it isolated Quebec. "A mistake was made in 1982," he said. "I doubt that I would have moved ahead in 1982 without Quebec. I wouldn't have signed the deal. I said nothing then. And I said nothing during my leadership because that would just unduly provoke people who would resent the statement. I said only then that I could well understand what happened in 1982 because Quebec had a separatist government. I left it at that." When Turner returned to public life he found a constitutional deal he did not like, a vision he did not share, and a party he could not unify.

Six years later, Turner would survey the wreckage of his stewardship and lament his broken career. It wasn't supposed to be this way. In the 1960s, he had been the bright hope of Canadian politics. Handsome, graceful and bilingual, he seemed to have it all. He was terribly Canadian. Raised in Ottawa, he went to school in British Columbia and vacationed in New Brunswick. His wife was from Winnipeg. He had gone to Oxford, where he was a Rhodes Scholar and a superb athlete. One of his classmates said of him, "We all knew John Turner would be prime minister of Canada one day. The only question was: for which party?" Turner returned to practise law in Montreal and won a seat there in 1962. He later represented an Ottawa riding, then practised law in Toronto, returned to Ottawa and won a Vancouver riding. If geography mattered, Turner was everyman's politician. But, in being from everywhere, he was from nowhere. Turner was so much of the whole country that one wondered if he understood any one part of it.

Turner left politics in 1976. He had asked for a chat with the prime minister to clear up problems, and left submitting his resignation. Trudeau, never much on career counselling, had cavalierly offered the crown prince a seat in the Senate. Turner was insulted and stormed out in high dudgeon. He said later that he left over policy differences on wage-and-price controls, another position he revised during his leadership campaign. There was more to his departure than a disagreement over policy. Turner knew that Trudeau was not going; the job he coveted was not open. Keith Davey, who would later fall out with Turner, advised him to leave politics in the mid-

1970s. As Davey tells it, Turner later developed a deep antipathy for the prime minister. "Turner had an absolute pathological fear and dislike of Trudeau," he said. "Their relationship became nonexistent when Turner left Ottawa. Neither had much respect for the other. Turner was not one of Trudeau's favourite players, but he didn't have much time to waste talking about it. Turner absolutely, utterly, totally rejected Trudeau." Another reason to quit was to make money. Turner told Eugene Whelan, a Trudeau loyalist, that he did not want to become "a financial eunuch" like other politicians.

The pretender with blue eyes and high ambition sought refuge in Toronto, where he spent nine years doing deals and hosting lunches, waiting for the main chance. There was little evidence that he thought much about the country. To many, just being John Turner was enough; all the whispering about his inevitable rise to the top would inevitably propel him there. As was true of Edward Kennedy when he ran for the presidency in 1980, Turner was never as popular as the day before he declared his candidacy. The problem was that he had waited so long that many did not know him; when he fumbled early and often, they wondered what the fuss was about. Suddenly, his march to destiny ceased to be inexorable. It began to fall apart for him the moment he stepped before the television lights on 16 March 1984.

The success at Meech Lake surprised Turner. Anticipating failure, he was in Montreal to criticize Mulroney's inability to accommodate Quebec. Now, the morning after, Turner had to respond to an agreement. He would have to reconcile his party's position and the new accord. When Parliament met at 11:00 a.m. on Friday, 1 May 1987, Turner was not at Question Period. His understudy, Herb Gray, asked only about the process. When the House reconvened in early afternoon, Turner looked and sounded as if he supported the accord. Brian Mulroney walked across the floor to shake his hand. The pictures on the television news that night seemed to show Turner congratulating Mulroney, which embarrassed Turner. "That's one of his favourite gimmicks," he says. "But when the prime minister of Canada walks across the floor, you cannot refuse to shake his hand. Are you going to turn your back on the PM on TV?" Later Turner told Bob Kaplan: "The next time you see Mulroney moving, let me know. I'm getting out."

Turner's support was not unqualified. In his remarks in the Commons, he congratulated Mulroney, Bourassa and the other premiers. He called it "a happy day for Canada and Quebec" because the province was a partner in Confederation again. While he had not read the text of the accord, he was satisfied with the recognition of Canada's linguistic duality and Quebec's distinctiveness as "a sound foundation on which to build our future." In the same remarks, he raised several key questions about the distinct society (Would it be in the preamble?); the spending power (Would it preclude national programs?); and the veto (Would it kill institutional reform?). He wanted to know if the federal government won anything in return for its concessions to the provinces, such as expanding minority language rights or withdrawing the notwithstanding clause. Both had been in his party's resolution. He also asked about the prospects of a full parliamentary debate. Immediately, Turner was sending out mixed signals. He had embraced the agreement while raising doubts about it. This ambivalence characterized his handling of the issue. On the one hand, the accord was marvellous. On the other hand, it was menacing. But what would the party do if it could not change it?

On television the following Monday, Turner broadened his questions to include aboriginal rights. He also attacked "the constitutional straitjacket" imposed by the requirement for unanimous consent for changing federal institutions. Donald Johnston, who was outraged by the accord, was cheered. He was confident Turner shared his reservations. At a meeting of his senior caucus members (including Raymond Garneau, Bob Kaplan and Lloyd Axworthy) at 1:00 p.m. on Tuesday 5 May, Johnston savaged the deal. He called it a denial of the kind of the country the party had stood for and a capitulation to Quebec nationalism. Garneau followed. "He just sat there chewing his lip, and then he just tore into us," Johnston remembers. "He has a bit of anglophobia, Raymond does, about the privileged English in Quebec. He has never understood the country or the constitution. He is a Quebecker first, a Canadian second. He told us we were the only people off-side on this. Everyone was saying what a great thing it was except John Turner. It was just awful."

The meeting degenerated into a shouting match. Axworthy was unhappy that the party's position, which he had been defending, was now changing. It was already clear that some members of the party saw little difference between their platform and the accord. (Eric Maldoff, for example, remembers attacking the accord the previous weekend in the company of senior Liberals. He thought it was inconsistent with the platform. Joyal and Garneau "were absolutely astonished that I was horrified," he said. "They thought Meech Lake was sufficient.") At the caucus meeting, each side questioned the other's good faith. "It seemed to be, 'This guy is a mouthpiece for Bourassa, this guy is a mouthpiece for Trudeau,'" says Kaplan, who supported the accord and wanted to call a national meeting of the party to debate it. The idea got nowhere because Turner thought opponents of Meech Lake would use it to undermine his leadership. Meanwhile, Turner asked caucus members to reserve public judgement. To satisfy Turner, Johnston left the meeting and called the *Westmount Examiner* to hold a column he had written attacking the accord.

If the special caucus of senior Liberals had been awful for Johnston, the Quebec caucus the next morning — Wednesday, 6 May — was worse. This was a regular meeting of the Quebec Liberals before the national caucus. Johnston describes it as the most difficult caucus in ten years in politics. "I really feel as if I'm sitting with a bunch of members of the National Assembly," Johnston told his colleagues in French. "Our perspective on Canada by definition has to be different from that of provincial members. Is this serving the national interest?" Johnston was roundly denounced by Garneau and André Ouellet. Ouellet called Johnston a "Westmount Rhodesian," what René Lévesque used to call unilingual English Montrealers. Johnston had no allies at the meeting. David Berger, who later opposed the accord, was not there. Sheila Finestone, who represented Trudeau's old riding, and Warren Allmand, another English Montrealer who voted against the patriation package because it did not offer enough protection to anglophone rights, supported the deal. At the national caucus meeting that followed, Johnston had more support. The caucus decided to study the question. Meanwhile, the Tories were set to exploit the division among the Liberals. That afternoon, they announced they would table a resolution in Parliament, supporting the accord in principle. The Commons would vote the following Monday.

Johnston was agonizing. Should he go public with his criticism, to salve his conscience, or remain silent, to preserve party unity? On Thursday, 7 May, Johnston learned that Turner and Gray had decided on their own that the party would support the resolution on Monday. Johnston, angry that no one had spoken to him, decided to resign as caucus critic on external affairs. In a letter to Turner, he wrote: "I hold views on the constitution and the Meech Lake Accord which I feel obliged to make known. I see long-term consequences flowing from the accord which could radically change the shape of the Canadian federation from a political, economic, and social point of view." He said his views might not change any minds but he wanted to be free to state them. He reminded Turner that he had always been loyal to him, "both as a leader and a friend, and dedicated to your success and that of the Liberal Party. That will not change."

The letter was written, but where to send it? Turner had gone to visit his ailing mother on the West Coast. Johnston tried repeatedly to contact Turner, an effort that made the antics of the Keystone Kops look like the Mounties' Musical Ride. Later, Kaplan met Johnston at a snack bar in the East Block and tried to talk him out of resigning. He invited Johnston to support the party's forthcoming amendments to the accord. (Turner, always one to seek advice, had asked him and Ouellet to canvass the caucus and to suggest changes.) Johnston turned him down. "I felt then that Johnston was finished with us, if it wasn't over one thing it was over another," recalls Kaplan. As Kaplan talked to Johnston, Herb Gray tried to placate Lloyd Axworthy, who was also unhappy. At that moment, the party was in danger of alienating two of its most prominent spokesmen.

Johnston did not hear from Turner that day. "The bastard never called me back," he says. On Friday, Johnston finally reached the leader at breakfast on Saltspring Island. (The two contradict each other on who called whom, when. Turner says the breakfast call was the first he heard that Johnston was trying to reach him. "Let's have no games on that," he says.) The transcontinental conversation was strained. Turner asked Johnston to be patient. "Don, wait until Monday!" he pleaded. "We'll talk. I can't talk from out here. I'm three thousand miles away." Johnston said that, if the party was going to approve the resolution in principle, there was no point in waiting. "This is not helpful," said Turner. "It's not fair." But Johnston would not be moved. It was 10:30 a.m. in Ottawa, and his letter was ready to be distributed. The media got it during Question Period, which surprised and angered his colleagues. Marchi called it "a bit of showmanship." When he and others left the Commons, they were peppered with questions about the party's divisions.

The imbroglio between Turner and Johnston reflected the growing split among Liberals over Quebec. "It ripped the party apart on linguistic lines," laments Michel Robert. "That was very damaging because, since Laurier became leader in 1896, the Liberal party had been the place of conciliation between the two groups." It also showed Turner's failure to manage dissent, and the personal cost to him and others of Meech Lake. "I am very fond of Don," says Turner. "He was my student at Stikeman & Elliott. I hired him. He was my tennis partner. But Don isolated himself from the mainstream of Quebec thinking." Johnston, for his part, says he tried to be fair to Turner. He regrets only the timing of his letter of resignation, not the contents.

Johnston was no longer alone in his opposition. As the debate began to intensify in the weeks before the agreement was sealed by the premiers at Langevin, some of his colleagues began to reconsider. On 11 May, the House of Commons debated a resolution supporting the accord in principle. There was no recorded vote, and the Liberals were spared embarrassment. Turner supported the resolution but restated his reservations, one of which was that the House was being asked to support an agreement that was not yet in its final form. "I want to make it perfectly clear that we do not interpret this motion as a blind endorsement of the statement of principles agreed upon at Meech Lake," he said. "At the same time, I view this as a general framework for discussion, not the final solution." His ambivalence was deepening. A party research paper summarized the position this way: "The Liberal response was positive in its attitude towards constitutional renewal: progress was necessary and desirable but there were clear limitations on the concessions which could be made to achieve it." That seemed to mean the accord if necessary, but not necessarily the accord. During that debate and those that followed before the meeting at Langevin, Turner hoped to persuade the premiers and the prime minister to accept changes. The larger question, though, still remained unanswered. What would the party do if the amendments failed, as they surely would?

In his remarks on 11 May, he spelled out his reservations. Entrenching two first ministers' conferences a year would create another level of government. The distinct-society clause did not recognize multiculturalism or aboriginal people. The limitations on federal spending power would limit new social programs. Still, having raised these and other questions, Turner supported the accord. He did not try to hold up the agreement in the hope of forcing changes, the way Joe Clark and Ed Broadbent tried to delay the patriation package in 1981. From Turner, there were no threats, just exhortations. "On two recent occasions, Quebec has said yes to Canada," he said. "Now is an opportunity for this country to say yes to Quebec."

While Turner was thrashing about in search of a position, he was in no mood for dissent. When David Berger assumed Johnston's mantle and condemned the accord, Turner fired him. Berger — a likable though little-known parliamentarian — was expendable. He allowed Turner to show that he was in control of the caucus. But sacking Berger won him no points. "It was mean," says Charles Caccia. "I don't understand it. Young David was honest and made some very difficult speeches in caucus. Here, Turner went after the youngest. It was unbelievable." Caccia, for his part, took a different tack than Berger's and Johnston's. Although unalterably opposed to the accord, he did not immediately attack it in public. In fact, Caccia was conspicuously silent in early May. "I thought you should fight from the inside, and respect the rules of the game," he explained later. Unlike Johnston, Caccia did not resign from the caucus (although he was later removed as environment critic). It never crossed his mind, making it harder for Turner to accuse Caccia and other malcontents of using Meech Lake to undermine his authority.

After the meeting at Langevin, Turner's problems intensified. Bad enough that Pierre Trudeau's broadside had raised doubts about the accord. Now the resolution would go to a parliamentary committee and return to the Commons for a vote. There would be no sliding, shambling or shuffling; the party would have to take a stand. As many as one-third of the caucus members were threatening to oppose the accord, which would fracture the party.

At a special meeting in early June, all the members of the caucus spoke, each offering his or her view of Canada. This was the Liberal party, they told themselves, the party that had always been the bridge between solitudes, and now it was crumbling. By all accounts, this was an emotional session that went from afternoon into evening. "If we support Meech Lake, where would we be?" asked Senator Jerry Grafstein. "Where would we stand? We would be nothing." On the other side, no less eloquent and no less passionate, were Jean-Claude Malépart, the streetwise populist from the east end of Montreal who would die of cancer before the debate reached its climax, and Raymond Garneau, who would lose his seat in the next election. They asked where the party would be in Quebec if it rejected the accord.

Towards the end of this catharsis, it was Turner's turn to speak, to sum up the consensus. He spoke for some time, arguing that the party must accept the accord. Sensing the opposition in the room, he said he would go over the head of the caucus to appeal to the party, that he was on the right side of history, that he would go to the aid of Quebec as had Laurier and King. What shocked his colleagues — not just his adversaries — was that he seemed to be reading a prepared speech. The dissidents thought he had not listened to them, that this long debate had been a sham. "I knew it was over for him then," says John Nunziata. "I turned to Sheila [Copps] and said, 'This guy is finished.' How could he continue if he didn't understand the party and the caucus?"

Turner calls this "a bum rap," explaining that he always brought to the caucus notes that he would edit during the debate. On this occasion, he listened for hours. He scribbled comments and replied to arguments. The allegation that he ignored his caucus still angers him today. Perhaps he was right. Perhaps the accusation was unfair. Perhaps it was a misunderstanding. But as so often in this debate, it was how it looked. "From that moment, there was poison in the air, almost bordering on hatred between those of us who dissented and Turner," remembers Caccia. "We could not believe he would betray the party."

That summer the House of Commons set up a special joint committee to study the accord and report to Parliament. The hearings were meaningless because Mulroney had said that nothing in the accord could be changed unless it were an "egregious" error. Of course, the committee never found one; the most enduring result of this process was the entering of "egregious" into the constitutional lexicon. Even if the outcome of this exercise was a foregone conclusion, the Liberals took it seriously. The committee gave them a forum to propose their own package of amendments, which, although they could not change the accord, would help put distance between the party and the government. Both the Liberals and the Tories ended up in the same unpleasant place at the end of the day, but if the Liberals could say they had taken a more scenic route, more of them might accept the inevitability of the destination. At root, the amendments were designed to placate the dissidents. They would be of more help to John Turner than to the constitution. The process was a shell game, a hollow within a hole.

André Ouellet knew all this ("The special committee was a public relations exercise for the government," he says), but played along

anyway. He and Robert Kaplan, who had been involved with the issue since the party resolution in 1986, were now asked to sit on the
committee and draft the party's package of amendments. It was no
surprise that Ouellet and Kaplan were chosen; both were supporters
of Turner and Meech Lake. A problem arose, however, when Don
Johnston demanded to appear. "Those bastards," Johnston says.
"They wouldn't let me testify. Ouellet and I nearly came to blows on
this." If Johnston wanted to testify, Ouellet said, other MPs would
too. He told Johnston: "You're behaving like a kid." The committee
decided that no parliamentarians would testify, but there could be no
doubt which parliamentarians they had in mind.

Meanwhile, Turner was trying to mend fences. While the committee was meeting in July and August, he individually invited members
of his caucus to lunch, usually at his favourite restaurant in Hull.
Turner, with his nineteenth-century sense of honour, politesse and
reason, wanted to talk things through. When it was Caccia's turn,
Turner asked why the two of them could not be friends. Caccia, who
is equal parts cerebral and emotional, was blunt. "In order to become
friends, there has to be an ideological bond," he told Turner. "Between you and me, there is none. Until we can establish a bond on
federalism, there cannot be friendship, as much as I regret saying
that." Caccia says the conversation was hard because Turner wanted
to bury the hatchet. The leader knew he was in trouble in caucus and
was asking for friendship. Caccia said no; such was his hostility to the
accord. The meeting was polite but cold. Turner had been rebuffed.
All he would say later was, "Charles Caccia is not the easiest man to
have lunch with, no matter what the subject." Caccia, for his part,
saw the emerging tragedy. "I felt sorry for the man because he was
trying to build bridges. I would have liked to reciprocate, but ideologically it was impossible."

Turner was encountering a similar coolness from others who
lunched with him. Nunziata says it was like going to the dentist: "He
wasn't there. I got the impression this was a burden, a responsibility." Nunziata, Marchi, Berger, Johnston and Caccia were joined in
their opposition to Meech Lake by Sheila Finestone, David Dingwall,
George Henderson, Russell MacLellan, Fernand Robichaud and
Keith Penner. On 9 September, the special joint committee reported
to Parliament and, as expected, endorsed the accord without any
changes. In the same report, the Liberals issued a minority view with
their own set of amendments. Warren Allmand proposed those

changes in the House on 1 October, but they were defeated on 26 October by a vote of 219 to 37. When a vote on the unamended accord was taken the same day, the moment of truth arrived for the Liberals. Eleven members — more than one-quarter of their forty-member caucus — voted against the resolution, which passed 242 to 16. Each had his or her reasons. For Dingwall, it was the process; for MacLellan, the decentralization of power; for Penner, aboriginal rights. "We sold the farm for a run-down, old half-ton truck," he moaned.

Insiders suggest that more Liberals wanted to oppose the resolution but voted with the party for the sake of unity. Some critics were urged to disappear or abstain. Sergio Marchi refused. "If I stayed away from that vote, I would be nothing," he recalls. "I would be no better than the alderman from North York that I used to be." This time there were no firings, no recriminations.

The Liberal amendments, as moved in the Commons, were appended to the report of the special joint committee. Kaplan and Ouellet did not oppose the majority report; they simply refused to sign it. They thought the Conservatives had ignored views expressed "time after time by independent witnesses" at the hearings. But they were not angry enough to reject the whole accord. They had, as Turner liked to say, kept their options open. In their minority report, the Liberals reiterated their general support for Meech Lake. At the same time, they denied the government's claim that the accord was "a seamless web" that would unravel with changes. There was still time, they suggested, to include women, aboriginal peoples and northern Canadians. Meech Lake could be changed. "We regret that the Prime Minister did not utilize this window of opportunity to complete more of the national constitutional agenda," their report says. "We are convinced that this was, and still is, possible."

The amendments were predictable. They called for the repeal of the notwithstanding clause and the "where numbers warrant" provision. They accepted the distinct society in the main body of the agreement — a departure from the party resolution — but wanted to recognize native peoples, multicultural and regional identities and the advantages of developing the economic union in Canada. They also gave Parliament a mandate "to preserve and promote" linguistic rights, and to confer more responsibility on provincial legislatures to protect linguistic minorities. Furthermore, the amendments made the Charter supreme over the entire act, not just certain parts of it.

Until the Senate was reformed, the Liberals called for election to the Senate for a nine-year term. They suggested breaking a deadlock in appointments to the Supreme Court by appointing judges from the Federal Court for one year. They wanted spending programs established by the "Parliament of Canada," not the government, and they wanted them "compatible with minimum national standards." They wanted to remove the Senate from the unanimity rule for amendments, allowing changes by seven provinces with 50 percent of the population. For the creation of new provinces, they wanted to leave power with the federal government. As for the national conferences ad infinitum, they returned aboriginal rights to the agenda, but put the fishery on it only for the first meeting. On balance, the amendments reflected a more traditional Liberal vision of the constitution, though not necessarily Trudeau's.

While they did not embody the party platform, the changes did try to come to terms with the accord in hand. All in all, it was an attempt to set things right without setting the accord on fire. "We have formulated nine amendments to correct serious flaws which we think need to be corrected," said Allmand when he introduced them in the House of Commons. "We do not believe that correcting any one of the flaws by way of any one of our nine amendments will in any way take away from the five conditions of Mr. Bourassa."

Allmand could say that, but the truth was his party's amendments would alter the accord. To allow the federal government to preserve and promote minority language rights in Quebec, for example, would allow Ottawa to intervene in Quebec, which is why the provincial government wanted sole power to preserve and promote the distinct society. When New Brunswick wanted a similar right for the federal government to be written into a parallel accord, it got nowhere with Bourassa. Similarly, Bourassa was reluctant to guarantee the supremacy of the Charter because that might limit the distinct-society clause. The other provinces, for their part, were unlikely to accept "minimum national standards" in their cost-sharing programs. That might reduce their flexibility to spend money as they chose when they opted out.

The vote in the Commons on 26 October was not the end of the parliamentary process. The resolution went to the Senate, where the Liberals used their majority to force a new round of hearings. One of the witnesses was Pierre Trudeau, who delivered a stinging denunciation of the accord, as he had the previous August before the Commons committee. The Senate committee then issued its own report, adopting a package of amendments identical to the one the Liberals had already moved. The Senate rejected the resolution, and it went back to the House of Commons for a second vote. On 22 June 1988, the Commons voted again. Again the party whip and others begged the dissidents to stay away. This time, the number of Liberal opponents dropped to six. Sergio Marchi abstained.

During those eight months between votes, and through the election campaign in the autumn of 1988, Meech Lake continued to consume the party. Within the parliamentary caucus and among the membership, there was a feeling that the issue had impaired the effectiveness of the leader. The difference of opinion was not over whether the constitutional question would overwhelm Turner, but over exactly how and when. Until his departure in 1990, Turner believed that his opponents were using Meech Lake to do him in. It was less principle than personality. They did not like him. They did not want him. They never had. Turner put it this way: "There was no doubt that for those who had never accepted my leadership in 1984, who were reinforced after the election that year, and had tried to unseat me in 1986 [that] Meech Lake gave these forces an intellectual legitimacy. Meech Lake became a shield for those opposed to my leadership for various reasons." In his darkest hour, Turner never doubted that he was right. "I paid a political price for Meech Lake," he says. "I paid a price for my concept of what was needed for the country. It might well have cost me the [1988] election."

One explanation for Turner's position is that he thought it was both good politics and good principle. After all, even his opponents conceded that Turner was saying in the 1980s what he had said in the 1960s. That argument is credible. It may also have been true, on the other hand, that he did not really believe in the accord but felt it was good politics, just as some suspected that he was not really opposed to free trade, but that position, too, was politically smart.

Others argued that the battle was greater than John Turner. Turner's most vehement critics on Meech Lake — Nunziata and Johnston — had supported him publicly during the leadership review in 1986. Caccia, who did not, refused to go public immediately after Meech Lake was announced. Had they really wanted to wound him, they could have attacked him earlier. They believed the party's popularity in Quebec was paramount to him and others. The argument of those who supported the accord was: "If we defeat Meech Lake, we lose Quebec." Or, "Meech Lake will do to us what the hanging of Louis Riel did to the Conservatives: consign the party to the margins of politics for decades." Turner had expressed these kinds of sentiments in private. So had Garneau, Malépart, Ouellet and Joyal. Eric Maldoff, who was not an active Liberal but was invited to help draft the party platform, remembers how Garneau and Joyal responded when Maldoff attacked the accord in early May 1987. "Both their faces fell," he says. "Garneau walked out of the room and came back and then laid on me the politics of this. 'Whether you like it or not, we have to endorse it [the accord] because this could break us away from the Quebec electorate for perpetuity.' Suddenly I was given all the low-ball arguments for doing things in politics."

Things began to deteriorate as the two camps dug in. The issue had moved off the floor of the Commons and into the Senate and the provinces, but it never went away. The accord became a lightning rod for all that was wrong with the leader. Indecision on free trade and cruise missile testing compounded Turner's image problems. Few in caucus believed in him any more. The summer of lunches had not helped. When Turner made impassioned speeches in the House, a coterie of Liberals rushed behind him to make the chamber look full on television. They applauded dutifully at the end. Below the surface, the cancer was spreading. "The opposition [to Turner] emerged progressively," recalls André Ouellet. "Turner realized that he was facing a more and more hostile caucus because of Meech Lake and those opposing him were using this pretext to be even more vehement against him. The anti-Turner movement now had a cause to more openly and more radically oppose him. It was a rallying point for some."

In their bitterness, the Johnstons and the Caccias had more credibility than the Marchis and Nunziatas. For Caccia, a parliamentarian and minister for two decades, Meech Lake was the end of a dream. It meant, as he said, undoing everything he had built. "Turner ruined our lives," he laments. "You would go home and it was the subject at breakfast, lunch and dinner. It became the dominant feature of life to an unhealthy degree. The decision generated internal anger. It meant twenty years of struggle thrown out the window." To Caccia, and some of the others, it would not have been as bad if this was solely government policy. But for the Liberal party to act as accomplice was to them unforgivable. "Can you live in peace?" Caccia asks.

"Can you forgive anyone? It's enough to make you climb a wall at midnight."

Turner believes that the ill-fated attempt to remove him in April 1988 was helped by the accord. It offered his opponents a moral fig leaf. A senior Liberal approached caucus members and asked them to sign individual letters urging Turner to resign. When he had fifteen letters, he would approach the leader. Ultimately twenty-two members agreed to sign, Nunziata and Marchi among them. "I knew I could be seen as a traitor," remembers Marchi, "but I was convinced deep down that, if John was to step aside, the party would be saved and we would be able to turn the country around. Meech Lake was my reason." When the letters were presented to Turner at Stornoway, he did not want to see them and was prepared to resign. "How can I go on?" he asked his assistants that night. But his staff steeled his will, he refused to quit, and the palace coup collapsed.

Bleeding from a thousand cuts, Turner limped into the election campaign in October. Meech Lake was not an issue. The fratricide, however, had consumed the party's resources, alienated its loyalists and drained its creativity. Beyond free trade, Turner had few ideas. He was a one-issue candidate who concentrated so much on the north-south issue that he forgot about the east-west issue. "I don't think we would be in opposition today if we had taken a position on Meech Lake," says Caccia. "In the last two weeks of the campaign, when we had nothing more to say, we could have opened up a second front in addition to trade and kept the momentum going." While the accord was not an issue, Turner admitted later that he resented Mulroney's attempts to exploit the party's differences in Quebec by suggesting that the Liberals might reopen the accord if they were elected. For Turner, this was a low blow. "I didn't enjoy his playing politics with this during the election, insinuating that if the Liberals were elected they would not ratify Meech Lake," he says. "After the political price I had paid, I didn't appreciate that. He started to politicize the issue, and that was a dumb move too. He only has a few friends, and on this issue, Broadbent and I were among them. Playing politics with the constitution of the country is a dangerous game."

Ironically, his fellow Liberals were saying Turner was doing the same thing: playing the constitutional card to woo Quebec. But the folly of that approach became evident on election night, 21 November 1988. When the returns were in, the Liberals had fallen from seventeen to twelve seats in Quebec. It was their worst showing since

Confederation. The bastion of the the Liberal party, the foundation of its success, had been routed. It had taken two elections to dislodge the party in Quebec, and now the humiliation was complete. For this once-proud organization, Meech Lake produced the worst of both worlds: a divided membership and fewer seats. If there was a victory here, it could only be called a moral one.

The other casualty of Meech Lake, besides the party, was John Turner. From the moment he returned in 1984, his world had been falling apart. The crown prince had returned to claim his throne, only to be foiled by hubris. Instead of the prize, he found purgatory: a fitful run for the leadership, a painful interlude as prime minister, and a disastrous election campaign. By all measures of leadership, he had failed: he could not unite his party, articulate a vision, form a government-in-waiting.

His failure was evident in Turner as pretender, when he reversed himself on Manitoba. It was evident in Turner as prime minister, when he named Liberals to patronage posts and blamed his predecessor. It was evident in Turner as candidate, when he called an election for which the party was ill-prepared. Finally, it was evident in Turner as leader of the opposition. He took contradictory decisions and he could not keep his staff. The party went broke. The word went out: the gentleman was lazy, hazy and rusty. Every few months a new Turner would emerge, promising new ideas and new style. Inevitably, however, the old Turner would return, sowing new doubts and undoing the work of all the publicists and pamphleteers. He would, as someone once noted, rise to a challenge and then slip back again. Ultimately, the resurrection of John Turner failed. He left public life unfulfilled — somewhere between not yet and not ever.

Turner blamed Meech Lake for many of his problems, and he was in part right. "It's an area which could have been managed better by the leader," says Ouellet, who was one of Turner's supporters. "Because of his style, he allowed this situation to deteriorate rather than improve." It is here that the indecision asserted itself. True, there is much to suggest that Turner was always sympathetic to provincial rights in general and the demands of Quebec in particular. It is a legitimate view, submerged during the Trudeau years, which the accord brought to the surface again. Determined to accommodate Quebec, Turner moved the party away from what he thought was Trudeau's rigid federalism. In the end, it might have worked if he had been a little shrewder; after all, political leaders do change positions and survive. He might have carried it off, for example, if he had broadened the process of consultation before Ste.-Hyacinthe and stuck to the party's platform later on. But Turner did not seek a consensus and was unable to accommodate dissenters.

When Meech Lake was announced, he might have been more cautious. Instead of withholding support, Turner was quick to endorse the accord. Over the course of the next month, he was enthusiastic, lukewarm, skeptical and critical. Worse than wrong, he was indecisive. He was accused of being weak and malleable in the hands of his Quebec advisers; many said his position was determined by the last person who talked to him. It was no surprise that Raymond Garneau was so often at his side at critical moments during the constitutional debate. Persuading Turner which way to go on the constitution required only that he be the last person to get his ear.

As a response to Meech Lake, Turner might have offered his party's platform. In those five weeks between Meech Lake and Langevin, when the accord was still in flux, his influence was greater than he thought. If his party had stood foursquare against the accord, explained its impact and stirred public opinion, it might have helped Peterson, Ghiz and Pawley win concessions at Langevin. Using the party platform as a basis of negotiation, Turner might have neutralized critics, focussed the issue and rallied support. At worst, the talks at Langevin would have broken down and Bourassa would have walked away, as he did at Victoria in 1971. (Bourassa himself says that, had the accord collapsed at that early stage, it would have been a setback but not a catastrophe.) Even after Langevin, Turner might have used his amendments to oppose the resolution. He could have argued that his reservations were over decentralization and the transfer of power to the provinces, not over accommodating Quebec and recognizing its distinctiveness. In other words, Turner could have mounted an effective opposition that might have cost him something in Quebec — where his party was weak anyway — while consolidating support in the rest of the country. In the subsequent campaign, he could have married his opposition to Meech Lake to that of free trade. He could have barnstormed the country, posing the question, *à la* Trudeau: "Who speaks for Canada?"

Turner was unable to do that. It all ended for him that November night, a personal tragedy, the able, attractive politician who lost it all. He withdrew gracefully, his dream in ashes, his ambition unrealized.

Until the end, he remained decent and honourable and earnest. But the issue would not go away with him. Long after his departure, the thunder of the Constitutional Wars would resound deep within the troubled soul of the Liberal party.

Pierre Trudeau:
How Northern Magus
Became Cincinnatus

ON THAT NIGHT HE WALKED IN THE SNOW AND FOUND HIS FUTURE, Pierre Elliott Trudeau recovered his freedom. The next morning — 29 February 1984, a day that arrives only once every four years — he announced his resignation. In June, at his party's convention, he offered a political testament and a parting pirouette, his last official acts of rebellion. Then he abandoned Ottawa for Montreal, where he joined a prominent law firm. He lived in an art-deco mansion on the side of Mount Royal and retreated to a glass country house in the Laurentians. After almost twenty years away, Trudeau rediscovered the rhythm of life *before* politics. More than at any time in his life, he seemed to know what he needed and what he wanted.

Citizen Trudeau accepted his obscurity happily. The only evidence of his activities were rumours in gossip columns, photographs on social pages, footprints in exotic lands. He refused honorary degrees if they meant delivering the convocation address. He gave no interviews, made no speeches, published no articles. Despite handsome offers, he refused to write his memoirs. Writing was hard work, he complained, and he had no need to justify his past. Besides, memoirs were for old people. True, when he resigned at age sixty-four he was younger and more fit than Winston Churchill had been when he had become prime minister. The face remained a mask of insouciance, and the eyes still engaged those who came under their steady gaze. The frame was strong and supple, disciplined by the daily swim in his pool. His sex appeal endured. He continued to be interested in young women, who accompanied him to Place des Arts or the Musée des Beaux Arts, and they continued to be interested in him. A poll in 1989 found him women's third most popular choice for a companion on a desert island. He was sixty-nine.

The job was a place to go. Every morning he descended the stone steps at the top of Pine Avenue and walked to his office on Boulevard de Maisonneuve Ouest. It was uncertain what a special counsel did, and there were mumblings at the firm of Heenan Blaikie that he was paid too much, as if this plutocrat needed the money. He would lunch at a few favourite restaurants, often with Marc Lalonde, his former minister of finance, and Tom Axworthy and Ted Johnston, his two former assistants. Occasionally Trudeau paid; often he did not. There remained a few close friends, but not many. Of the old circle, he still saw Jacques Hébert, whom Trudeau had made a senator, and Gérard Pelletier, who had served in his cabinet. Jean Marchand, the fiery unionist who had accompanied Trudeau and Pelletier to Ottawa in 1965 as one of "the three wise men," was dead. Trudeau's associates remained protective, a kind of Praetorian Guard, and refused to say much about him out of respect or fear. Senator Leo Kolber, a wealthy businessman, was a frequent travelling companion. Few could explain their relationship other than that Trudeau liked to go in style and Kolber always saw to that.

There seemed to be no metamorphosis of Trudeau once he entered private life. The man remained an anachronism and an eccentric. He still thought you ought not get in a car with an ice-cream cone because — *quelle horreur!* — that wasn't done in the family Packard in 1931. The tongue was still biting and mirthless. There remained in him something of the pugilist — some called it the schoolyard bully — who had a curious need to affirm his superiority. It was the dark side of his character, and it explained much of his success. Some said he had mellowed in retirement but there was still the smirk, the snicker, the shrug. Age did not bring self-deprecating humour. Unlike Lester Pearson, he could never tell a joke on himself because that might diminish him. At three score and ten, Trudeau continued to command respect more than affection. Unlike Louis St. Laurent, no one would call him "Oncle." He might become frail, grey and owlishly wise, but he would never be an Eisenhower or an Adenauer. He did not want to be. The role of elder statesman, sipping sherry in a leather wingback chair, was anathema to him. In retirement, he would never be retiring.

His life revolved around his three teenaged boys, to whom he was a doting father. Keith Davey remembers a visit with Trudeau a few months after he left office. Trudeau showed him a briefcase full of letters and invitations, including one from the United Nations inviting the former prime minister to visit for the day. "This looks good, Pierre," exclaimed the senator. "They'll fly you there and back. Why don't you go?" The response was flat. "Easy for you to say, Keith," Trudeau said. "If I go away, who would give the boys their Latin that night?"

Another career seemed to hold no interest for him. One associate said that Trudeau would have liked to teach law, as he had before entering Parliament in 1965, and was disappointed that the Université de Montréal had not offered him his old job. Nor was he asked to join boards of directors, though, given his disdain for business, it is not hard to understand why. There had been talk of a position in an international organization, but here, too, nothing happened. He rejected an offer from a foreign government to act as adviser, and he declined Mulroney's request to join a prestigious international panel on South Africa. He did not want to be blamed if it failed.

As he continued to refuse roles other than those he had chosen for himself, Trudeau moved from the recent past to the distant past, returning to the life of the professional dilettante. He was now something between a dandy and a grandee. He defied the laws of convention as easily as the laws of life; he proved that you could go home again. In this light, his renunciation of politics was not surprising. Those who thought he would come to the aid of his party misunderstood him. Did they think he would address the Rotary Club in Hamilton? Trudeau had never cared much for the party, which was always more an instrument than an end, and leaving politics meant leaving it. His life had always been a set of watertight compartments of people, places and preoccupations — student, nomad, rebel, aesthete, athlete, politician, father, elder. Politics was just a phase. He did not disown his past, rather he placed it in perspective. He still honoured public service. "There's no more noble *métier* than politics," he told a friend a few months after he left office, insisting that he had no plans to return. "But the only thing that would drive me back is the constitution."

The constitution and Pierre Trudeau had become synonymous, like the House of Commons and the Peace Tower. The association gave him an enduring authority on the subject. During the patriation debate, a frustrated Jean Chrétien once complained: "You know, I wasn't born only to talk about the constitution!" Perhaps Trudeau was. John Roberts, one of his ministers, observed that the constitution represented "the distillation of his intellectual position." He had studied it, taught it, written about it. If Robert Bourassa knew the arithmetic of federalism, Pierre Trudeau knew the grammar. This was the only issue that truly animated him in government. Nothing came closer to a political *raison d'être*. Always, the interest was less nomenclature and nuance than rights and freedoms.

Trudeau was Canada's constitutional compass. For two decades, his philosophy on the role of the state, on the rights of people, on the future of Quebec, on the powers of the provinces and on the meaning of language had become conventional wisdom. His idea of Canada — a pluralist, egalitarian society endowed with a bilingual government — became known as the "Trudeau Vision." Although it was not his alone, his endurance and eloquence allowed him to claim paternity. There were those who knew more than Trudeau did and there were those who had been at it longer, but none had been prime minister for sixteen years. Trudeau set the tone, tenor and tempo of the debate. He was to the constitution what Bobby Orr was to hockey — the player who controlled the play, and could, on a good day, determine the outcome of the game itself.

On the constitutional compass, Trudeau represented True North. His philosophy had been forged in a lifetime of thought and practice. So clear was the vision, so strong the commitment, that it became the standard against which all others were measured. "Two nations," "special status," "a community of communities," "sovereignty-association" and "the distinct society" were competing doctrines judged in relation to his own. In his era, the question was to what extent other views of federalism differed from his. Those that deviated a few degrees from True North — say, a modest devolution of power to the regions — were open to debate. Those that deviated a lot — say, the creation of "two nations" — were rejected brutally and quickly. The problem with the Meech Lake Accord, for Trudeau and his acolytes, was that it set the compass needle 180 degrees from True North. It was not a retreat from his position, but a reversal. No wonder the prince so abhorred it.

Trudeau watched silently from Montreal as the debate over the accord unfolded in May 1987. He had been dismayed by his party's hasty endorsement. His conclusion was instinctive and categorical: the accord meant the dismantling of the country. He did not have to wait for the phone call from Mulroney offering to send Norman

Spector and André Burelle to Montreal to brief him. A three-hour apologia, even from Burelle, his trusted former assistant, would simply harden his stance. He talked to Donald Johnston and encouraged his opposition, hoping that he would arouse public anger. When he did not, Trudeau reconsidered. "I must do something," he told Gérard Pelletier. His reasoning was simple: "Nobody was objecting to Meech Lake and I thought somebody should object." But he was reluctant to speak out. He had taken a vow of silence, almost monastic, when he had left office nearly three years earlier. He felt strongly that leaders have their chance in government and should give others theirs. But what was different here was that this was not just any issue, and he was not just any politician. This was the constitution, the one issue he had always said could bring him back. Dante had warned that the hottest places in Hell were reserved for those who remain silent in time of crisis. Feeling the heat from the Inferno, Trudeau reached for pen and paper.

There was no need for soul-searching or deep research. He could find his way by dead reckoning. Trudeau wrote his essay himself, checking references with Tom Axworthy. He showed it to Pelletier, who suggested that he soften the tone. Pelletier approached *La Presse,* while Jim Coutts, Trudeau's former principal secretary, offered the English translation to the Toronto *Star.* Michel Roy, the editor of *La Presse,* also raised concerns about the tone, but Trudeau refused to change a word. The article appeared in both newspapers on 27 May 1987, six days before the premiers reconvened in Ottawa. The night before, Trudeau attended a dinner in Toronto honouring G. Emmett Cardinal Carter. While the presses were running in Montreal and Toronto, he sat at a head table with Brian Mulroney, John Turner and David Peterson. One of them — it is not certain who — congratulated him on his self-restraint on Meech Lake. Trudeau broke bread with his adversaries and smiled tightly. About the little surprise that awaited them in the morning, he never let on.

The article was a searing polemic, informed by logic, inflamed by hyperbole. It was the first time Trudeau spelled out his objections. Over the next three years, until the drama played itself out, he would return to these arguments in appearances on radio and television, in testimony before two parliamentary committees, and finally in a book on his government. The tone was reminiscent of the Trudeau of *Cité Libre* in the 1950s, the intellectual journal that flayed the rightist government of Maurice Duplessis and the Union Nationale. Here,

Trudeau returned to youthful logician, historian, ideologue, pamphleteer. The words were poison darts; the arguments *reductio ad absurdum*; the mood black. Trudeau believed the accord represented the end of his Canada. If saying that meant being a little nasty and lobbing a few Molotov cocktails, so be it.

Under the accord, bilingualism was a dead letter: "Those Canadians who fought for a single Canada, bilingual and multicultural, can say goodbye to their dream," he warned. "We are henceforth to have two Canadas, each defined in terms of its language." The Charter of Rights was impotent: "For those Canadians who dreamed of the Charter as a new beginning for Canada, where everyone would be on an equal footing and where citizenship would finally be founded on a set of commonly shared values, there is to be nothing left but tears." The other parts of the accord — on immigration, the Supreme Court, the amending formula, the limitation of federal spending power — were a sell-out to the provinces: "It doesn't take a great thinker to predict that the political dynamic will draw the best people to the provincial capitals, where the real power will reside, while the federal capital will become a backwater for political and bureaucratic rejects." For Trudeau, the accord could appeal only to those who hated bilingualism, the Charter and a strong central government.

Trudeau saved his heavy artillery for Brian Mulroney. "What a magician this Mr. Mulroney is, and what a sly fox," he exclaimed. "He has not quite succeeded in achieving sovereignty-association, but he has put Canada on the fast track for getting there." Between 1984 and 1987, Mulroney had wooed the provinces to the table with a host of concessions, he said, and then sealed the deal by giving away more federal powers. "What a dark day for Canada was this April 30, 1987!" wrote Trudeau. The accord was particularly galling, he said, because it was all so unnecessary. He denied Quebec was ever "out of the constitution" and argued that every time Canada had wanted to patriate the British North America Act, Quebec had demanded more concessions, or a form of special status, as a condition of approval. He acknowledged that it was unfortunate that patriation did not include Quebec, but Quebeckers still supported the package in 1982 even if their separatist government did not. "A gamble lost, a gamble won — big deal!" he wrote of the Patriation Round. "Quebec public opinion, with its usual maturity, applauded the players and then, yawning, turned to other matters."

Trudeau turned his wrath on the nationalists and provincialists in

Quebec, whom he called "perpetual losers." Because they did not have the stature to succeed in Canada, he said, they sought refuge in a ghetto in Quebec. If they didn't have the rights of French Quebec to protect, they would have no reason for being. "That bunch of snivellers should simply have been sent packing and been told to stop having tantrums like spoiled adolescents," he raged.

What particularly angered the former prime minister was that Ottawa had reopened the issue. Until 1982, the federal government had to make concessions in every round of talks to get the provinces to patriate the constitution. But, after 1982, he argued, it enjoyed the advantage. With the constitution patriated and the Charter entrenched, the provinces had lost their bargaining power. Talks could then take place without blackmail or precondition. Even a union of the ten provinces could not force the government's hand. "With the assurance of a creative equilibrium between the provinces and the central government, the federation was set to last a thousand years," he boasted. "Alas, only one eventuality hadn't been foreseen: that one day the government of Canada might fall into the hands of a weakling. It has now happened. And the Rt. Hon. Brian Mulroney, PC, MP, with the complicity of ten provincial premiers, has already entered into history as the author of a constitutional document which — if it is accepted by the people and their legislators — will render the Canadian state totally impotent. That would destine it, given the dynamics of power, to be governed eventually by eunuchs." (In French, Trudeau called Mulroney *un pleutre,* a term suggesting weakness as well as cowardice.)

With the same brush, Trudeau tainted the current premiers, Joe Clark, Robert Stanfield, Allan Blakeney and Jean Lesage. He did not mention John Turner by name, although his guilt was implicit. Trudeau raised the old shibboleths — nationalism, separatism, provincialism — and denounced them all. He took aim at the other visions and accused Mulroney of embracing them all. He repeatedly reaffirmed the need for a strong central government.

His "paper," as he called it, invited critics to focus on style rather than substance. Arthur Tremblay, the Conservative senator who had known Trudeau since they attended Harvard together in the 1940s, was shocked at the language and thought it would have little impact. Later, he concluded it aroused public opinion and gave the opposition stature. That the accord was flawed many accepted; the doubt was whether it was as bad as Trudeau said it was. His analysis assumed the worst. He presumed, for example, that high-court judges nominated by the provinces would champion regional interests, as if it were a certainty. The boast of the constitution's lasting a millennium — which evoked Hitler's Thousand-Year Reich — was infelicitous. So was the sprinkling of sexual references, such as "eunuch" and "impotent."

The attack was reminiscent of Trudeau's earlier taunts and jeers: *Just watch me. Why should I sell your wheat? Where's Biafra? Go on and bleed. Eat shit.* Former prime ministers did not behave like this. They did not attack their successors and they did not speak indelicately. Now, owing nothing to anyone, Trudeau railed at those who would desecrate his Canada. He had spent a lifetime breaking other people's rules. Now, in breaking his silence, he was breaking his own. Yet it was that very silence — that exquisite, eloquent silence — that gave his remarks their fury and force. Trudeau had always understood the importance of timing. His interventions during the referendum debate, so carefully rationed and contained, had been calculated for maximum effect. Even his opponents conceded that they had turned the tide. This time Trudeau's remarks unleashed a firestorm. They angered the prime minister, unsettled the premiers, comforted the dissidents and sowed doubt among Canadians. The first ministers signed the Meech Lake Accord a week later, but, on 27 May, the critics found voice.

Initially, Trudeau's broadside may have actually stiffened support for the accord. The western premiers, meeting at their annual conference in Saskatchewan, reaffirmed their endorsement. Howard Pawley said the accord conformed to his idea of Confederation "because it strikes a fair balance of rigid centralism on one hand, and the other extreme of provinces having over-dominant roles." A week later, behind closed doors, Pawley argued that the constraints on spending power would weaken the federal government, and he complained that Mulroney had not spoken for Canada. David Peterson, who had once called Trudeau "a millstone around his neck" (a comment Trudeau remembered six years later), also claimed to be unmoved by the attack. "The benefits of having Quebec in now far outweigh any minor discomfiture one may have with certain of the provisions," he said. Trudeau's "strong and rigid" view of Canada, he added, was not in keeping with "some of the realities of our federalist system." A week later, that "minor discomfiture" over the distinct-society and the spending-power clauses brought him close to scuttling the accord. This unacknowledged influence on Peterson may be the reason Bourassa did not blame the premier for his opposition to the accord, but rather "that bastard Trudeau."

Mulroney, who had been wounded most grievously, was livid. He bristled at being called "a weakling" and "a sly fox," and even resented the lack of warning. But more wounding was the sense of rejection. Mulroney had liked and admired Trudeau and wanted to be liked in turn. "One thing about the old Trud," Mulroney told L. Ian MacDonald before he became prime minister, "he sure has a lotta class." MacDonald wrote in his biography of Mulroney that the two "shared many views of the country, and always would." Trudeau, for his part, had been favourably disposed to Mulroney. He thought that the Tories would "not have the brains" to nominate him as leader in 1976. Later, Trudeau invited him to 24 Sussex and suggested he run for the Liberals. "We tried to get him into the cabinet," remembers Keith Davey. "We wanted to make him minister of labour. He was very interested in it and it almost happened." Later, when Mulroney entered Parliament as leader of the opposition, Trudeau greeted him warmly. For the next ten months, their relationship in the House of Commons was so civilized that partisans on both sides complained that each was being too nice to the other. Many believed in 1984 that Trudeau saw Mulroney as his natural successor, even if he was a Tory. He thought him an honourable person, a strong federalist, a defender of minority rights — a worthy custodian of his legacy.

If, after Meech Lake, Trudeau felt that his successor had betrayed the country, Mulroney felt that Trudeau had betrayed him. The anger was deeply personal. Some suggest that Mulroney always resented Trudeau's deification. Despite winning the Tory leadership, carrying Quebec and routing the Liberals, Mulroney still thought that he walked in Trudeau's shadow. His insecurity came out in complaints about his press coverage, how "the boys" would have been kinder to Trudeau. If a crowd was not big enough, the applause not loud enough, he was sure to draw the comparison. "If it had been Trudeau, they would have called it Trudeaumania," he once moaned to his press secretary. The sense of inferiority was reminiscent of Lyndon Johnson's attitude towards the Kennedys, a family LBJ tried to love and, once rebuffed, came to loathe. From the day Trudeau's polemic appeared, Mulroney's words became harder, his anger finer.

That simmering hostility helps explain his fixation on Trudeau at the opening of the meeting at Langevin. It also explains his effort to upstage Trudeau's appearances before parliamentary committees and, later, to discredit his record and paint him as the author of Quebec's isolation. "It was so bad after the first attack [27 May] that had Trudeau died the next morning the prime minister could not have delivered a eulogy at his funeral," recalls a former senior adviser to Mulroney. "He would and could not because it would have been pure hypocrisy."

After setting the fire a week before Langevin, Trudeau fanned the flames. Over the next two days, he appeared on English and French radio and television. The conversations were less interesting for what they said about the accord — Trudeau reiterated his opposition — than for what they said about him. He explained that he was speaking out because he feared the premiers and the prime minister were determined to ram through this constitutional change while no one was paying attention. "In a sense, they are politically astute because I don't think the Canadian people are very interested in this subject," he argued. "They've heard a lot about the constitution and I think they would rather get it over and done with." When asked why he had intervened, Trudeau gave a simple reason: he wanted his children to know that he had not been silent during the dismemberment of the nation. He didn't want his boys to say, "You were there, Daddy. What did you do about it?"

If the style was offensive, that was politics. "Well, I meant them to be offended," he said in response to a question. "I think they're doing something basically wrong, and I'm saying so in strong language." From Trudeau, no remorse, just a scowl. When Peter Gzowski asked him on "Morningside" if he felt isolated, he replied, "Well, I'm like Garbo. I rather like to be alone. And that doesn't bother me." He had always been independent. Solitude was natural for him. As a youth at Old Orchard Beach in Maine, where his family used to vacation, he was known to tuck a book under his arm and disappear for the day behind the rocks and sand dunes. He remained, as Richard Gwyn called him, "the northern magus," a political magician, as well as "the single combat warrior" who was eager to fight and usually won.

Now the warrior was returning for the last great battle of the Constitutional Wars. His polemic in May was the opening shot of a three-year campaign. There would be other fights on other days. In between, he would go home and rest. He was like Lucius Quinctius

Cincinnatus, the general and statesman of ancient Rome, who left a successful career in the army to become a farmer. He preferred the plough to the sword. When the army was imperilled, as it was in 478 B.C., he took command, saved the day and returned home. He was summoned again a few years later to put down a revolt, then went home again. Trudeau, too, left a successful career in public life to go home. But when he sensed danger, as he did more than once, he returned to defend his vision of the country.

Three months after his outburst, Trudeau surfaced again. The Special Joint Committee on the Constitution, that panel of MPs and senators studying the accord in summer 1987, had begun public hearings. Its mandate was to examine the amendments and report to Parliament. The committee was sensitive to charges that its review was a sham because it could make no changes. Moreover, the members objected to allegations that they planned to hear only supporters of the accord. Trudeau, the most prominent of the critics, would help legitimize the hearings. Perhaps that is the reason he hesitated before accepting their invitation. His appearance was scheduled for the afternoon of 27 August 1987, in the Railway Committee Room of the Centre Block. The former prime minister was one of several witnesses that day.

The room was packed with admirers anticipating a tour de force. Many had lined up early to get a seat. Tom Axworthy, Senator Jerry Grafstein, Charles Caccia and Jacques Hébert were there. Trudeau — clad in light summer suit with *boutonnière* — did not disappoint. He said he did not have a brief and not much to read, then talked for half an hour and answered questions for two and a half hours. Trudeau was known for speaking extemporaneously, with only a few notes, a talent he had perfected in public life. But that did not mean he was not ready. "The presentation looked more spontaneous than it was," Axworthy remembers. "There was enormous preparation. The arguments were all arranged, the points and the citations were clear."

The argument continued the line of attack he had begun in May. His theme was that Canada must be more than its provinces, that there had to a national will greater than the narrow allegiance to the regions. He cited Henri Bourassa ("le *grand* Bourassa," he sniffed, in pointed reference to the Quebec premier), who had championed national patriotism over provincial patriotism, a loyalty to the nation greater than a loyalty to Ontario or Quebec. Without it, there would be no nation. Trudeau feared the accord would weaken the centre by weakening the executive, the legislature and the judiciary. "They undermine and eat away at our Canadian sovereignty, in a way, by submitting these three fundamental arms or divisions of the modern state to a kind of remote control by the provinces," he said. He cited provincial participation in the Senate and judicial appointments and the establishment of federal-provincial conferences as examples of the growth of provincial power. The provisions on immigration and the spending-power clause would also weaken the resolve of the federal government. Both were a power grab by the premiers. "It is their job to try and get more powers, more money, more jurisdiction . . . for their provinces," said Trudeau. "All politicians — and you are politicians — think they can govern better than anyone else; provincial politicians are no exception. So, the more they can grab for themselves the more we see provincialism developing at the expense of . . . national patriotism." Of the premiers, his voice dripping with vitriol, he said: "You scratch my back, I will scratch yours — and if you do not scratch my back, I will scratch your face."

The most serious threat to the sense of nation, he argued, was the distinct-society clause because it would make Canada a league of princely states. At root, Trudeau found the clause duplicitous. Either it meant something or it did not. If it meant nothing, that would anger Quebec and produce some "nasty surprises" later on. If it did mean something, it would undermine the Charter, which had proclaimed equal rights for all Canadians. Here, as with the spending-power clause, the modifications made by the premiers at Langevin after his diatribe in May were obviously inadequate. The Meech Lake Accord, as Trudeau saw it, was a licence to broaden provincial power. His underlying thesis was that the provinces would always ask for more. Mulroney had bought peace in 1987 the way Chamberlain had bought peace in 1938. The naive man with the black homburg and the umbrella waved a piece of paper and claimed a new world; Mulroney waved his own piece of paper and proclaimed a new country. For Trudeau, Meech Lake was Munich. This was not peace but appeasement. "It was said that with the accord . . . finally peace had been restored to federal-provincial relations," said Trudeau. "Yes, peace! But at what price? By giving the provinces everything they wanted."

His performance was electrifying. The eyes darted and the eyebrows arched. The hands drifted to the heavens as if to deliver benediction. He shrugged often, his signature of defiance. He shuffled. He shifted. He gestured. He seemed to draw energy from the memory of other battles. He was combative and contemptuous, scholarly and scornful. After all, this was the constitution, *his* constitution. He had a proprietary claim to it. Now the castle had been stormed and the crown jewels stolen.

It was the betrayal of his vision that cut most deeply. By 1987, after eighteen years of bilingualism, the country had accepted the French fact. It had also embraced a charter that would confer the same rights on people everywhere. If francophones had schools and language, they would not have to hide in Fortress Quebec. Trudeau said it was working; anglophones in Calgary were enrolling their children in French immersion programs and accepting French on the cereal box. But Meech Lake would reverse that by promoting linguistic ghettos. After the idea of the bilingual country had become a reality, after English Canada had accepted French as an official language, Quebec wanted more powers to defend French. It wanted to become "a distinct society," responsible for promoting and preserving French, while the rest of the country would do far less. "I say that [Meech Lake] is really welshing on the deal," Trudeau lamented. "And it makes me unhappy."

Trudeau spoke and the crowd applauded. Arthur Tremblay thought the Liberals had packed the room with their supporters. When co-chairman Chris Speyer leaned over and asked if he should silence the cheering, Tremblay shook his head and whispered, "Don't even try." The partisans in the stately Railway Committee Room erupted regularly, applauding each time Trudeau made a point. When Trudeau finished his presentation and began to answer questions from committee members, the tension rose. The tiger was now among the titmice.

Robert Kaplan and André Ouellet — the two Liberals on the committee — were uneasy about Trudeau's appearance. Both were former cabinet ministers who now supported the accord. Ouellet decided simply not to show up that day. "It was not fear, just a question of *délicatesse,*" he says. "Here is a man with a totally different view. Why should I confront him? He doesn't need me to challenge him." Ouellet had advised Kaplan not to ask questions, arguing that it was inappropriate for former ministers who now endorsed the deal to do so. Kaplan disagreed. "I didn't want to argue with him," he recalls. "I wanted to pick issues where the things he would say would be helpful to our position, which was that the [Liberal] amendments were good." Kaplan, concerned that Trudeau might "take me apart," proceeded gingerly with the opening question. He asked Trudeau to explain why Quebec was isolated in 1981, and Trudeau was happy to oblige. Kaplan politely followed with innocuous queries on contemporary Quebec. The former prime minister was gentle.

He was more testy with others. When Conservative Leo Duguay questioned his tone, he was unapologetic: "I suppose some of the things I said were offensive. That is the way I write. I am not always a pleasant person." He had taken abuse as prime minister, he said, and he "never went home and cried about it." When New Democrat Pauline Jewett insisted the accord was sensitive to Quebec, he countered: "You say you are showing compassion and understanding for Quebec. I find that a bit condescending. I do not need your compassion." When Liberal Jean Robert Gauthier asked how much better *he* could have done in striking a deal, Trudeau insisted that he would have bargained; Mulroney had not. "But when I negotiated, I asked for something in return, did I not? I asked for the Charter, the patriation of the constitution, the strengthening of the Canadian common market?" The parliamentarians landed only glancing blows. Conservative Charles Hamelin asked him earnestly: "Mr. Trudeau, have you perchance become the new Galileo of 1987?" New Democrat Lorne Nystrom, citing the overwhelming support for the accord, wondered aloud: "Are all these people wrong while you are right? Are all these people just weaklings and snivellers?" Trudeau reminded him he was defending the centre, as had every prime minister before him. "Read your history, man," he advised. "That is the history of Canada."

Trudeau knew he could not win there and he didn't care. He wasn't talking to these parliamentarians, these nobodies, as he once called them. He was doing what he had always done: going over the heads of the politicians to the people. If they too chose not to listen, that didn't matter either. He would talk to history. Only once in three hours of bravura was there a moment of self-doubt. He asked himself if perhaps — just perhaps — his dream of a bilingual country had been an illusion. "[Maybe it was] a noble dream," he said haltingly. "It was just a bit of poetry, but it is not realistic. Maybe I am passé. Maybe there is a new Canada now."

"Before Trudeau appeared before the committee, I thought Meech Lake was almost inevitable," said Jerry Grafstein. "When he finished, I said, it may change." The government wasted no time playing down the impact of Trudeau's appearance. In one of those coincidences, Mulroney chose that day to shuffle a couple of ministers in his cabinet and that night to keep Parliament in session beyond normal hours. The late sitting meant that Trudeau's testimony was not broadcast on the national parliamentary channel until early morning. The government need not have worried. By summer's end, the prospects for passing the accord remained unchanged. The premiers had signed the deal in June, and Quebec became the first province to ratify it three weeks later. The other provinces were committed to endorsing it. Public opposition still had no one to rally around. Trudeau returned to the farm.

Almost eight months later, on 30 March 1988, Trudeau got another chance to say his piece. Things had changed by the time he appeared, eleven months after the accord was signed. In August, opposition had been limited mainly to interest groups representing women, aboriginal people, minority language activists, Northerners and ethnic Canadians. Now Frank McKenna and his newly elected Liberals were in office in New Brunswick, and they opposed the accord. In Manitoba, the New Democrats had been defeated in the legislature and an election had been called. In Parliament, the Liberals had moved their amendments. Public support for the accord was dropping.

This time Trudeau's forum was the Senate. After the House of Commons had approved the accord in October, it had moved to the red chamber for debate. Most of the senators shared his antipathy for the accord. While they could not defeat it, they could use their suspensive veto to delay its passage for six months, until 23 April. (Ironically, before Trudeau and the provinces changed the rules in 1982, the Senate could have used its veto to kill the accord.) The Senate formed its own committee and held its own hearings. Again, the former prime minister was invited to testify.

Trudeau spoke in the chamber itself, addressing all the senators. He was seated in the centre, an island in an ocean of red, at a mahogany desk lined with inlaid burgundy leather. His suit was blue, his tie paisley, his rose prominent. The visitors' galleries were almost full. So were most of the seats, filled by many of the senators Trudeau had appointed. Notably absent was Lowell Murray, the goverment House leader. His fellow Tories rarely joined the applause that punctuated the presentation. The venue was more imposing this time, but there was less drama than at his appearance before the Commons.

Having spoken in French in August, he used English this time. A francophone journalist in the gallery shouted, *"Parlez français!"* and was thrown out. Trudeau stopped, defended his use of English and continued.

Trudeau's first appearance lasted three and a half hours; the second, five and a half hours. Jacques Hébert complained that the former prime minister was rushed in the Commons and promised the Senate would give him more time. In its length, Trudeau's presentation was reminiscent of speeches by members of the Politburo. Again he arranged his points, marshalled his arguments, sounded the alarm. The theme was the same: the accord was a monstrous mistake.

This time Trudeau moved from content to context. He put the constitutional debate into historical perspective and defended his record. A good part of his presentation was a history of federal-provincial relations, which might have been called "How the provinces asked for more." He traced their repeated demands for power, explained the reasons that he and other prime ministers had resisted them, and described how Brian Mulroney had broken with history in making the concessions he did. To buttress his argument, he reviewed provincial demands in intergovernmental negotiations over twenty years. At points he answered critics, such as former Parti Québécois minister Claude Morin, who said that he had broken his promise to renew federalism after the referendum of 1980. "There was no point in winning the referendum if we were going to give those who had lost [it] everything they were trying to get by winning it," he said. He also recounted, in detail, the concessions he had offered the provinces at different times over the years, challenging those who said those concessions were the same as what was in the Meech Lake Accord. Once again, Trudeau was using history to speak to history.

What made Trudeau's testimony somewhat different from his earlier comments was his prescription for changing the accord. He suggested that it go to the Supreme Court for a reference, a course that Bourassa had rejected. He also suggested that the Senate send it back to the House with amendments, and that, ultimately, an election be called. "I think we should take our chances," he said. "Let the people decide." (Ultimately there was an election and the Tories were returned, but the issue was free trade, not Meech Lake.) His mood was heavy with resignation. "If the people of Canada want this accord, and that is not beyond the realm of possibility, then let that be part of the constitution. I, for one, will be convinced that the Canada we know and love will be gone forever, but, then, Thucydides wrote that Themistocles' greatness lay in the fact that he realized Athens was not immortal. I think we have to realize that Canada is not immortal; but if it is going to go, let it go with a bang rather than a whimper."

Not with a bang, but a whimper. T. S. Eliot had talked about the end of the world, P. E. Trudeau was talking about the end of Canada. His was a portrait etched in acid and framed in black. Here again was Trudeau's scorn: "Mulroney and his whole cabinet were no match for Mr. Bourassa and his intergovernmental affairs minister. He [Bourassa] realized who he was dealing with and moved in for the kill." Here again was the contempt: "It [the accord] should be put in the dustbin." Here again was the disdain: "For the provinces the renewing of the constitution could only mean one thing: transferring more powers to the provinces. The people of Canada could not have their own constitution until their national government accepted its own dismemberment." Here again was sorrow: "That dream [bilingual Canada] will be gone. So, in vain, we would have dreamt the dream of one Canada."

Trudeau did not stop the accord or save the country that day in March. Nor could he. But he helped consolidate an intellectual opposition that would find focus in the dissenting provinces, and ultimately spread to the country at large. Before the Senate and the House of Commons, he had issued a *cri de coeur* that could come only from a disenchanted son of Canada. Even if this accord he loathed came to pass, he could say that he had tried to stop it. His children would know where he stood when the country began to fall apart, as he was sure it would.

Once again Trudeau returned to Montreal and to silence. His anger did not cool; it just simmered beneath the mask, melting the ice-blue core. On this subject, everyone knew, he was beyond persuasion. He raised his sons, went to work and travelled the globe. Still, the discontent bubbled. The rage would flare and fade, just long enough to remind skeptics that it was still there. It took different public forms. There was, for example, an angry exchange of letters in 1989 in *La Presse*. Claude Morin, the former Parti Québécois sage, accused Trudeau of deceiving Quebeckers in the referendum of 1980. Trudeau's response was withering in its scorn for nationalists, whom he called "cry-babies and blackmailers." Or in a response to columnist Marcel Adam, he said, "It would be better for Canada if the Meech Lake monster went back and drowned itself in the watery depths from which it should never have raised its hideous head."

There were always conversations with past and present players, and meetings with some of the accord's opponents, such as Clyde Wells and Bryan Schwartz. Whenever the subject arose, it triggered misgivings, remonstrances and regrets. Old allies in the Constitutional Wars who were now supporting the accord were reminded of their folly. Roy McMurtry, who had been attorney general of Ontario when the province had been one of those that backed the patriation package, remembers "getting shit" from Trudeau at a testimonial dinner in 1988. After charming McMurtry's young daughter, Trudeau was less flirtatious with her father. "I haven't heard you say anything in opposition to Meech Lake," said Trudeau. "That's because I'm not in opposition," replied McMurtry. "What!" Trudeau replied icily. "After all that we fought for!"

No one was beyond reproach. Trudeau tangled with Gordon Robertson, the former clerk of the Privy Council, and Jack Pickersgill, the former cabinet minister, at a weekly lunch of retired politicians and public servants. Trudeau had heard about the round table and asked if he could come. Inevitably, Meech Lake came up. When Pickersgill and Robertson attacked his position, Trudeau urged them to read Bourassa's remarks to the National Assembly, where they would find the true meaning of Meech Lake. By this time Trudeau had become so intractable that former colleagues believed he simply did not understand Quebec any more. No doubt he was one of the few remaining francophone federalists in the province. Of his former ministers, only a handful (Jean Chrétien, Marc Lalonde, John Roberts, Charles Caccia, Donald Johnston among them) supported his position. The rest did not. Francis Fox, Monique Bégin, Jean-Luc Pepin, Serge Joyal, Bill Rompkey, André Ouellet, Robert Kaplan, Jacques Olivier, Lloyd Axworthy (with reservations) and others endorsed the accord. Bégin, for example, even confessed her guilt over Quebec's estrangement in 1982. Her *crise de conscience,* however, had not been wrenching enough to force her to leave the cabinet.

These conversions puzzled Trudeau. As one former minister put it, Trudeau was puzzled by André Ouellet's criticism, calling it, in French, "the kick of the donkey." Ouellet shrugged and said: "I have been a provincialist all along. Maybe Trudeau is disappointed.

Frankly, I'm too modest to think that he's bothered by my stand. I don't think he gives a damn where I am." It's possible that Trudeau didn't give a damn about Ouellet, whose advice on constitutional matters he never sought. But it is hard to believe that these defections did not trouble him "after all that we fought for!" Trudeau did not expect support out of personal loyalty. What puzzled this Cartesian was that people could think one way then and another way now. It was the inconsistency he could not fathom. Keith Davey, a Trudeau loyalist to his dying breath, ascribes the sea change in others to either blindness or opportunism. He heaps scorn on the Serge Joyals ("He's a closet separatist") and the Francis Foxes ("He always goes for the main chance"). He suspects Trudeau shared his views. "Sure, some of those guys are heading to the high ground," he says. "They think it's a safe place to be because those are the cards they have to play. I don't respect those guys and neither does Trudeau."

As the debate intensified, Trudeau seemed more alone in Quebec. Some compared him to Cassandra shouting from a rooftop, or, more pointedly, to Sir Wilfrid Laurier in the evening of his life, out of touch and out of step. A friend tried to organize a party to celebrate Trudeau's seventieth birthday on 18 October 1989. To mark the occasion, he proposed inviting seventy of Trudeau's friends. After contemplating the guest list, the friend dropped the idea; the constitutional question was too sensitive. Within the elite of this small society, the accord had become a wound. "The feeling is that this is a family," said a former Quebec minister. "When we federalists fight each other in Quebec, we weaken our position before other Quebeckers. We don't like to do that." Trudeau, he said, had lost the respect of Liberals because he had fought the issue outside the party, and he had painted a world with Meech as *Götterdämmerung.* "It's not the end of the country," he sighed. "And Trudeau is not the only brain in the country."

For Trudeau, though, there was never any question of compromise. He never really believed that he was passé. He always felt he was right. The change of heart among his colleagues was their response to a temporary, faddish phenomenon. John Roberts suggested Trudeau believed in Arthur Schlesinger's cycles of history: what goes down today will come back up tomorrow; that liberalism and conservatism, or centralism and provincialism, go in and out of fashion. Trudeau accepted the validity of what he did and he knew that one day it would be understood. The monolithic opposition in Quebec did not perturb him because he always knew the Quebec nationalists were against him and that their view dominated. That he could be wrong this time — when the cause was shared not only by the chattering classes of the intelligentsia, the media, the artists, but now by the business community — did not bother him. Throughout, Trudeau remained rigidly consistent, splendidly isolated, utterly self-assured. He did not spend his days brooding on a mountaintop, obsessed with defectors and traitors. If it came to that, he would rather go skiing.

And so with his Canada still under siege, Cincinnatus left the plough one more time. It would be the final battle of the campaign. He had launched his first sally in May 1987 with his vicious essay. His second volley had come before the two parliamentary committees in August 1987 and March 1988. Now, after lying low for almost two years, he used the publication of his book to attack the accord once again. By March 1990, however, denouncing the accord was like shooting someone committing suicide. Manitoba and New Brunswick were demanding changes, and Newfoundland was preparing to rescind its resolution of support. As the clock began running out, many were warning that the end of the accord would mean the end of Canada. Trudeau now reentered the fray, on this, his farewell tour.

Whatever Trudeau's reluctance to write his memoirs, whatever his disavowal of the need to correct the past, he could not abide the distortion of his record. In 1988, he and Tom Axworthy decided to ask their former colleagues to write about the achievements and failures of their government. Trudeau would edit the essays with Axworthy and write one of his own. The result was *Towards a Just Society: The Trudeau Years*. It was to have been published in fall 1989 but was delayed until the following spring. The timing was accidental but nonetheless exquisite. The organizers planned a three-day book tour. Of course, the book was about the Trudeau years, all sixteen of them. Of course, only 4 of 404 pages dealt with Meech Lake. Of course, there were fourteen other contributors. And, of course, for three days in March the only author was Trudeau and the only subject was Meech Lake.

"We'd like to generate a little Trudeaumania," declared Jeffrey M. Goodman, the publicist who planned the tour with the precision of a royal visit. Trudeau launched the book in Montreal on Tuesday, 21 March, with a press conference. That night he appeared in taped in-

terviews on English and French television broadcasts on both national networks. "There is no way you could turn on the television in
Canada and not see him," said Goodman. The next day, in Ottawa,
he held a press conference and attended a lunch with old associates.
On Thursday, the last day of the tour, he addressed high-school students in Toronto and hosted a cocktail party at the Royal York Hotel.
If this road show happened to take place during the Liberal party's
leadership race and as the debate over Meech Lake boiled, that was
coincidental. Skeptics could not help but wonder if this was
Trudeau's long-awaited return from exile, his flight from Elba.
Surely not. Those rumours remained farfetched, but loyalists still en-
tertained the prospect of a restoration. "I don't think he would like to
come back at all," said Jacques Hébert, who was Trudeau's eyes and
ears in the Liberal caucus. "But if there were a great movement in the
whole country to find someone to speak for Canada, well, why not
the old Pierre back for a little while?"

The contents of his book — not to mention Trudeau's thoughts on
the accord — were already well known. In the last chapter Trudeau
discussed the values that had shaped his career. Towards the end,
with biting sarcasm, he excoriated Mulroney for failing on both free
trade ("a monstrous swindle") and national reconciliation. He thun-
dered: "Alas, by now it is clear that, barring a sharp and unlikely
change of course, our Great Helmsman is indeed steering Canada toward peace and reconciliation — the kind to be found in the grave-
yards of the deep."

The book offered Trudeau's version of history. It held that national
unity was strong when he left office in 1984, that separatism was in
retreat, that the constitution was set for generations. Trudeau never
mentioned that the Parti Québécois was elected twice during his term
of office, that Quebec was refusing to participate in constitutional
conferences, that it was exempting its legislation from the Charter.
No matter. The partisans just wanted him to banish the contortion-
ists and the confederates once more, with feeling. This time, Trudeau
dealt less with the substance of the accord than with the consequences
of its failure. He called the rising chorus of separatist threats blackmail and did not predict independence for Quebec. But if it happened, he would live with it. "If Quebec separates, let us separate,"
he said. "I'll not hang myself in a loft." Later, he said: "Canada is not
eternal. The United States is not eternal. Heaven knows, we know
the Soviet Union is not eternal. Things change. But let's not play

games with them." He said that another referendum would be the only way to consult Quebeckers and he was convinced they would choose Canada, even if the nationalists would always favour an independent Quebec. What was telling here was his prediction that nothing dramatic would happen if Quebec did leave Canada. The province would not go bankrupt, as some claimed, and Canada would not be absorbed by the United States, as others claimed. Life would go on. In a sense, he was helping legitimize the independence movement he so despised, by defanging it. In French, they called this process *banaliser*.

And so it went for three days, as the prince travelled from Montreal to Ottawa, to Toronto. Trudeau repeatedly corrected distortions of his record. "We wanted to write our own history so that people know what we did and why we did it," he said. "And if it was wrong, it'll stand there to be condemned, and if we tell any lies they'll be denounced. We lived that history, we helped to make it, and we want it to be there." They might call him dated but they were the ones with no sense of the past. "They call us yesterday's men," he said. "They say we represent yesterday's ideas and values. All I can say about that is perhaps it is better than today's men, who have no ideas and no values."

At every stop, he showed he had lost little of his sharpness. At the National Press Theatre in Ottawa, never one of Trudeau's favourite haunts as prime minister, more than a hundred news organizations turned out to see him, proof that "yesterday's man" could sell tomorrow's papers. In the final minutes of his news conference, a West German journalist asked him to compare the return of nationalism in Canada to that in Europe. He responded with an erudite answer on the essence of the state and the meaning of unity. Afterwards, a tearful translator emerged from her booth. "You just don't see that any more," she said.

In Toronto, he stood on stage at a high school, outsize Canadian flag behind him, slender microphone before him. In the crowd, among hundreds of adolescents who were not yet born when he took office, were Charles Caccia and Keith Davey. Goodman opened the session, noting that the *New York Times* and the *Times* of London were there, and that the all-news channel was carrying it too. "The whole world is watching," he crowed. Trudeau liked answering questions from the kids. The answers were the same on Quebec, Meech Lake and everything else. What was striking here was the body language. The head and hands in synch, the legs fixed on stage, the thumbs almost hooked in the belt. It was not quite the return of the gunslinger, but it was close. A student called him "Prime Minister" and he liked it. Another said he was the only one since 1968 worthy of the title. He liked that, too. The students had been warned not to ask him embarrassing questions, such as the joy of sex at seventy. No doubt he would not have had any trouble with that one, either.

That night Brian Mulroney addressed the country on national television, and Pierre Trudeau, for the first time that week, did not make "The National." Was this the last of the great ovations? A day before, broadcaster Barbara Frum had interviewed him. At the end, she said, "It's been fun." *Fun?* Had the former prime minister become an old eccentric, a curiosity?

History would show, and his opponents would concede, that he had played a critical role in killing Meech Lake. He had spoken out early, drawn skeptics to his side, and conferred legitimacy on a ragtag opposition. When he raised objections — this strongman from Quebec who had established bilingualism, patriated the constitution and won the referendum — English Canada began to question its enthusiasm for the accord. Trudeau ensured that Jean Chrétien, who was inclined to compromise, was four-square against the deal, at least in his public declarations, when he ran for the Liberal leadership. At the same time, Trudeau encouraged Clyde Wells in his opposition, assuring him that killing Meech Lake would not destroy the country.

Out of office, Trudeau remained influential. Chrétien was leading the party. Allan MacEachern, the Liberal leader in the Senate, was frustrating the Conservative agenda. And Wells, though no intimate of the former prime minister, was challenging executive federalism. Each, in his way, was championing the old vision of Canada. No wonder Mulroney seethed with resentment.

The prince returned to Montreal, back to the farm, to a province in turmoil where he was again alone. Never had all the elements of society seemed so arrayed against him, never had he seemed so out of season. As French Canada embraced the distinct society and English Canada rejected bilingualism, his dream was in ruins. While he could talk of the cycles of history, he was now caught up in them. No one could deny the death of the accord had revived the forces of independence. The nationalists he had fought before would fight again, better armed and more confident of their success. Perhaps he and his followers, the few of them who were left, could still preach his ideal.

Perhaps they could fight another referendum. But could they pull it off again? He had won the battle for Meech Lake, but had he not lost the war for Canada? In the face of growing adversity, Trudeau offered a sigh, a shrug and a wave. Ever resolute, ever mysterious, he disappeared into the mists, offering only a favourite passage from T. S. Eliot:

> I grow old . . . I grow old . . .
> I shall wear the bottoms of my trousers rolled.
>
> Shall I part my hair behind? Do I dare to eat a peach?
> I shall wear white flannel trousers, and walk upon the beach.
> I have heard the mermaids singing, each to each.
>
> I do not think that they will sing to me.

The Three Horsemen
of the Apocalypse

WHEN THE PREMIERS SIGNED THE ACCORD ON 3 JUNE 1987, THEY AS-
sumed that it would be approved quickly. They had solemnly agreed
to seek ratification "as soon as possible." In fact, the annual constitutional conferences prescribed by the accord were to begin by 31 December 1988. While the amending formula gave the provinces three
years to ratify the accord, that was considered unnecessary. Like so
many generals in so many wars, the first ministers naively expected
this battle to be over by Christmas — if not by this one, then by the
next one. Mulroney said later that few understood the implications of
the time limit. "I thought, and many people thought, that within a
matter of months after the signing all provinces would have ratified
it. Nobody anticipated that governments would change, signatures
would be repudiated, and all of a sudden a simple, straightforward
document of unity would become a catch-all for everybody's wish
list as governments changed across the country."

At the time, speedy passage was a safe prediction. There were majority governments in Ottawa and in nine provinces. In Ontario, the
only minority legislature, both the Liberals and the New Democrats
supported the accord. Only a few provinces planned public hearings.
Of course, there would be elections within the next three years, most
imminently in Ontario and New Brunswick. It was widely believed
that David Peterson would win and that Richard Hatfield would lose.
But even the defeat of a signatory did not raise the alarm. That in June
1990 the first ministers would be negotiating frantically to save the
accord was inconceivable that spring.

It started well enough. Robert Bourassa returned home in triumph.
"Quebec has won one of the greatest political victories of its history,

a victory recognized beyond doubt by most objective observers as one of its greatest in two centuries," he declared. Richard French, who was in his cabinet at the time, remembers watching Bourassa enter the National Assembly the day after Meech Lake. "I had never seen him so moved, so obviously emotional. He was tremendously proud of himself. It was exhilarating, like winning an election. He was shaking." Quebec became the first province to ratify the accord less than three weeks after the meeting at the Langevin Block. The National Assembly met in Committee of the Whole and held four days of debate. (Quebec was the only province to hold hearings on the accord between Meech Lake and Langevin.) Both Bourassa and Gil Rémillard testified. The matter could be handled with dispatch, they implied, because everyone in the province liked the deal except the Parti Québécois and Pierre Trudeau.

The day the National Assembly gave its approval — 23 June 1987 — became a watershed in the story of Meech Lake. As the first province to ratify the accord, it started the clock running. When the premiers and prime minister rushed to save their house of cards three years later, 23 June became a flashpoint. Under the threat of a deadline, the country seemed as perishable as a bottle of milk in the noonday sun. Suddenly, Canada was "best before 23 June." The date was important for other reasons. Saint-Jean Baptiste Day, Quebec's provincial holiday which had often been an occasion of nationalist outpouring, was 24 June. When it looked as though the accord was going to die in 1990, politicians, policemen and money traders awaited 23 June in fear. The federal Liberals, for their part, had other reasons to contemplate 23 June. That was the day they would pick their new leader, a date cleverly chosen so he or she could avoid declaring a position on Meech Lake on the grounds that it would be *fait accompli* by then. Or so they thought.

There was no reason, in that steamy summer of 1987, to doubt those rosy predictions. The special parliamentary committee was struck and began to call witnesses. Only opponents of the accord complained that the hearings were held in July and August, when no one was paying attention. More important, only a few questioned the logic of scrutinizing a package of amendments that could not, in reality, be changed. It was a bit of a charade — a public-relations exercise, as André Ouellet said — and an unconvincing one at that. When criticism of the accord began to take root in 1989, the hearing process became symptomatic of the lack of public participation on Meech

Lake. What the committee did do, however, was to offer a forum for disaffected groups to express their opposition. With all three political parties and all the provinces in agreement, the committee was all the critics had.

As co-chairman Chris Speyer put it, the committee's role was not to make "a final decision," but to help Parliament make a more informed assessment. It was told to report by 14 September. The committee held five and a half weeks of hearings in July and August, during which it received 301 written submissions and heard 131 individuals or groups. The members said they had had enough time and had heard enough witnesses, rejecting criticism that they did not travel or give petitioners enough time to prepare. These were legitimate grievances. The larger complaint was that the committee heard what it wanted to hear. Bryan Schwartz of the University of Manitoba, for example, charges that the committee found time to hear more supporters than critics.

Certainly, many noted Canadians spoke in favour of the accord: Gordon Robertson, former secretary to the cabinet; Lowell Murray, Norman Spector and Frank Iacobucci, the three federal officials on the dossier; former Conservative leader Robert Stanfield; Eric Kierans and Jack Pickersgill, former Liberal ministers; Peter Meekison of the University of Alberta and Gérald Beaudoin of the University of Ottawa; Solange Chaput-Rolland, a former member of the National Assembly; and Yves Fortier, the prominent Liberal lawyer. While no one suggested a *quid pro quo,* at least four of them later accepted government appointments. Beaudoin and Chaput-Rolland were put in the Senate, Fortier was named Canada's ambassador to the United Nations and Iacobucci was appointed chief justice of the Federal Court of Canada.

But, the committee also heard criticism of the accord from representatives of minority language groups, labour, women, ethnic Canadians, Northerners and aboriginal people. A range of interest groups — from the National Action Committee on the Status of Women to the Canadian Ethnocultural Council — raised concerns. Farmers, nurses, public servants, day-care advocates and anti-abortionists had their day. In addition, a number of opponents of the accord appeared: Pierre Trudeau; Senator Eugene Forsey; Al Johnson, the former president of the CBC; Deborah Coyne and Timothy Danson, both constitutional lawyers; Izzy Asper, a prominent Manitoba Liberal and businessman. The heads of territorial governments appeared, as did the opposition leader in New Brunswick, Frank McKenna.

The trouble with the committee was not so much who it heard as what it could do. The committee became a pageant of opinion, providing a forum for the erudition of Eugene Forsey, the scorn of Pierre Trudeau, the passion of Solange Chaput-Rolland, the anger of George Erasmus, the experience of Gordon Robertson. But as long as the committee could not recommend changes, what good was it? From the very beginning, the government had forsworn any changes unless they were "egregious errors." If the committee had any doubts about the difficulty of amending the amendments, Lowell Murray set it straight on the first day of its public hearings. "In seeking to resolve Quebec's concerns while meeting the shared objectives of all eleven governments, the accord is a seamless web and an integrated whole," he said. "It represents a finely balanced package — the product of negotiation and compromise. As such it should not be tampered with lightly." Nonetheless, he encouraged the committee to scrutinize the agreement. If it found real flaws, the government and the provinces would look at them, "bearing in mind that any change would have to meet the test of unanimity." Here, Murray was enjoining the committee to do its work well, but not too well. If it pushed too hard, learned too much, raised too many questions, and proposed too many solutions, the ball of wool would unravel.

It was thus no real surprise that the committee endorsed the accord in its report on 9 September 1987. On each of the accord's provisions, it found no cause for concern. It concluded that the amendments were a compromise and "no one should expect absolute perfection in a compromise." The committee argued that the fears about the accord were unfounded because they presumed the worst. It said that any flaws in the accord "must be serious and must be likely," and in its judgement, none were. The report was endorsed by the Conservatives, who had a majority on the committee, and the New Democrats. The Liberals abstained and moved their own amendments.

As the accord came to a vote in the House of Commons in October, events were moving ahead on other fronts. At the end of August, the premiers met at their annual conference in Saint John and rejected calls to reopen the accord. On 23 September, Saskatchewan became the second province to ratify. There were no public hearings. "We didn't see the need for them," says Grant Devine. "We were in favour of it. The opposition was in favour of it. People could call their members about it." Meanwhile, David Peterson had won a huge majority in Ontario, guaranteeing the accord smooth passage. But while the lone minority government had disappeared in Ontario, trouble was brewing in New Brunswick. Richard Hatfield, his reputation in tatters and his government under siege, insisted on seeking reelection. The premier shrugged and said, "I can't imagine doing anything else." Hoping to recover the popularity that had kept him in office since 1970, he waited until late in the fifth year of his mandate to call an election. In the end, King Richard succumbed. On 13 October, hubris was punished with nemesis. The Conservatives lost every seat in the province; the numbers resembled elections in one-party states. For the country, the significance of this defeat was not the end of a vainglorious premier and his tired government. It was the beginning of the end for the accord.

Meech Lake was not an issue in the election campaign that brought the Liberals to power in New Brunswick. But McKenna's position on the accord was clear. As opposition leader he had been against it from the day it was announced. He called his campaign a referendum on the accord and he promised changes. In the three months between the signing of the deal and the calling of the election, two realities were evident in New Brunswick: the Liberals were going to win power, and they were going to oppose the accord. Why, then, did Hatfield not pass the resolution, as had Quebec, before he dissolved the legislature? One explanation was that Hatfield refused to believe he could lose the election, perhaps the greatest exercise in self-delusion since Hitler issued invitations to a banquet celebrating the fall of Leningrad. Another was his presumption that McKenna was bluffing. Whatever the reason, Hatfield's failure to pass the accord was critical. New Brunswick revived the opposition and ensured the debate would be protracted.

The new Captain Canada, as some were quick to hail him, was Frank J. McKenna. That he should arrive on the national stage when he did was the happenstance of history. McKenna brought more than a passing interest in the constitutional question. On April Fool's Day, 1970, he submitted his senior thesis to St. Francis Xavier University. The fifty-eight-page paper, called "Changing Canada's Federal Constitution: The Background," traced the evolution of the amending process of the BNA Act. The style was descriptive, the analysis thin, the conclusions guarded. Nonetheless, it won top marks. Seventeen years later the heart of McKenna's thesis — that the provinces would play a decisive role in changing the constitution — seemed ironic and prophetic.

Now a general in the Constitutional Wars, McKenna was the only premier to oppose the accord. Time was on his side. The deadline for ratification was three years away. McKenna, shrewder than his self-effacing, folksy manner suggested, knew the meaning of time. He understood that an agreement fashioned in secrecy and haste could dissolve in the glare of public scrutiny. Until McKenna, the critics had no standard-bearer. No wonder his arrival was greeted enthusiastically. Here was a premier who had not signed the accord and who had — or so he could argue — a mandate to change it. Fundamentally, he wanted Quebec to accept the constitution but thought the price was too high. As he saw it, Meech Lake would weaken women's rights, limit minority language rights outside Quebec and impair the ability of the federal government to offer national social programs. Moreover, he thought the revised amending formula — the subject of his undergraduate thesis — would make Senate reform impossible. That McKenna was now using the unanimity rule to re-open the accord was another irony of this exercise in nation-building.

Still, McKenna never promised to scuttle the accord. He told the parliamentary committee that he would hold public hearings and consult the people. To speak before they did would be presumptuous, he said. It would be irresponsible to declare that he would reject the deal because that would limit his bargaining power. Nobody would talk to him. But nor would he promise to accept the deal. That would hurt his credibility, too. Said McKenna: "I would go to the ballpark and the rest of the players would say, 'Mr. McKenna, you forgot to bring your bat. How can you negotiate with us? You have already told us you are prepared to sign the accord whether any changes are made or not.' I must keep the leverage I have; and I intend to keep the leverage I have." That he did until the end. At the committee hearing, a frustrated MP tried to smoke him out. "Come on, Mr. McKenna," snapped Charles Hamelin. "It seems to me you are a possible threat to the accord." McKenna answered: "It seems to me I am also a possible source of comfort to many Canadians who feel improvements can be made."

Beyond seeking these changes, the premier's position was ambiguous. Unlike John Turner, who had embraced the accord and then proposed amendments, McKenna was maximizing his influence by deferring his decision. He was as cool and unfathomable as the currents of the Bay of Fundy. Naturally, his position began to raise questions that autumn: would he have the courage to say no if he were alone in the end? Would he risk the antipathy of Quebec, which would forever blame him for thwarting its aspirations? Would he resist Mulroney's blandishments and punishments?

McKenna was forthright, disciplined and ambitious. Despite his success, he looked more like an adolescent than an adult. His presence did not always match his position. He would talk thoughtfully about the constitution and the economy, his authority belied by a halting speech and a boyish grin. He had always been precocious. Elected premier at age forty, he had been in the legislature since 1982, and party leader since 1985. The fourth of eight children, he was born in 1948 and grew up on a dairy farm in Apohaqui, in southern New Brunswick. As the story goes, he milked cows before school and did chores afterwards. He played six varsity sports, chaired the student council and won a scholarship to St. Francis Xavier in 1966. It was there, at Mulroney's alma mater, that McKenna began to make his mark. He was named the outstanding sophomore and junior, became the first student on the board of governors and won a handful of academic awards. As president of the student union, he led a student strike and helped bring liquor on campus. McKenna showed early an interest in the constitution and in the process of government. He lectured in political science at graduate school, worked on parliamentary issues for Allan MacEachern when MacEachern was president of the Privy Council and spent another summer in the constitutional-law unit in the Prime Minister's Office. In law school, he led his class in constitutional law and wrote a journal article on offshore mineral rights. As a lawyer he argued cases in constitutional law.

All this did not make McKenna a constitutional expert. Yet his roots in New Brunswick and his education at St. Francis Xavier did expose him to people like John Stewart, who taught him Political Science 420: The Government of Canada. Stewart, later a senator, preached the John A. Macdonald doctrine of Confederation — that the federal government, not the provinces, is supreme. McKenna called himself a federalist in that tradition. Those who believed in McKenna and feared Meech Lake hoped his commitment to strong national institutions would prevail. Fundamentally, McKenna believed that Ottawa must protect linguistic minorities and foster economic equality. Much of that belief came from McKenna's sense of place. New Brunswick was the only officially bilingual province in Canada; minority rights meant something. Many of the province's francophones — who represented 34 percent of the population — opposed Meech Lake because they feared that it would dilute the Charter.

The other reality about New Brunswick was that it was one of the poorest provinces in Canada, more vulnerable than others to economic pressure. It relies heavily on equalization grants and transfer payments. Per capita, it was the third-highest recipient of federal aid in 1988. Much of this was statutory, but much was not. A defence contract, a new federal building, a sewage plant, a few grants, loans and subsidies — all were tools of persuasion in the hands of the federal government. It was expected that all manner of carrots would be offered to win McKenna's support, and it would be hard to resist them. The influence was subtle. By one account, when McKenna telephoned Mulroney to tell him that New Brunswick would endorse the free-trade agreement, Mulroney replied: "Frank, I'm glad to hear that. Particularly because we are going to be making an announcement on the frigate program this Friday and I very much want it to go to New Brunswick."

It was unlikely, when he was first elected, that the government would force McKenna's hand. When Ottawa pressed him for an early decision, he demurred: "Ultimatums mean nothing to me." McKenna took his time, unfazed and unhurried. He would await the outcome of the federal election. He would strike a committee to examine the accord and allow his legislature to discuss it, but not to vote on it. He would watch the debate, marshal his arguments, solicit support. And then, if he was still alone, he would decide whether his contribution to constitutional reform would be to stop it.

McKenna's refusal to pass the accord enhanced his prospects of winning changes. The longer he waited the more likely he would be to find allies. Delay bought time. When his position softened in the last months of the debate, some of his supporters felt betrayed. But accepting the accord later did not diminish the importance of his early opposition. By taking a stand then, New Brunswick kept the issue alive and preserved options for new governments in Manitoba and Newfoundland. In a sense, Frank McKenna made Gary Filmon and Clyde Wells possible — a reality that became apparent only seven months after his election.

On 8 March 1988, the government fell in Manitoba, brought down by a lone disgruntled backbencher. The New Democrats, who had had a razor-thin majority in the legislature since their re-election in 1986, were defeated on a motion of non-confidence. Howard Pawley resigned as party leader and an election was called for 26 April. The Conservatives, led by Gary Filmon, began with a commanding lead and were expected to win a smashing majority. They won only a slender minority — twenty-five of fifty-seven seats. The Liberals, under Sharon Carstairs, became the official opposition. They had gone from one to twenty seats, and were poised to take power next time. The New Democrats, led by Gary Doer, a youthful former cabinet minister, were reduced to twelve seats. The Tories had won and lost, the Liberals had lost and won and the New Democrats had lost and lost.

At first, the new government in Manitoba seemed no threat to the accord. The Conservatives were committed to supporting their federal cousins, and the New Democrats were committed to honouring their signature. Together they appeared to have enough votes to pass the accord. The Liberals were another story. Led by the helium-voiced, indefatigable Carstairs, whose personal popularity was largely responsible for their resurgence, they promised to defeat it. Indeed, the day after the election, Carstairs declared: "Meech Lake is dead." Her sabre-rattling meant little as long as she was isolated (although she claimed there were enough dissident Tories and New Democrats prepared to break party ranks and reject the deal). Filmon formed a government and promised to introduce the resolution in the legislature, hold public hearings and propose its ratification. But there was more to it than numbers. The discontent over the accord ran deep in Manitoba. Filmon knew the accord was political dynamite; he could win the legislature but lose the province. The issue could bring down his government at the next election. The voters who had made the Liberals the official opposition could also make them the government on this issue. Perhaps that was why Filmon waited almost eight months before introducing the motion. Perhaps that was why he privately promised the New Democrats in 1988, as one Tory insider put it, "not to let Sharon Carstairs see the voters for two years."

If Filmon had been handed a hot potato, he could thank Howard Pawley. The premier had been under pressure to reopen the issue for months before his government fell. In December 1987 he had received a letter from seventy-five prominent party members urging him to reject the accord and renew negotiations. Pawley agreed the accord was flawed and promised to await the round of public hearings. In the interim, to ensure he wasn't isolated, he asked Frank McKenna to withhold his support in New Brunswick. By the time Pawley's government fell, the House of Commons, Quebec, Saskatchewan and Alberta (its legislature ratified 7 December) had already passed the accord. The federal government thought his dawdling was a response to the free-trade deal, which Pawley opposed. Federal officials resented his linking the constitution and free trade, which no other province had done. They had expected that the accord would be adopted quickly in Manitoba, though Pawley had always promised public hearings and could have used those to justify a retreat. By the time his government fell, he had delayed consideration of the question and was musing about a free vote. "The big blow to the accord was Pawley hoisting it when free trade came in," recalls a senior federal adviser. "He put it on the back burner in early 1988, and he failed to live up to the agreement. I think that the delay will be looked upon as a turning point in the whole thing."

Enter Gary Albert Filmon, the buttoned-down, barrel-chested hydraulic engineer. Neither the party nor the province was sure he was up to the job. Manitobans were so skeptical that they denied him the majority government that pollsters confidently predicted was his at the outset of the campaign. The lack of confidence from the party had plagued Filmon since he had won the Conservative leadership in 1983. Filmon had inherited the party from the austere Sterling Lyon, who had been defeated after one term in office. Filmon was unable to unseat the New Democrats in 1986, despite the fracas over French language rights that played into his hands. Critics within the party said he was too moderate and too meek; Filmon argued he was just misunderstood. They put out rumours and wooed Jake Epp, Manitoba's senior minister in Ottawa. Filmon circled the wagons, silenced the critics and won the election.

That kind of persistence was the hallmark of Gary Filmon, a self-made man born in 1942 to a family of modest means in north Winnipeg. He excelled in high-school sports, particularly basketball. At the University of Manitoba, he studied hydraulic engineering. After graduating, he ran his father-in-law's business college. Filmon entered politics as a city councillor in 1975 and was elected to the legislature in a by-election in 1979. Later, he served as minister of consumer and corporate affairs in the last nine months of the Lyon government.

Filmon was a natural member of the Premiers' Club. He was solid, stolid, earnest and energetic. His values were free enterprise and self-reliance, his world was the community. Like Grant Devine and Don Getty, for Filmon the family was the centre of existence. He loved his children, his cottage, his golf and his racketball. He liked Ronald Reagan and Duff Roblin. On the face of it, he came to public life with no clear-cut cause. Indeed, he entered politics because he was angry that the New Democrats had imposed a new business tax; that seemed to be enough. But he was not dogmatic. He could propose pay equity for civil servants and more funding for day-care centres — liberal positions in his own party. He could oppose the extension of French-language services in Manitoba in 1984 and broaden them in 1990. Unlike the two other premiers who arrived after Meech Lake, he had no interest in or experience with the constitution. History was not a strong suit either; he could, for example, visit Charlottetown and declare that Prince Edward Island entered Confederation before Manitoba. Yet, whatever these limitations, he managed his political crisis deftly and survived the shoals of minority government. In this, the absence of a deep-seated philosophy was an advantage.

In August 1988, three months into his term, Filmon was telling friends the Meech Lake Accord was not an issue in Manitoba. If it was not entirely true then, it was less so by late autumn. The resolution to ratify the accord had not even been introduced in the legislature, yet support was already beginning to evaporate. The New Democrats dealt it a body blow on 24 November, three days after the federal Conservatives were re-elected with a majority. Although the New Democrats had had reservations about the accord since Pawley signed it, they had never said what they would do if their concerns were not met. Now Gary Doer was worried. He said the election ensured that free trade would go ahead. The agreement posed a threat to social programs, and so did the accord. Canada could not afford both. Carstairs was gleeful. Doer was prepared to join her as pallbearer at the accord's funeral.

Filmon had told Mulroney that, whatever the realities of his situation in Manitoba, he would try to pass the accord. His personal relationship with Mulroney was not strong but he wanted to build it. Manitoba had suffered under the New Democrats, he thought, largely because of their frosty relations with Ottawa. Filmon, a Tory and a believer in free enterprise, would change that. If he would help the federal government on Meech Lake, he reasoned, it would help him the way it helped Grant Devine. By December, Filmon decided to discharge his obligation. For two days he consulted his advisers, preparing a speech that laid out his position. He chose to table the resolution to ratify the accord the week before the legislature rose for Christmas. "It was good timing for us," he says.

Still, the issue was troublesome for Filmon. If he put the accord to a vote, his fragile government could fall, precipitating a snap election it might lose. Filmon did not want to be the Joe Clark of Manitoba. Hence, it was altogether possible that the premier was already looking for a way out of this dilemma when he rose in the legislature on Friday, 16 December 1988. Caught between the expectations of federal Conservatives in Ottawa and the exigencies of opposition parties at home — between the national question and his political survival — he had to make a choice. That day, he chose the accord. His support, as expressed in his long, carefully crafted speech, was neither qualified nor conditional. He endorsed the process, denying the deal was made in haste ("Far from it"). He endorsed the purpose ("Meech Lake makes it possible for Quebec to join the Canadian family"). He endorsed the distinct society ("It is nothing more than a restatement of reality"). He endorsed the limitation on federal spending power because it reflected provincial diversity. He endorsed the provisions on the Supreme Court, the Senate and the federal-provincial conferences. He said the accord would make changes easier by providing "the beginnings of a road map for ongoing constitutional renewal."

In fact, his most critical comment on the accord was on the danger of changing it. "Were we to change or amend this resolution, it would be undoubtedly lost," he said. "Let there be no pretending or posturing. If this House changes the Meech Lake Accord, we have abandoned and lost the accord and the new beginnings it stands for." There was no doubt that Friday in Winnipeg where Gary Filmon stood on the question. "The significance of Meech Lake goes beyond the specific constitutional changes that it will achieve," the premier said. "The real significance of Meech Lake goes to the heart of the idea of co-operative federalism. After fifteen years of conflict, confrontation and mistrust, Meech Lake marks a new beginning for federalism." In his remarks, Filmon mentioned Pierre Trudeau twelve times, arguing that Meech Lake marked a break from the clashes of the past.

There it was. Filmon — statesman, nation-builder and profile in courage — had introduced a resolution that could defeat his government and end his political career. Yet Filmon had done it, he maintained, because it was good for the country. In Ottawa, Mulroney was delighted. He thought Filmon's speech was the most spirited defence of the accord he had heard made by a premier, and he called to tell him. "Great speech," Mulroney said. "Great defence of Meech Lake." Filmon accepted his congratulations and left for the weekend.

The day before Filmon made his speech, in another of those exquisitely timed coincidences of which this story is made, the Supreme Court of Canada ruled on a controversial part of Quebec's language law. A challenge to the sign language provisions of Bill 101 had been in the courts for years. The law, which was passed by the Parti Québécois in 1977, ordered all commercial signs to be in French only. It had been challenged in the lower courts, which declared the law unconstitutional, and was appealed to the Supreme Court. Bourassa had campaigned on a promise to allow bilingual signs. He said that the government would "respect the right to put signs in languages other than French while taking into account its obligation to respect the rights of the French-speaking majority." Had he acted immediately, he would have had the latitude to allow English signs; his large majority and the climate of goodwill would have made it little trouble. Bourassa himself noted polls showing only 12 percent of Quebeckers wanted French-only signs. But when he took office in 1985, he delayed; he said he would await the ruling of the Quebec Court of Appeal. On 22 December 1986, the Court of Appeal struck down the restriction on signs. Again, only a year after his election, Bourassa could have acted. His popularity was still high. The premier chose to appeal to the high court. In doing so, the practical man did an impractical thing: he foreclosed his options.

Everyone in Quebec City knew that the Supreme Court would strike down the sign provisions sections of Bill 101. Richard French, the Quebec minister of communications, asked Bourassa to examine other options that would allow him to honour his election promise. On several occasions in cabinet committee, French suggested a major program to encourage the use of French in technology, education, popular music, television and immigration services. Having shown its commitment to the language, French argued, the government could be more generous on signs, which he did not think were a threat to the language anyway. Bourassa was uninterested. As the province awaited the decision, French was filled with foreboding. He knew the court would strike down the law, that the government would have to respond, and that it would break its promise to his constituents. He would have no choice but to resign. He was so sure of it that a year before the court decision he warned newcomers to his staff that they would eventually be working for another minister.

He was right. On 15 December, the court struck down the requirement of French-only signs. At the same time, it ruled that the province could legislate against English-only signs, even that it could require "marked predominance" for the French language. The ruling seemed like a compromise, and offered Bourassa an out. The French fact would be displayed, but the rights of the English minority would be protected. The Supreme Court had reaffirmed the right of Quebec to promote its distinct identity, the *raison d'être* of the distinct-society clause of the accord. Yet it also said that right did not justify the exclusion of another language and the limitation of minority rights.

Bourassa rejected the accommodation. The government had been contemplating its response for months. On the Thursday the ruling came down, the premier huddled with his cabinet and caucus, and later called a special session of the party. The critical question was whether to invoke the notwithstanding clause, override the Charter of Rights and bring in new sign legislation. The discussion went on for three days.

In Ottawa, federal officials watched all weekend. The more they learned, the more they worried. They thought the court decision was generous but suspected that public opinion in Quebec would be hostile. In conversation with their Quebec counterparts, they warned of the threat to Meech Lake if the government overrode the Charter. But they knew their arguments would not carry much weight. They could not promise Bourassa that, if he accepted the court's ruling, New Brunswick and Manitoba would accept Meech Lake. What they did know was that support would erode in both provinces if he rejected the ruling, still not much of an incentive to a government worried about its own political standing. By Saturday, the word from Quebec City, as one senior mandarin put it, was that "things were going ratty. The caucus was hawkish."

The Liberals wanted the notwithstanding clause. Norman Spector telephoned Mulroney at home to tell him Bourassa was prepared to suspend the Charter. Mulroney talked to Bourassa, but Bourassa would not move. He had made up his mind. David Peterson also called Bourassa. He warned him he would lose his anglophone caucus and he would lose Meech Lake. Again, Bourassa refused to budge. You are not the premier of Quebec, he told Peterson, how would you know? Peterson, who liked Bourassa, concluded he would rather deal with him than Parizeau. But he had no illusions as to the damage. "The notwithstanding clause was a stake through the heart of Meech Lake," Peterson says.

On Sunday, Bourassa announced that he would table Bill 178. The law would maintain French-only signs outside whereas bilingual signs — with French predominant — would be permitted on the inside of stores and businesses. Like the Supreme Court, he, too, thought he was offering compromise. Naturally, francophone nationalists said it went too far; naturally anglophones said it did not go far enough. The next day a hard rain began to fall. From the rest of Canada, there was condemnation. "What a fearful price this country pays for its Robert Bourassas," mourned the *Globe and Mail,* the voice of the establishment. "His years of dithering and frittering, dissimulation and weakness — followed by Sunday's bold decision to do the wrong thing — condemn us all to a diminished union." Once again, as he had in the mid-1970s, Bourassa was embroiled in a storm over language. "Who is the real Robert Bourassa?" asked *La Presse.* "Is he a nationalist, a federalist, an unconditional ally of the anglophones or a separatist who doesn't realise it? Does he have a backbone or is he a reed that bends but does not break?"

The subsequent response in Quebec and in the rest of Canada was a body blow to the accord. Although Quebec's action had nothing to do with Meech Lake, the symbolism was devastating. When Bourassa moved to suspend fundamental rights, he lost whatever goodwill the accord had fostered. The mood shifted, the opposition grew, the chemistry changed. Throughout this weekend of trial, Bourassa remained unflappable and unyielding. He said then, as he says now, that he did it to maintain "social peace." "What choice did I have?" he asks. Even Richard French, who quit over the issue, believed that Bourassa had little alternative at the time if he wanted to maintain his popularity. The premier's reasoning was simple. By opting out of the Charter (including the Quebec Charter of Rights), he consolidated his support among Quebeckers without affecting the prospects of the accord. "There would have been strong opposition to Meech Lake anyway," Bourassa says. "Others were blocking it anyway. I don't think Clyde Wells would have agreed with Meech Lake whether or not we would have used the notwithstanding clause. Or New Brunswick. Maybe it would have changed in Manitoba."

In Manitoba, things had changed over the weekend. The news from Quebec had caused an uproar in the keystone province. On Monday, Filmon tried to telephone Mulroney. Just before he was to go into his legislature, Lowell Murray returned the call. "I'm going to withdraw the resolution," Filmon told Murray. "You can't do that!" replied Murray. "Well, I'm doing it," said Filmon. "The decision is made." He told Murray he had tried for two hours to reach Mulroney, but no one had returned his call. Before speaking to Murray, Filmon had asked Carstairs and Doer to agree to withdraw the resolution. Either leader could have forced it into committee, but the fear was that, in the overheated climate, public hearings would become a forum for prejudice. Later, Filmon formally withdrew the resolution from debate and urged Mulroney to call a first ministers' conference to defuse an emerging constitutional crisis. When he had introduced it three days earlier, Filmon said that the accord symbolized the obligation of all governments to protect minority language rights. If Bourassa could breach those rights, all bets were off. "I believe the decision made yesterday by the Government of Quebec to restrict minority language rights in that province violates the spirit of the Meech Lake Accord," he told a hushed chamber. "In these circumstances, I have concluded that the debate on the resolution now before us and the public hearings would not serve a useful purpose and may invite an anti-Quebec backlash."

The opposition parties immediately offered their support. "Democracy can only function when the majority concedes some of its privileges and its rights to the minority, be it the English-language minority or the French-language minority," said Sharon Carstairs, speaking in French. "The Meech Lake Accord jeopardizes these rights and, for this reason, we have a duty to stop it." She argued that these rights, which were guaranteed in the Charter, would be undermined by the "distinct-society clause." Gary Doer agreed that Bourassa had broken "the balance between the rights of the majority and the rights of the minority."

Over the weekend, Filmon spoke to Bourassa three times. Filmon had always thought that Bourassa's response to the court ruling would be "measured and moderate." He never expected that

Bourassa would override the Charter. Bourassa called him on Saturday to tell him that he was considering using the notwithstanding clause. Filmon told him it would have "serious implications" in Manitoba and urged him to reconsider. On Sunday, Bourassa told him he had made up his mind; Filmon again warned that it would have "very, very serious impact" in his province but did not tell him he would withdraw the resolution because he had not decided to do that. Later that day, however, Filmon heard Bourassa's remarks at his press conference. "He said if Meech Lake had been in place he would not have to utilize the notwithstanding clause," remembers Filmon. "It clinched it for me. It gave credence to all the arguments that people had that charter rights were impinged upon by the Meech Lake Accord. They now had evidence." While Bourassa did not say that directly, he did concede "there is a third level of protection [for French language rights] which may be added with the ratification of the Meech Lake Accord." (When Filmon was later challenged on that point by Mulroney and Murray, he produced a transcript of Bourassa's remarks. Bourassa, Filmon says, has not denied his interpretation.) On Monday, after consulting his caucus, Filmon telephoned Bourassa with his decision. "His reponse was just so totally pragmatic, as it always is," Filmon remembers. "'Well, Gary, I did what I had to do,' Robert said. 'You do what you have to do.' If he was upset about it, he certainly did not let on."

With the weekend developments, the balance shifted again. Filmon had cast his lot with Doer and Carstairs. Manitoba had aligned itself with New Brunswick. Meech Lake had now become entangled in provincial politics and language hostility. For the next eighteen months, as Filmon struggled to keep his government afloat, he would continue to oppose the accord. His reservations would include elements of the accord he had applauded earlier. Suddenly, Gary Filmon was more interested in burying the accord than in praising it. By using the notwithstanding clause to limit minority language rights, Bourassa had given him an opening through which to rush for the high ground. Of course, Filmon could never admit that. He explained later that he always thought accommodating Quebec was a worthwhile objective, which is why he had introduced the resolution in the first place. He always had concerns about the accord — his speech did raise the prospect of changes to be made in the future — but he was prepared to proceed with the ten days of legislative debate and a round of public hearings. "It [Bill 178] altered the way I looked at Meech Lake. It did not fit in with the mood . . . [with] the concept of eleven first ministers getting together and agreeing this was for the good of the nation, that we were going to be more generous with each other. The whole climate changed."

The climate had changed not only in Manitoba. In Quebec, three of Bourassa's four anglophone ministers quit on 20 December, the day before a bill restoring French-only outdoor signs was approved in principle by the National Assembly. It was a wrenching decision for the trio of ministers. Richard French, who had the only job he ever wanted in the cabinet, called Bourassa to tell him he was resigning. Bourassa asked him if he wanted to come over to talk about it; French said there was nothing to discuss. Herbert Marx, the public security minister, also left cabinet. "It is impossible for me to make a 180-degree turn," he said. "I just can't do it." Clifford Lincoln, the minister of the environment, had tried to find a way to stay and when he could not, he delivered an emotional farewell. "In my belief, rights are rights are rights," he told the National Assembly in a much-quoted speech. "There is no such thing as inside rights and outside rights. No such thing as rights for the tall and rights for the short. No such things as rights for the front and rights for the back, or rights for East or rights for West. Rights are rights and always will be rights. There are no partial rights. Rights are fundamental rights." Some of his colleagues, including members of the Parti Québécois, wept as he spoke, and afterwards they rushed to his desk to offer their congratulations.

In Ottawa, all Brian Mulroney could manage was that he was "disappointed" with Bill 178 because it "offended" the Charter. The language he used was weak because he knew that Quebeckers supported Bourassa and he did not want to jeopardize his suppport there. The federal Liberals felt no such constraint. By now, having broken with Bourassa on free trade, they condemned the use of the notwithstanding clause. The election over, their Quebec fortress in ruins, they had nothing to lose. For three days in Question Period, John Turner lashed the government for refusing to condemn Bill 178. He rounded on Mulroney for allowing Lucien Bouchard — then secretary of state responsible for protecting minority language rights — to sit in the cabinet after he had endorsed Quebec's decision. Bouchard, for his part, avoided the House of Commons that week.

To Turner, this was a turning point in the debate. "Once Bourassa used the nothwithstanding clause, although the language law was a different issue, the climate immediately began to deteriorate," he says. "He had broken his electoral commitment to the English-speaking minority and his party, and the PM's failure to respond weakened the resolve of many Canadians for that accord. Although it was not strictly relevant, it contaminated the public perception of Meech Lake. That was the critical point." By March 1989, Turner recalls, he could see it slipping away. He told Mulroney, "You didn't respond to Bourassa. The climate is changing. What are you doing about it? Who is speaking for the accord?"

The notwithstanding clause not only reversed Manitoba's support, it made Meech Lake topical. Public support, which was never deeply committed to Meech Lake, began to fall steadily for the next year. English Canada began to associate Bill 178 and Meech Lake. Of course, one had nothing to do with the other. Or did it? The impact was psychological.

Bill 178 was probably the greatest threat to the accord in this period, but it was not the only one. The previous spring, both Alberta and Saskatchewan, after Quebec the only two provinces that ratified Meech Lake, moved to limit the rights of their minority language groups. The Supreme Court ruled in February 1988 that all laws in these two provinces had to be in English and French because the relevant part of the Northwest Territories Act of 1886, under which they were established, was still valid. The ruling was considered a victory for francophones. On 25 April, the Conservative government in Saskatchewan repealed the law and passed Bill 2, which allowed the cabinet to decide what statutes would be translated. French was permitted in the courts and in the legislature, but would not be part of the official record. There was money, however, from the federal government for translation and for the establishment of a bilingual institute.

In Alberta, francophones got even less. On 22 June, the Conservative government said it would allow French to be spoken in the legislature with the permission of the Speaker, and in the courts with interpreters. But there would be no translation of statutes. Quebec refused to criticize either government. Indeed, Quebec later closed the circle by intervening in a case brought by Franco-Albertans for more control of minority language school boards, on the *government's* side. Only a few months later, Quebec invoked the notwithstanding clause. Taken together, the suspicion grew that Bourassa remained

silent or actually opposed to expanding rights on the understanding
that if the western provinces could curtail the rights of their linguistic
minorities with impunity, he could do the same in Quebec.

Predictably, these unholy alliances over language rights bred cyni-
cism. By the end of 1988, the accord was less than eighteen months
old and not yet ratified, but here was its spirit. English Canada was
becoming more English, and French Canada more French. A bilingual Canada would find little support among the premiers; no wonder they had refused to promote that characteristic at Meech Lake. Of
course, Bourassa could argue that the English-speaking minority in
Quebec was far better treated than the French-speaking minority in
other provinces. He was absolutely right. But these setbacks to minority rights within six months of each other, in provinces where the
accord was most strongly supported, seemed a foretaste of Meech
Lake. It only deepened the fears of its critics.

There were questions about the meaning of the distinct-society
clause since the parliamentary committee had held its hearings. On 28
September 1987, Joe Ghiz and one of his senior ministers, Wayne
Cheverie, went to see Robert Bourassa in Montreal. At the meeting,
which was a well-kept secret, Ghiz suggested that his government refer the question directly to the Court of Appeal of Prince Edward Island. The court could rule on the legal implications of the clause for
the Charter and for the distribution of powers — the two key concerns — and lay all doubts to rest. He thought a ruling would dispel
doubts and ensure speedy ratification by the remaining provinces. "If
we were right in our thinking — that it didn't undermine anything —
and if we could allay these fears through our Court of Appeal, then it
could go," says Cheverie. Bourassa told them he wasn't interested in
the court's interpretation, and the idea was dropped.

Those fears notwithstanding, eight provinces had ratified the accord by the middle of 1988. Joining Quebec, Saskatchewan and Alberta were Prince Edward Island (13 May 1988); Nova Scotia (25
May 1988); British Columbia and Ontario (29 June 1988); and Newfoundland (7 July 1988). Only half the provinces had public hearings;
in some that did not, the debate was limited. British Columbia, the
worst example, held only six hours of debate, which Liberal leader
Gordon Wilson called "pathetic." By the time Newfoundland approved the accord, it was more than a year old. Quebec had become
anxious that the process was taking too long and thought Ontario
was dawdling. But the real problem was British Columbia. Bill

Vander Zalm, who had been the last hold-out at Meech Lake, was still unhappy. "We toyed with not doing it," says a former senior official. "There were times we said, 'Let's not do it because Ottawa was screwing us around. Maybe forget it. Let it drag on.'" But Ottawa was pressuring Victoria, and Vander Zalm was persuaded to ratify because he promised he would. "The premier had always felt he had gone against his instincts," said the official. "He never did it with a full heart. As the months passed, he felt Ottawa was shafting us. The delay in ratification was deliberate. We played it to the nth degree." That ambivalence helped explain Vander Zalm's wavering on the accord. In June 1989, for example, he suggested it be re-examined. In January 1990, he called the accord "unacceptable" to his province. Still, he never withdrew his support.

By spring 1989, antipathy to the accord was hardening. New Brunswick was pushing ahead with its public hearings on the matter. Manitoba, governed by the minority triumvirate, was preparing to form its own task force to examine the accord. The federal government seemed unfazed by the gathering opposition in both provinces. Federal officials had almost no contact with New Brunswick, and relations had cooled between Filmon and Mulroney, who felt betrayed by Manitoba's reversal. The antagonism between the province and the federal government was one of the reasons for the delay in establishing the Centre for Sustainable Development in Winnipeg, which Mulroney had promised at the United Nations in 1988. Mayor William Norrie complained that the rift had imperilled other federal projects in Winnipeg. If Manitoba could hold up national reconciliation, Ottawa seemed prepared to hold up provincial rehabilitation.

In April, with the accord already in deep trouble, matters got worse. After ten years in office, Brian Peckford retired as premier of Newfoundland. Unlike Pawley's government, Peckford's had ratified the accord, but that would not matter. In the subsequent election, Newfoundlanders chose a new party, the Liberals, and a new premier, Clyde Wells. More than any of his fellow premiers, Wells influenced the debate as the accord entered its final year. He was the third horseman of the apocalypse.

In Clyde Kirby Wells, Q.C., B.A., LL.B., M.H.A., the opponents of Meech Lake had found a new exemplar. Pierre Trudeau remained their champion, but he remained powerless. Wells was Trudeau in power, a comparison the premier found flattering. He would sound the trumpet, rally the troops, mount the charger, swing the mace. He would banish the satraps, snivellers, weaklings and eunuchs. He would speak for Canada. That Wells should arrive when he did was another one of those imponderables of this saga, more fateful than the emergence of his soulmates in Manitoba and New Brunswick. Greater things were expected of Wells because of his independence and intellect, which made him suspicious of the premiers in general and the accord in particular. His pride and passion would electrify the last stage of the constitutional endgame.

To a greater extent than any of his colleagues, Wells had studied the constitution and thought about federalism. He was born in 1937 at Buchans Junction, Newfoundland, the second of nine children of a freight handler with the Newfoundland Railway. He was not born a Canadian and did not become one until Newfoundland joined Confederation in 1949. He attended Memorial University in St. John's in the 1950s, where he majored in government and history, and studied law at Dalhousie University. His view of the country was shaped by K. C. Wheare, a political scientist at Oxford who argued that the fundamental principle of the federal state is the equality of its constituent parts. Although Wells did not attend Oxford, he became one of Wheare's devotees, and his attachment explains his lifelong commitment to an elected Senate.

His law practice was largely commercial, and largely in litigation. "I spent all my time in the courts," he remembers. There was scarcely a constitutional case of the last two decades involving Newfoundland that he missed. His most significant role was arguing the federal side when Newfoundland challenged Ottawa's right to patriate the British North America Act in 1981. He also argued the federal case on the ownership of offshore mineral rights. "Newfoundland is a province just like the others," said Wells at the time, rejecting the provincial claim to ownership of the seabed. The federal government won. His reputation grew. "Clyde knows as much about the constitutional law of Canada as any person alive today," says Ed Roberts, a friend and a former Liberal colleague.

At the urging of Premier Joey Smallwood, Wells entered politics in 1964. He was minister of labour in 1966, at age twenty-eight, but resigned from the cabinet in 1968 (along with then Liberal John Crosbie) in opposition to the premier's plan for a refinery at Come By Chance. It took courage for an ambitious politician in Newfoundland to stand up to Smallwood in those days. And it showed an early willingness to preserve his integrity, even if it meant being an outsider, that became the hallmark of his career. In 1971, he resigned his seat. He returned to private practice and renewed his interest in the constitution. In 1977 and 1978, he was Newfoundland's representative on the Canadian Bar Association's committee on constitutional reform. In the association's report he again showed his independence. He dissented from the report because he did not like the proposed "House of the Provinces," a body chosen by the provinces to replace the Senate. He thought it would undermine the national will and become "a constitutional nightmare." Around this time, he even began to draft a model constitution for Canada. It was an intellectual exercise that soon frustrated him, and he abandoned it. Recognizing Quebec as a distinct society was not a part of it, not even in the preamble.

After sixteen years out of politics, Wells won the Liberal leadership in 1987. He was not convinced he wanted the job, and insisted on an honorarium from the party to compensate for his loss of salary. The Liberals had been racked by division. Of the seven party leaders since Smallwood, Wells was the only one to win an election. In April 1989, he won a majority government, ending seventeen years of Conservative rule.

From the beginning, Wells seemed an unlikely premier. He was brighter and sharper than most of his counterparts. He did not believe in lacerating the federal government, a ready target for a premier. More pointedly, he had ideas about the provinces and the federal government that were antithetical to the traditional provincial view. He had the temerity to challenge the role of the premiers, even to argue for less authority for the provinces. One of the reasons he so favoured an elected Senate — his *idée fixe* — was that it would correct the imbalance in the federation. "The first ministers have moved into that vacuum because they have political legitimacy," he says. "You then have people elected who have a provincial responsibility, exercising national legislative power and developing national policy, so naturally it will be disjointed and twisted and contorted to their different points of view, and seldom takes into account the national interest." He says the reason his view is unusual today is because the premiers have won power and influence through executive federalism. "Once you give people power, or they feel power, power becomes self-serving, and it becomes more important," he says.

Wells was a formidable presence. He had thick hair, cornflower eyes and a complexion said to turn red when he was angry. He liked

to ski and sail, and there were times in the debate he would rather
have done either. As a lawyer, Wells was described as solitary, stub-
born and sometimes sanctimonious. As a politician, he was said to be
honest, pedantic and thoughtful. "Wells is really a priest, not a politician," says a professional associate. "He is miscast. He has a princi-
pled view, about which he is absolutely doctrinaire. His conscious-
ness that he is right, even though he says he may be wrong, is so
profound that it is unbelievable; it is theological and dogmatic." Everyone conceded he had self-confidence and talent, and no doubt his
style was more restrained than that of his three flamboyant predecessors. The place he was most comfortable was the courtroom. He
loved the majesty of the stage, its traditions, its decorum, its drama.
Now, as he was sworn in as premier on 5 May 1989, he prepared for
the biggest case of his career.

It had long been clear that Clyde Wells had deep reservations about
the accord and that they would make him its most formidable oppo-
nent. He had declared his position shortly after he was elected leader,
only three days after the deal was signed in Ottawa. In a speech to the
Newfoundland House of Assembly on 18 March 1988, a few months
before the province ratified the accord, he laid out his objections,
threatening then that his government would rescind any resolution of
support were it elected. He reiterated those views during the election
campaign the next year, and again after he became premier. The accord was unacceptable. Strangely, however, Wells heard nothing
from the federal government for the first six months he was in office.
Until November 1989, there was not a letter, a telephone call or a
visit from Brian Mulroney or Lowell Murray. He did hear from his
former colleague and old friend, John Crosbie, who told him,
"You've got to stop this foolishness about Meech Lake." He also
wrote Mulroney when one of his ministers told him that Barbara
McDougall, the employment and immigration minister, had suggested they could do business on other matters only if Wells had "a
different position on Meech Lake." An angry Wells called the prime
minister, and Mulroney promised to check into it, but that was the
last he heard.

No doubt Ottawa was determined to keep its distance. "We did
not want to give him the impression we were prepared to accommodate any change," says a senior federal official, who concedes it may
have been a mistake. "But I'm not sure you would have changed his

mind by going down to see him." The silence exacerbated the frustration in St. John's and set the tone for the relationship that followed. That coolness, however, did not stop Wells from shaping his intellectual opposition. In speeches, interviews, debates and papers, he continued to attack the accord. That autumn, he hired Deborah Coyne, a redoubtable critic of the accord. Coyne — a young constitutional lawyer described as brilliant and dedicated — left a job of only a few months in Toronto to join Wells as adviser. (He had read one of her articles in a scholarly journal.) Her presence reflected the depth of his opposition to the accord, but her critics wrongly assumed she was the reason for his opposition.

Meanwhile, the constitutional carousel was turning in the two hold-out provinces, which were proceeding with public hearings. In New Brunswick, the Select Committee on 1987 Constitutional Accord began its hearings in January 1989. Before it adjourned to write its report, it had received 182 briefs. While that legislative committee was at work, an independent, all-party task force was doing the same in Manitoba. By the time it retired to gather its thoughts in the summer, it had heard more than 300 presentations. The process radicalized the province in its opposition to the accord, and cemented consensus on the changes needed.

As it happened, the summer of 1989 was a lull in the Constitutional Wars. The battle lines were drawn, and the two sides taunted each other, but refused to come out to fight. Ottawa watched silently as the three horsemen mounted their steeds, donned their armour and assembled their weaponry. It decided the time was still not right for a meeting, and it cancelled a constitutional conference scheduled for September in Prince Edward Island, where the Fathers of Confederation had met in 1864. Apparently, Mulroney thought it was too early for the first skirmish. As the clock ticked, however, it became apparent discussion of the issue could not be postponed indefinitely.

A Roll of the Dice

THE GOVERNMENT CONFERENCE CENTRE, A NEOCLASSICAL, GRANITE temple at the centre of Ottawa, is a mirror of the nation's character. It faces the Château Laurier Hotel, a bastion of tradition and enterprise; it borders the Rideau Canal, a symbol of commerce and security; it sits in the shadow of the Cenotaph War Memorial, a monument to sacrifice and honour. For half a century, it was a railway station, the hub of a far-flung country. When the trains stopped coming in 1966, Union Station, as it was known, fell into disuse. Enterprising merchants wanted to tear it down and build a shopping centre. The government saved the building and chose a function no less glorious: a permanent forum for federal-provincial conferences.

In its new incarnation, it has been the site of many battles of the Constitutional Wars. Here, Pierre Trudeau fought the premiers until nine of them agreed to patriate the constitution in 1981. Here, Brian Mulroney invited them to celebrate and sign the Meech Lake Accord in 1987. Inside, in what was the large waiting room, history and practicality mingle. Rows of Corinthian columns hug the walls, a sea of red carpet lapping at their feet. Arched windows reach for the ceiling, adorned with inset rosettes. At the far end, an irregular quadrangular conference table, covered in blue leather, straddles the room. At each public meeting — and there have been many here — the prime minister sits with his back to the wall and is flanked by the premiers in order of precedence. Behind him, in several rows, sit federal and provincial officials, shaded by the flags of Canada, the provinces and the territories.

By autumn 1989, Mulroney could no longer avoid public discussion of the accord with the premiers. With the deadline of 23 June

1990 eight months away, positions were hardening. Manitoba and New Brunswick had published their committees' reports proposing amendments to the accord. Newfoundland had issued a position paper. Manitoba and New Brunswick were refusing to ratify, while Newfoundland was preparing to rescind. Bourassa and Mulroney continued to insist that the accord was "a seamless web" and could not be touched. As the premiers gathered in Ottawa on 9 November 1989, the battle lines were drawn.

Formally, the conference was on the economy, not the constitution. It was the annual gathering of the first ministers, the fifth since the meeting in Regina in 1985. Discussion of the accord was consigned to the second half of the second day, after talks on the environment. Before the conference, Mulroney had already begun playing down expectations. The first ministers would discuss the general sales tax, interprovincial trade barriers, deficit reduction, interest rates, education and the environment. Meech Lake? As little discussion as necessary, said federal officials. The feeling was that it would not yield much except to keep everyone talking, and there was no certainty it would do even that. As they gathered, it was apparent the premiers were going to work on the dissenters, particularly the new premier from Newfoundland. "It will be a first first ministers' conference for Wells," said David Peterson. "I think it will be important for him to learn about the atmosphere in the rest of Canada; it will be important that he understands the history of Meech Lake." The tone was revealing, the subtext clear: the premiers who had written the accord understood the chemistry of constitution-making; Wells, the neophyte, did not. He would learn, he would understand, he would yield.

The accord dominated the discussion at the private dinner in the wood-panelled members' lounge of the National Gallery. Wells said later that his reception at his first first ministers' conference had been "warm" at the dinner, but not "hot." Others called the encounter "bruising." The dissident premiers were told that they were playing with the future of Canada, a warning that they would hear often over the next eight months. Wells came in for particular abuse because of his insistence on rescinding his ratification, something his caucus had wanted him to do the previous June. Deborah Coyne was getting the same treatment at meetings of officials. But Wells was unyielding. A memo from one of his officials advised: "It is best and wisest to be up front about what everyone expects to come out of the negotiations:

that the existing accord is dead and the sooner we adopt to the post-Meech world the better." It was on Wells that attention was focussed at the dinner. Although Filmon said he supported Wells, he was largely ignored — part of the federal strategy to isolate Newfoundland, to make Wells hold the dagger. At one point, Frank McKenna told Wells: "Clyde, you're no fucking constitutional expert!" He also said Wells's referendum idea — Wells had talked of holding a referendum in Newfoundland if he was the lone hold-out — was ridiculous. Other premiers were also critical. Later, Joe Ghiz came to his defence. "I know Clyde Wells," he said, "and you're not going to change his mind." Wells emerged from the meeting exhausted, his complexion a deeper scarlet than usual. He managed a pinched smile, which suggested to one of his assistants, "We did it. We survived. We told them that we will rescind, that this must be reopened."

It was clear that the other first ministers would use these private sessions to cajole, coax and co-opt the skeptics. As Grant Devine put it, with oatsy charm, the new premiers were forced to spell out their positions without circumlocution. "We'd say, 'Explain yourself, please. What are you talking about here? You can say that on TV because a lot of folks don't know what's in the constitution. But don't say that to me. Now, what are you talking about, Slim? Either put your money where your mouth is or stop saying that. You don't BS me and I won't BS you.'"

The public never knew what went on behind closed doors at these meetings, but there was no doubt the pressure on the dissenting premiers was unrelenting. Perhaps that was why Clyde Wells was so eager, then and in the next few months, to move into public session.

Because Newfoundland was the last province to enter Confederation, Wells was the last of the premiers to address the opening session of the first ministers' conference. He spent most of his forty-one-minute speech on the economy, lamenting Newfoundland's chronic disadvantages in Confederation. In the last few minutes, he turned to Meech Lake. He asked his colleagues "please" to stop misrepresenting his views on recognizing Quebec as a distinct society, arguing that he did not oppose it as long as it did not confer legislative power. He also challenged Mulroney's repeated claim that the rest of Canada would never have left Ontario out of the constitution, as it allegedly did Quebec in 1981. Wells argued that the country would have isolated Ontario if it, too, had demanded special status. But he insisted he was not rejecting Quebec. "I am rejecting a Canada with a Class-A province, a Class-B province, and a Class-C province," he said. During his remarks, Robert Bourassa left the room. He said later that he had gone to retrieve a report, but Gil Rémillard intimated that the timing of his departure was no coincidence.

When Wells finished speaking, Mulroney chastised him for even considering excluding *any* province. He asked: "Where do you think you would get the right to say that 'we' would have proceeded without the most populous province and impose on that province a constitution that it felt was unacceptable and not in their interest?" Mulroney argued that he could never do that, that a constitution must bind the whole country, and excluding one part would destroy its purpose. "When you said we would proceed without Ontario if Ontario had demanded something we thought was unreasonable or a special status, that is where you and I separate fundamentally in terms of a vision of Canada," Mulroney told Wells. "For me a constitution without Ontario is no constitution at all."

Wells grimaced. "That is not accurate," he told the prime minister. "I say to you, without hesitation, that no province in the nation has the right to hold up forever the rest of the nation, and if Ontario were in precisely the same position in 1982 as Quebec was in 1982 . . . that Quebec could be let out of Confederation at any time, then I have no quarrel with treating Ontario exactly the way we treat Quebec." Wells said the amending formula in the constitution allowed changes to be made without the approval of Ontario or Quebec, but not without both. At this point, David Peterson jumped in. "My friend," he said, turning to Wells, "you must reflect very carefully on your own logic that no one province holds up the constitutional development of this country. Your own logic is not working in your favour." Then, he turned to Mulroney: "Ontario is part of the constitution and it is going to continue to be, Prime Minister. Do not use me as an example any more, will you?"

Mulroney responded to Wells. He reminded him that Canada had brought Newfoundland into Confederation in 1949 because the country had "foresight and leadership," and that Canada was better for it. He suggested, pointedly, that without that "openness and generosity" the country would not survive in 1989. Wells did not like that either. He thought Mulroney was painting a false picture of the past, and here, as this exchange on live television continued, he let him have it. "I cannot allow the suggestion to remain on the table that my attitude is somehow that I do not want Quebec to be part of the country or that I am not being generous in making sure that Quebec is a full constitutional participant," he said, "and frankly, Prime Minister, you should check the historical facts before you use the example to which you have just referred. It happens to have nothing to do, no relevance to the constitutional issues that are involved in the Meech Lake Accord." Mulroney said that he did not mean to suggest that the entry of Newfoundland into Confederation had anything to do with the Meech Lake Accord. Then he changed the subject.

The exchange lasted twelve minutes and was the most telling of the conference. Mulroney learned that Wells was not afraid to challenge him on the facts or questions of principle. The new premier from the newest province was ready to state his case forcefully and defend himself persuasively. There was something else at work here. Just as Trudeau had been in the room at the Langevin Block that morning in June, a black spectre haunting Brian Mulroney, he was in the hall of the Government Conference Centre that afternoon in November. A similar confrontation between two headstrong advocates in the same city had taken place twenty-one years earlier. Then, too, the subject was special status for Quebec. On 6 February 1968, Pierre Trudeau, the justice minister and future prime minister, had challenged Daniel Johnson, the premier of Quebec. The occasion was the first ministers' conference on the constitution. Trudeau sat on the right of Lester Pearson in the ornate, gold-flecked Confederation Room of the West Block. In that clash of wills, also carried on national television, Trudeau asserted his support for a bilingual Canada and guaranteed rights for all citizens. Johnson countered that the only way to resolve the national-unity crisis was to grant Quebec special powers, which would make French and English Canada equal. Trudeau responded coldly. He repeated what he had been saying for two decades: no special status, one Canada, two languages. If not, there would be two separate nations. The tone was icy. Instead of referring to each other as minister and premier, Johnson contemptuously called Trudeau "the member from Mount Royal," his federal riding, and Trudeau called Johnson "the deputy from Bagot," his provincial riding.

Mulroney was not Johnson and Wells was not Trudeau, but there was an eerie sense of the past in that hall. Wells did not call Mulroney "the member from Charlevoix," and Mulroney did not call Wells "the member from Bay of Islands." Still, there was personal tension, and a touch of history. Wells said he had not expected the confrontation with Mulroney, and he did not provoke it. He had wondered whether to use all the references to Meech Lake at the end of of his speech and, during the course of the day, he decided that he should. After the exchange with Mulroney, he was pleased by the analogy to Trudeau. The country was again talking about the place of Quebec, the alignment of its regions, the role of the federal government. It was as if, after all those years of Trudeau federalism, nothing had changed. By the end of the twelve minutes, Wells had become a national figure. His office was flooded with calls and letters and flowers. That Thursday, 9 November, was Wells's birthday. It was also, incidentally, the day the Berlin Wall fell.

The conference ended inconclusively. The prime minister declared it a "constructive and helpful meeting" and announced that Lowell Murray, his constitutional emissary, would make another round of visits to the provincial capitals to try to find common ground. He would focus on Senate reform as an incentive for the second round of talks. If there was progress, a conference would be held on 1 November 1990, after passage of the accord. Senate reform was now seen as a kind of panacea, a *quid pro quo* to satisfy the complaints of the other provinces. Mulroney, under questioning from reporters, tried to cast it in the best light. Why would Murray be packing his bags unless there was something to discuss? "He is a busy man," said Mulroney. "He has better things to do with his time than run around the country, unless there is a willingness to dialogue." But that willingness was doubtful. The premiers muttered the usual pleasantries, but, on balance, rarely had so many said so much about so little. Manitoba and Newfoundland were showing no signs of relenting. In fact, the autumn chill seemed only to freeze their positions.

In Manitoba, the all-party task force, which had been examining the accord for months, had forged a common front among the three parties. Either Sharon Carstairs and Gary Doer had succeeded in boxing in Gary Filmon, or Filmon had succeeded in co-opting his two opposition leaders. (Carstairs said the task force effectively made Meech Lake, once exclusively her issue, a government issue. "It neutralized me," she conceded.) A triumvirate was dictating Manitoba's position on Meech Lake. The federal government would have to deal with three Manitobans, not one. The three wanted changes to the accord, and if they did not get them, the accord would die in their legislature.

The report of the task force, released in October, said it all. It did not nibble at the edges of the accord, leaving the foundation intact, as did the legislative committee in New Brunswick. Rather, it took dead aim at the heart of the accord: the distinct-society clause, the spending-power clause and the amending formula. Instead of the distinct-society clause, it proposed a "Canada Clause" recognizing the distinct nature of Canada and the contribution of aboriginal and multicultural Canadians. The task force recognized Quebec as "a distinct society" but said that recognition should not be used to override the Charter. It also said that all provinces, including Quebec, should "uphold" rather than "preserve and promote" the character of Canada. Instead of unanimity on the amending formula, it suggested seven provinces with half the population. As for the provision on spending power, it simply dropped that clause.

"The simple fact is that the accord, as it now stands, cannot and will not be approved by the legislature," said Filmon. Carstairs remained unswayed by warnings that killing Meech Lake would fuel separatist sentiment in Quebec. "I am not going to be forced into amending my constitution because someone holds a threat over my head." Both said there was time to reopen the accord, but rejected the suggestion that a parallel or companion accord — a separate agreement with additions or deletions to the original one — would be a suitable instrument. All this was tough talk, born of hard electoral considerations. It left little room to manoeuvre. Whatever the triumvirate's claims to reasonableness, their suggestions undermined the essence of Meech Lake. Robert Bourassa could not accept Manitoba's proposals without scuttling the accord. Either Filmon, Carstairs and Doer were sabre-rattling for political consumption, or the accord was truly dead in Manitoba.

In New Brunswick, which released its report the same week, the tone was much softer. The legislative committee asked for modest changes, none of them affecting the sections on the distinct society, the spending power or Senate reform. It asked only to protect women's rights, not the whole Charter, from encroachment by the distinct-society clause. It endorsed the spending-power provision as it was, and unanimity for Senate reform. New Brunswick did agree with Manitoba on dropping the need for unanimity among the provinces to make territories into new provinces, and recommended that both territories should have representation on the Supreme Court.

By the end, however, the exclusion of the North was seen as easily fixed, at least in the next round. The report was a mandate for Mc-Kenna to negotiate a parallel accord, something he had been talking about. Despite its conciliatory tone, however, the committee still wanted some changes. "We cannot share the drafters' belief in the fragility of the accord — a seamless garment that must not be altered. Rather we see it as a constitutional cloak of great durability, once a few loose strands are in place." For this task, McKenna offered himself as tailor.

The premier said the committee's proposals were "almost identical" to the points he had been arguing since the very beginning. That disappointed critics in his province, who said McKenna had sold out to play the great conciliator. "It's gone to his head," complained Anne Crocker, one of the original opponents of the accord. As much as McKenna denied it, his position had shifted since his appearance before the parliamentary committee in August 1987. While he had always left himself an opening — he had never promised to kill the accord — there was little doubt that he had retreated. In his testimony to the committee, he had expressed reservations about spending power, advocating that Parliament set national objectives. He wanted Parliament to promote, not just preserve, the linguistic duality of Canada. He wanted a more flexible amending formula than unanimity. He wanted changes to the nominating procedure of the justices to the Supreme Court, arguing that allowing the provinces to nominate judges would add "a distinctly political flavour to the nomination process."

Because as opposition leader McKenna had wanted fewer changes than had Filmon or Wells, his reversal was not as great. But his shift on Meech Lake began with the committee report. It allowed him to distance himself from his early opposition. In November 1989, shortly after the first ministers' conference, he said the only real difference between his two positions was on the spending-power clause and the amending formula — and that was the committee's decision, not his. But no doubt he was dismayed by the bad deal he inherited. "The trouble with Meech Lake is that it was passed. I wasn't there, but I have to live with it." In moderating his opposition to Meech Lake, McKenna was not alone. By the time the first ministers reconvened seven months later in the Government Conference Centre, Gary Filmon, Sharon Carstairs, Gary Doer — and Clyde Wells —

would also narrow their criticisms to the accord. There were many conversions on the road to Ottawa, but McKenna's was the earliest and the most enthusiastic.

Of the three opponents of Meech Lake, Wells was the most implacable. After the November meeting, it was apparent that McKenna would eventually come on side. The government knew Manitoba was a problem but hoped that Filmon would call an election, win a majority and ratify the accord. Ottawa believed that Filmon's opposition was a matter of politics, not principle. At the same meeting, Filmon was told by David Peterson: "Gary, if you had a majority, you'd have passed this by now." Filmon reacted angrily. There was also a sense among federal officials that however defiant, either Sharon Carstairs could be brought around by Jean Chrétien, her old friend, or Gary Doer could be persuaded by Ed Broadbent, the former leader of the federal NDP.

Wells was a different story, which is probably why Mulroney ignored him until shortly before the first ministers' conference. The more the issue was discussed that autumn, the more determined Wells appeared. The premier put his objections in a letter to his colleagues before the conference. The heart of Newfoundland's objections remained the distinct-society clause, what it called the creation of special legislative status for one province. "No federation is likely to survive for very long if one of its supposedly equal provinces has a legislative jurisdiction in excess of that of the other provinces," Wells wrote. His great concern was the possibility of laws further limiting the rights of English Quebeckers, such as Bill 178, which would divide the country. "Canada would inevitably evolve into two linguistic enclaves and the end of the nation, as we know it, would not likely be far off." He suggested the most effective way to ensure the survival of the French language and culture in North America was not by isolating Quebec but by strengthening bilingualism.

Second, Wells rejected the requirement of unanimity in the amending formula, saying that it would put Canada "in a permanent constitutional strait jacket." His greatest fear was that the accord would kill Senate reform. For Wells, institutional reform was the key to the kingdom; without it, Newfoundland and other small provinces would never have influence at the centre. In the "Triple E Senate," which Wells endorsed, he proposed a veto on linguistic and cultural amendments for Quebec senators.

Third, Wells wanted changes to the limits on federal spending power. He argued that the accord would make it impossible to establish new social programs with minimum national standards, and that such programs were critical to Newfoundland, the country's poorest province. He foresaw Quebec and Ontario opting out of national programs and demanding financial compensation, reducing the government to chief cashier of Confederation. "Inevitably, we will end up with a patchwork of programs across the country with different standards, and a steadily weakening commitment to reduce disparities and promote equal opportunities for all Canadians especially in the poorer, disadvantaged regions. Equally inevitably, this will steadily weaken our sense, however fragile, of national community."

Spending power, the veto and the distinct society were not Newfoundland's only concerns. Wells objected to the idea that the province would submit lists of nominees to the Supreme Court, which "effectively cedes the power to appoint judges to Canada's highest court to certain of the provinces." He objected to the immigration clauses, because they "unacceptably weakened" the ability of the federal government to set immigration policy. He attacked entrenched first ministers' conferences, which he called an inappropriate forum for provincial influence on national policy.

What Wells had articulated in his letter to Mulroney on 18 October — and at the first ministers' conference and in a raft of statements, speeches, letters, debates and interviews — was a philosophy of federalism that was unusual, if not extraordinary, for a premier. Wells simply refused to embrace provincialism. Here was a premier with a first truly national view from a province. He did not need twelve minutes on national television to show that his philosophy was different from that of virtually all his colleagues, even those who, like Peterson, had not necessarily asked for new powers at Meech Lake. Nor did he need the twelve minutes to show that he was more of a federalist than Brian Mulroney. Read his lips, or read his speeches. At root, he wanted a return to the Canada of Pierre Trudeau — and of Lester Pearson, John Diefenbaker, Mackenzie King, Wilfrid Laurier and Sir John A. Macdonald — the Canada of a strong federal government and provincial representation in national institutions. His view of the distinct-society, spending-power and immigration clauses was remarkably Trudeauesque. That his colleagues were not listening and that the vision was said to be passé were no matter to him. Indeed, there was something strangely symbolic in the emergence of St.

Clyde of Buchans Junction, girding himself to slay the dragon. As the Trudeau vision had been consigned to the margins of the debate, its lone advocate among the premiers had been consigned to the margins of the conference table. But neither the demise of the vision nor the weakness of his province would deter Wells. From November to June, he would dominate the debate, and eventually become its most troubled and unpredictable player.

After the federal-provincial conference, public interest in the Meech Lake issue began to grow. Perhaps it was the power of television, or the threat of the deadline: 23 June 1990 was no longer an abstraction. By year's end, events accelerated. Robert Bourassa had been re-elected with a majority in Quebec, accompanied by a resurgent Parti Québécois, a development that strengthened his hand in negotiations. Each of the three dissenting provinces had completed its studies, expressed its objections, proposed its changes. Lowell Murray was again looking for common ground. The prime minister was denouncing the patriation package of 1981 and warning about the danger of losing Meech Lake. His anxiety was echoed in part by John Turner, who was soon to resign as opposition leader, and Ed Broadbent, who had departed as NDP leader. The Liberal leadership race had opened in earnest, and the party was divided along linguistic lines, as was the country itself. By January, Canada was entering a season of recrimination.

Why the sudden interest in an issue people had contrived to ignore? Canadians are a phlegmatic lot, unlikely to become excited about much of anything. The passion they showed in the free-trade debate of 1988 was unusual. The constitution is not a left-right issue or a pocketbook issue. It is esoteric and complex and theoretical. Quotas and duties are easier to understand — they can be quantified — than periods and preambles. Now, as the life was ebbing out of the accord, Canadians were becoming alarmed.

In early January, like a New Year's baby, Friends of Meech Lake was born. It was a non-partisan group to rally support for the accord. Its leading members were former politicians, among them Robert Stanfield, the former leader of the Conservative party; Stephen Lewis, the former ambassador to the United Nations; and Solange Chaput-Rolland, a Tory senator. The real goal, though, was to mobilize the academic community to support this vision of Canada, to show that Meech Lake was not a shabby political deal, but, rather, an accommodation that would serve as a foundation for a renewed nation. The accord was not just an effort to appease Quebec, but a response to a change in the country. The consequences of failure were unspeakable. "In all my years in politics in Canada, I've never been more concerned about the future of my country," said Stanfield. A few weeks later, another group of distinguished persons — Canadians for a Unifying Constitution — presented themselves with the same purpose. Its members included former premiers Richard Hatfield and Brian Peckford, former Bank of Canada governors Gerald Bouey and Louis Rasminsky; former Ontario attorney general Roy McMurtry; and former clerk of the privy council Gordon Robertson.

What was remarkable about these groups — the first of their kind — was that they had taken so long to organize. (An organization opposed to the accord — the Canadian Coalition on the Constitution — had appeared in 1987 but was inactive by 1990. It had been founded by Deborah Coyne, then teaching law at the University of Toronto.) That the two pro-accord groups should appear in 1990, while an anti-accord group should dissolve, reflected the slide in the accord's popularity. In 1987, no had thought this kind of drum-beating and tubthumping would be needed. Similarly, by 1990, an organization opposed to the accord was unnecessary; most of Canada already was.

What truly reflected the deteriorating situation, however, was the intervention of the business community. Surely if business leaders were speaking out, the situation had to be serious; in the past, business showed interest in the constitutional question only when it became a crisis. That business people were reacting now suggested that the danger was threatening the bottom line. The strongest call for support for Meech Lake came from the business community of Quebec. It argued that the accord was a reasonable compromise and would allow Quebec to prosper within Canada. Its failure would isolate Quebec and put it on the road to independence. The most dire warning came from Claude Castonguay, a former senior minister in the Bourassa government, and now the chairman of the Laurentian Group Corp., one of the largest companies in Quebec. "We are like the couple, so much immersed in recrimination and pettiness that they are getting to the point where the only way out is divorce," he said in a speech in February. "Divorce while living under the same roof, perhaps, because of the children, but divorce all the same." If the accord failed, he warned, Quebeckers would never forgive the rejection. They would begin looking for alternatives to the *status quo*.

Furthermore, many of Castonguay's colleagues in the Québécois business community would lead the way. As Bourassa had said, their loyalty to federalism was not unlimited. Because they had fought for the "No" side in the referendum in 1980 did not mean they would do so again. In fact, many of them said that, if the accord failed, they would consider other, more militant, options. These declarations, in winter 1990, were ominous. They were the loudest voices of the chorus of doom, and they were not to be dismissed. In the past, the nationalist forces had always been led by the intelligentsia, the artists, the media and some of the politicians. Now the entrepreneurial class, the new gods of the new Quebec, had signed on. If business executives — who were characterized by caution and restraint and timidity — had thrown themselves into the struggle for the distinct society, who could resist? The world had changed since 1980. Now, when the revolution came, Quebec knew which side of the barricades business would be on.

At first, their conversion was suspect. Here they were, pinstriped establishmentarians, talking the language of leather-jacketed rebels. "We have to give ourselves a new economic structure, with political autonomy and an economic union with the rest of Canada," said Bernard Lemaire, the president of Cascades Inc., one of Quebec's largest forest products companies. "We're ready. We won't be scared twice." The tone of the English community, though no less worried, was different. It, too, warned of the consequences if Meech Lake failed. But they disagreed with many francophone business people who thought that an independent Quebec would cause no disruption to the economy. The Business Council on National Issues, the voice of Canadian business, warned that the demise of the accord would bring economic harm. More important, though, its president, Tom d'Aquino, dismissed his colleagues in Quebec who thought a transition to independence would be smooth. "It's an act of lunacy to say separation would have a negligible impact or no impact at all," he said in March 1990. "These people who believe that you just wave a magic wand and tomorrow it's business as usual are dreaming."

Yet, that winter, many were talking about business as usual. The Toronto-Dominion Bank said Americans should not be afraid to invest in Quebec if Meech Lake failed, though it did not discuss the economic repercussions of independence. But Merrill Lynch & Co., the Wall Street investment house, and the Bank of Montreal both argued that separation would not be damaging. The report by the Bank of Montreal — written by a junior analyst — suggested that the separation of Quebec and Canada would be as painless as the "non-event" of Norway's separation from Sweden in 1905. There were, of course, some in the Quebec business community who were skeptical about the repercussions of independence, and Castonguay attempted to distance himself from those who foresaw no economic disruption. But the emerging message was that Quebec's economic élite was strong and confident. Theirs was no longer a society of farmers, loggers and clerics, but engineers, scientists and entrepeneurs. Quebec was competing in the world with Canada, and it could do so without Canada.

As the prospects of Meech Lake faded, economists began thinking the unthinkable. There was much talk about the economics of an independent Quebec — its ability to pay its share of the national debt, the viability of its own currency, the distribution of assets, the negotiation of new trade agreements, the establishment of customs. Few doubted that Quebec could survive; after all, countries with less means had. Quebec could indeed take its seat at the United Nations between Qatar and Rumania, even if it might have no more influence than either of them. Those who celebrated Quebec's economic prosperity never did address why Quebec, despite its sound economic growth in the 1980s, still had a lower provincial product, lower provincial personal income and twice the unemployment of Ontario in 1989. Nor did they explain, in that heady winter of 1990, the growing difference between interest rates on Quebec and Ontario bonds. No matter. Those sunny forecasts of the economists, endorsed by the investment houses, could only fuel the juggernaut. Indeed, the impact of that spate of optimistic forecasts — three, each within a week of the other — was the reverse of the Brinks Affair in 1980. On the eve of the Quebec Referendum, a flight of capital from Quebec — symbolized by a column of Brinks armoured cars trundling to Ontario — was an unsettling signal from bankers to Quebeckers considering sovereignty-association. This time, as Canadians prepared to kill the Meech Lake Accord, those cheerful reports reassured Quebeckers that, if it failed, they could make it on their own.

By winter's end, public opinion in English Canada showed no signs of softening on Meech Lake. A Gallup poll on 8 March 1990 reported that only 24 percent of Canadians thought that the accord would be "a good thing" for Canada. In June 1989, the figure had been 31 percent. In 1987, to a slightly different question, the response was 56

percent. The warnings of the prime minister, the appeals of eminent
Canadians, the fears of economic weakness for Canada or the blithe
optimism of Quebec — none could convince English Canada that the
accord was a step towards national renewal. Now, in fact, it had become a sword of division. Instead of opening their hearts to Quebec,
Canadians were hardening them. English began turning on French,
and French on English. The sour face of Meech Lake had begun to
show itself.

If the symbol of the national distemper was Meech Lake, the cata-
lyst was language. It exploded on 29 January, when the city council
of Sault Ste. Marie, Ontario, made itself unilingual. The resolution
made English the city's official language in the conduct of all business, including dealings with the province and Ottawa. Sault Ste.
Marie was then the largest municipality in the province to declare itself unilingual, though not the first. Over the winter, some forty-
seven municipalities, including Thunder Bay, made themselves unilingual. They said they could not afford French-language services
any more. True, they comprised only 47 out of 839, and there were
33 others, including Toronto, that reaffirmed bilingualism. But it
was a gratuitous, untimely slap at francophones — a run on the bank
of tolerance when its reserves were already low.

The good burghers of Ontario were quick to say that they meant
no offence to francophones. It was just a question of money, they
said; this French business was getting expensive. That the extension
of any new bilingual services, as mandated in certain areas where the
province's 500,000 francophones live, was paid for by the province
was not very persuasive. In fact, the French Language Services Act
did not even apply to municipal services. Still, they wanted to send a
message to the province: "We won't be pushed around." The trouble
was, they also told franco-Ontarians: "You're not welcome here."
That was how their action was interpreted in Ontario, and more im-
portantly in Quebec, which had already come to see the rejection of
Meech Lake in deeply personal terms.

If the link between the municipalities of Ontario and the debate
over Meech Lake was not immediately and absolutely clear, Brian
Mulroney was quick to draw it. In early February, the Liberals and
the New Democrats proposed a parliamentary resolution reaffirming
support for bilingualism and minority language rights. The idea was
simple and straightforward: the Commons would show its repug-
nance for the wave of intolerance. The biggest council of them all
would send a message of its own. But Mulroney could not resist a

little partisanship. It was not enough for Parliament to "support, protect and promote" the linguistic duality of Canada. He insisted that the resolution also say that the promotion of bilingualism reflected the spirit of the Meech Lake Accord and the Official Languages Act. Mulroney was being mischievous. He knew the accord was divisive among Liberals and New Democrats. The original resolution had been worded simply to make all-party support easy. By drawing in Meech Lake, Mulroney had muddied the issue. The resolution died. It was a perplexing ploy from Mulroney, who had been a staunch defender of francophone rights in Manitoba in 1983, even if he was less vocal in defence of anglophone rights in Quebec in 1988.

The parliamentary resolution, like the municipal resolutions, was seen as symbolic, and symbols had become critical in the debate over Meech Lake. The towns, villages and hamlets that spurned a bilingual regime that did not apply to them did not necessarily want to be mean-spirited. Similarly, the desecration of the Quebec flag by bigots in Brockville, Ontario, did not represent the feelings of most Canadians, but the footage of the event was played repeatedly in Quebec, as if it did. The discussion was no longer rational. It had moved from the merits of the accord to the perception of its impact or the consequences of its demise. When the townsfolk of Ontario declared themselves unilingual, they angered Quebeckers. And when the politicians of Quebec limited English signs, they angered English Canadians. Both actions may have been misread. Neither had anything to do with Meech Lake and everything to do with Meech Lake. Between the two solitudes, the crevice had become a chasm.

The conflagration over language soured the national mood. By March, with scarcely a hundred days to the deadline, the situation had the touch, taste and sound of a crisis. Time was running out. The players were posturing. For months, perhaps a year, the ship of state had been listing. Since the election of Clyde Wells in April 1989, it was obvious something was wrong. Then, suddenly, in the first week of March, the media made it official. On the same night, both the CBC and CTV evening news referred to "the constitutional crisis." There it was. And if the country needed a diagnosis of its malaise, it had only to read the declaration on the cover of *Maclean's*: "Canada in Crisis: How the Nation Could Break Up." Audrey McLaughlin, the new leader of the NDP, began using the term. Canadians now had reason to worry.

If Meech Lake had become a crisis, the federal government seemed

to want it that way. Four months had passed since the first ministers'
conference in November. Little had changed. Lowell Murray, the
travelling salesman of Meech Lake, had visited all the provinces, offered nothing new and returned home with an empty order book.
Meanwhile, the country had become more intemperate. Mulroney
continued to ignore Newfoundland; Wells said he had little contact
with Ottawa. More pointedly, Ottawa had ignored or alienated its allies in Ontario, Alberta and British Columbia. The strategy seemed
to be to let the crisis build, call a first ministers' conference and bring
in the Great Negotiator. It had become a constitutional endgame. If
that was the situation the government wanted, by early March, it had
come to pass.

In his Speech from the Throne, Wells renewed his threat to rescind
his province's ratification. Actually, he had repeatedly promised to
rescind the resolution — the accord had been passed by the House of
Assembly on 7 July 1988 — since the November conference. He said
he had to restate his intention because the federal government was not
taking his demands seriously. Moreover, Wells was disturbed by
rumours that the federal government was trying to isolate him
through secret negotiations with New Brunswick and Manitoba.
Mulroney did little to cool passions. He said that he did not have to
answer to Wells and told him to mind his own business.

Wells was not wrong. The federal government was shunning him
while courting Frank McKenna. "For two years they ignored me,"
McKenna says. "It was as if I was talking to the wall. They seemed to
say, 'There, there, he'll come around in the end.'" In January,
McKenna had rejected Murray's entreaties to lead a rescue mission,
telling him that saving Meech Lake was Ottawa's responsibility. Besides, Newfoundland and Manitoba were "allies" in opposing the
deal, and the problem was the intransigence of the other provinces.
That resistance had faded now. On 21 March, the first day of Canada's second constitutional spring, the country's newest nation-
builder rose in the restored Victorian slendour of the legislature of
New Brunswick to offer a modest solution for saving Canada. He
read two resolutions: one moving ratification of the accord, the other
making it subject to certain conditions. Then, in a speech carried live
on Canada's all-news channel, he offered an alternative of his own.
McKenna proposed a package of amendments to the accord that
would ensure that women's rights could not be overridden by the
accord; drop unanimous consent for the creation of new provinces;

establish the right of the federal government to promote, not just preserve, linguistic duality; place native issues on the agenda of the next
round of talks; and order public hearings on any future constitutional
amendments. All of this would be contained in "a companion resolution" to take effect at the same time as the accord. "It is time we spike
our guns with flowers," said McKenna, who had gone from the
voice of protest to the voice of conciliation.

The proposals marked another turn in the debate. They became the
current to spark talks that had been stalled for months. Beyond that,
they represented division among the three dissenters. McKenna was
now a dismounted horseman. After two and a half years of doubt and
delay, he had virtually embraced the accord. Between August 1987
and March 1990, his objections to the accord had softened. His proposed changes on sexual equality, the admission of new provinces
and aboriginal rights were not controversial. The proposals did not
affect the distinct society, the spending power, immigration, the Supreme Court or the question of unanimity on Senate reform. The
most contentious proposal was reaffirming the role of the federal
government in promoting bilingualism. While that would cause
problems in Quebec, which resisted the idea of Ottawa's promoting
English there, the rest were secondary items. It was fussing on the
fringes.

McKenna's proposals had been written in New Brunswick and Ottawa. Some parts had been in the works six months, others for three
weeks. Ottawa was intimately involved, and it, in turn, briefed Quebec. McKenna himself did not speak to Bourassa. His old allies of
January — Newfoundland and Manitoba — were not consulted either. In fact, in the period before the proposal was released, McKenna
did not return calls from Wells. The day after the proposals were ta-
bled, Newfoundland served notice of motion to rescind ratification.
Wells said the proposed parallel accord probably wouldn't be enough
to satisfy him. Filmon worried that it left unanimity for Senate reform intact. At the very least, McKenna's proposals did leave room
for Newfoundland and Manitoba to add their concerns. "It's digest-
ible to everyone," said McKenna hopefully, "but some provinces
will require a few hard swallows." Having unveiled his plan, Mc-
Kenna left for Ottawa and Toronto to sell it.

The dance of the dialectic continued. While McKenna was on the
road, the western premiers were meeting on the West Coast. Vander
Zalm was optimistic, as always, and Grant Devine called the plan

"doable." He should know, he allowed, because he was there in 1982. That was not true — he had nothing to do with the deal in 1981 and became premier three weeks after patriation in 1982 — but it made him sound authoritative. In Ottawa, Murray said the McKenna proposals were a good start. The government would consider them, which was taken as a good sign. Given that the government helped write them, this was a strange kind of progress. Even Pierre Trudeau, who was promoting his book that week, found something nice to say. He still hated the accord but gave McKenna "A plus" for trying to change it. This theatre of the absurd had become vaudeville.

On 22 March, the day after McKenna's proposals, Brian Mulroney went on national television — only the second time he had done so in five and a half years in office — to announce that the government would put McKenna's resolution before Parliament and refer it to a special committee for study. His speech was sentimental. "I love Canada — all of Canada," he said. The premiers greeted Mulroney's suggestion enthusiastically, but Bourassa warned there would be no renegotiation of Meech Lake; it had to be passed before there could be any other talks. The parliamentary committee, chaired by Conservative Jean Charest, would hold hearings and call witnesses. Frank McKenna would be the first to testify. The government seemed to embrace the McKenna plan, but was not certain. By week's end, the constitutional dossier was in a frenzy. After months of inactivity, the pace was dizzying. On Friday night, as the crisis entered a new stage, McKenna rushed home to join his legislators in a hockey game against the legislators from Quebec. Gary Filmon left for the Orient.

With less than three months to go before the deadline, all the actors were on stage. In Newfoundland, the government was positioning. In New Brunswick, the government was mediating. In Manitoba, the government was posturing. In Quebec, the government was brooding. In Ottawa, a committee was studying. And in the audience, Canadians were agonizing. Most still did not know much about Meech Lake even though they were being told that the fate of the country turned on it. By the time the Charest committee opened hearings on 3 April, the constitution had become daily fare. Meech Lake was a household word. It was affecting bond prices and interest rates and futures, both financial and personal. A distress hotline in Montreal, for example, reported that more and more callers were blaming Meech Lake for frustration and fear. It was creating a new vocabulary; "to meech" now meant to divide. It was giving rise to anxiety. At an academic conference at the University of Ottawa, a student cried as she talked about Canada. As Clyde Wells reaffirmed his opposition to Meech Lake, Senator Gérald Beaudoin shook his head and whispered to a colleague, *"C'est la fin du tout. C'est la fin du pays."* As this strange hysteria took hold, the constitutional maelstrom was inspiring songs, poems and epithets. "Meech Lake is a junk bond," said writer Mordecai Richler. "I *am* Meech Lake," declared Larry Zolf, the dishevelled, balding satirist. "I *am* a distinct society."

It was as if a strange contagion had afflicted Canada. Sharon Carstairs makes a goodwill visit to Robert Bourassa in Quebec City, only to find herself portrayed as a member of the Ku Klux Klan in a newspaper cartoon. Carstairs gets no apology and all Bourassa can say is that he has been the subject of far worse caricatures in western Canada. Later, in reporting on his discussion to the reporters, he says, "I exposed myself to Madame Carstairs for an hour." When anglophone reporters break up, he asks: "Why you laugh? Why you laugh?" There are other curiosities. John Buchanan, who has been becoming more shrill in his condemnation of critics of Meech Lake, warns that Atlantic Canada might have to join the United States if Meech Lake fails. Later, he qualifies his declaration. In Parliament, John Nunziata, campaigning for the Liberal leadership, calls separatists "traitors." It sparks a row. He does not apologize. Joe Clark writes an odd essay in which he calls the 1981 patriation agreement "a ticking time bomb." Clark does not remind anyone that he and his party had voted for it then, and had been proud of their contribution. Other voices caution reason. In one of the more eloquent appeals of these months, Bob Rae, the opposition leader in Ontario, calls for understanding and reason.

As for the committee, it was obvious it would serve purposes other than to study a resolution. If Quebec had already refused to accept any changes to the accord, either then or later, what was the point? The point, of course, was to legitimate the process. If there was anxiety over how the deal was done, then strike a committee, call public hearings, hear a few people. A month of televised hearings would help dispel the perception that the accord was cooked up by eleven men at a lakeside lodge. It would also have another effect: it would draw out the process and leave little time for any changes to the accord. The prime minister could then think it over and call a first ministers' conference. Meanwhile, the crisis would build, the pressure would mount, the stakes would rise. It was the gambler's approach to nation-building — one that Brian Mulroney undoubtedly favoured.

But as the committee began its hearings, there was little immediate reason for optimism. On 5 April, the Quebec National Assembly passed a motion reaffirming that Meech Lake must be passed unchanged. Early the next day, Newfoundland rescinded its resolution of ratification. Manitoba continued to refuse to proceed with an unamended accord. Mulroney, after placing McKenna's resolution before Parliament, said the next day that he did not necessarily endorse it. If this exercise was to succeed, Wells and Filmon would have to accept less, Bourassa would have to accept more. It was improbable. Later, in describing the climate in which it had to work, the committee said, with a touch of understatement: "The political situation was very difficult."

As much as McKenna and Mulroney argued that the resolution before the committee could be handled in a companion accord, that it did not reopen the real accord, the claim was dubious. The companion resolution would not only add to Meech Lake, as McKenna said, it would change it. That might not be enough to satisfy opponents but enough to anger allies. Allowing the federal government to create new provinces on its own contradicted the accord, which required agreement from all eleven governments. More important, giving Ottawa the right to promote bilingualism could circumscribe the distinct-society clause.

Nonetheless, the good ship *Charest* sailed ahead, bow pointed into the wind, leaving critics astern. After seeing McKenna, it heard a host of other witnesses, many of whom had long been involved in the debate. There were representatives of women, aboriginal people, labour, multicultural groups and the new pro-accord lobbies. The committee travelled to the Yukon and the Northwest Territories, to Vancouver, to Winnipeg and to St. John's. On the way, it heard not only from the people but from politicians. Peterson, Wells, Ghiz and Buchanan testified, a rarity before a parliamentary committee. When it completed its hearings 4 May, it had heard 160 witnesses and received 800 submissions. Predictably, there were accusations that the hearings were stacked. "What am I, leftovers?" asked Izzy Asper, on learning he had only ten minutes in Winnipeg. The committee argued, however, that it could not accommodate everyone, and it had to pick those who would be most helpful in examining the companion resolution.

In its unanimous report on 18 May, the committee made twenty-three recommendations. In the end, the sheer number — one more than the twenty-two demands of the Parti Québécois in 1985 — helped discourage their acceptance. But if it was not the number, it was the substance. The committee had no trouble addressing the admission of new provinces, the eligibility of Northerners for court appointments and putting aboriginal rights on the agenda. Nor was it particularly dangerous to suggest discussing minority language rights in the next round or committing New Brunswick to respect linguistic duality. By now, these were motherhood issues. What was troublesome was the committee's allowing the federal government a role in promoting the linguistic character of Canada and asserting that the distinct society did not override but could influence the Charter of Rights. In addition, it proposed that aboriginal and ethnic Canadians be recognized in the body of the constitution, a nod to Manitoba's "Canada Clause."

As much as it could, the report tried to be all things to all people. No one province had gotten everything it wanted, but everyone got something. "I really think we have found a way out of the mess," enthused New Democrat Lorne Nystrom. But the very same day, in Quebec City, an exasperated Robert Bourassa reiterated that he would accept no changes. And Liberal MP Jean Lapierre, predicting the reaction of many of his confrères from Quebec, called it "an English Canadian shopping list" that had turned the Quebec Round into the "Canada Round." The Charest report, in seeking compromise, had shown that no compromise was possible. The best efforts of parliamentarians to accommodate the fundamental concerns of Newfoundland, Manitoba and New Brunswick — all without reopening the accord — was seen as an assault on the fundamental concerns of Quebec. What seemed reasonable in English Canada was reprehensible in French Canada. The report and its reaction were a microcosm of the misunderstanding that the Meech Lake Accord had tried to bridge.

If there was any hope for the Charest report as a basis of an agreement, it ended the moment Lucien Bouchard got wind of it. Bouchard, the dark-haired *enfant terrible* of Canadian politics, had passions for Quebec as deep as the gorges of the Saguenay River. He was the kind of nationalist who drove his pregnant wife across the river to Hull to ensure she gave birth in Quebec, not Ontario. For months, he had been simmering about Meech Lake. While

Bouchard's outspokenness had been a problem for Mulroney since Bouchard had entered the cabinet in 1988 (where, as secretary of state with responsibility for both official languages, he had supported the use of the notwithstanding clause in Quebec), his frankness had become particularly irrepressible that spring. In April, he had stirred up a tempest when he had suggested that Canada would have to choose between Newfoundland and Quebec. Then he entered into in a slanging match with Liberal MP John Nunziata, who had called separatists "traitors." Mulroney had always stood by Bouchard, whom he had known since law school, had made ambassador to France, and had lured into politics in 1988. Now Bouchard was environment minister and Quebec lieutenant, two senior jobs in the government. But, as time began to run out for Meech Lake, Bouchard's impatience boiled over.

The breaking point for Bouchard came on 20 May, the tenth anniversary of the Quebec referendum. Bouchard, who had campaigned for the "Yes" side, was in Paris on holiday. He sent a sentimental telegram to the national council of the Parti Québécois, which was meeting in his riding. The telegram praised René Lévesque and those who fought for Quebec sovereignty. Jacques Parizeau read it to the meeting. The telegram itself was an inappropriate gesture for a federal minister to make although not necessarily a fatal one. But when Bouchard returned home, infant son in his arms, he was unapologetic.

The prime minister had been angry for three days; he could not understand how Bouchard, an astute, street-smart colleague, could have said what he had at a critical point in the debate over Meech Lake. He called Bouchard on 21 May and asked him to come over, but Bouchard said parting would be easier without seeing each other. Mulroney insisted and Bouchard went by. By one account, Mulroney ushered him into the den, closed the door and asked him to retract what he said or apologize. Bouchard said no. Then Mulroney said, "I will have to ask for your resignation." Bouchard replied, "I was just about to offer it. Mulroney told him, "Lucien, you may have just killed Meech Lake."

The next day, in his letter to Mulroney and at a news conference, Bouchard unleashed his demons. He said the Charest report would destroy the accord, and warned of "a trap" for Quebec in attending a first ministers' meeting. He accused the hold-out provinces of "hypocrisy" and excoriated the federal government for making an alliance with those who would humiliate Quebec. A man who had represented Canada abroad, and taken an oath as parliamentarian and minister, declared federalism dated, and pronounced a form of sovereignty as the solution. With bitterness oozing from every pore, he decamped with a warning for English Canada: "When we say something will happen the day after June 23 if Meech is not passed — well, just believe us. Read our lips, because we mean business."

It was in his letter — "Mr. Prime Minister" — that he turned venomous. Although some had said that Quebec was too willing to forgive "the iniquity of 1982," and although Bourassa had reduced "to the bone the price of Quebec's forgiveness," Quebec was still treated badly by English Canada, which had exhibited "intolerance" and "racism." Why, he said, Quebec could not even praise "the nobility and generosity" of René Lévesque without antagonizing English Canada. "The mere mention of the right of self-determination gives them a rash," he scoffed. Bouchard said that he could not abide the Charest committee's key recommendations on the charter, on the distinct society and on the abolition of the Senate veto because they altered the accord. Moreover, he said they would isolate Quebec. The victim of 1982, he spat, would not be the culprit of 1990; Quebec would not be portrayed as the province that scuttled the effort at national reconciliation. It was now apparent that English Canada could not take Quebec's minimum conditions seriously, and it was time for a new beginning. "Whoever starts to negotiate on his knees is very likely to end up flat on his face," he said.

With his resignation, Bouchard had altered the contours of the debate as it entered its final month. In its impact, his public renunciation of the accord was reminiscent of Charles de Gaulle shouting, "Vive le Québec libre!" It rattled the stock market and knocked half a cent off the Canadian dollar. Moreover, Bouchard had made it virtually impossible — if it ever had been possible — for Bourassa to make concessions on Meech Lake. If a star member of the cabinet found any changes to the accord unacceptable, how could the premier of Quebec entertain them? Now the smallest change would be seen as a capitulation, the most minor concession as a sell-out. Because of Bouchard, Quebec would have even less room to manoeuvre. In the long term, Bouchard had struck at Mulroney's strategy of national reconciliation. There were few tears in English Canada for Mulroney; he had ridden the back of the nationalist tiger, and now he had ended up inside. Nor were there tears for Bouchard — petulant, impetuous and demagogic. Bouchard had taken "*le beau risque*" but was never comfortable with it. He had tried federalism, found it wanting, and now he was going home, with honour and enthusiasm.

Reeling from the Bouchard resignation, Mulroney assessed his options. By month's end, the premiers were calling for a first minsters' conference. If the prime minister did not call one, David Peterson threatened to invite the premiers to Toronto. Lowell Murray had been meeting the dissident premiers, but he still refused to recommend a first ministers' conference. Mulroney himself summoned all the premiers individually to Ottawa for another round of consultations, another round of photographs outside his front door, another round of apocalyptic predictions. Meanwhile, the phone lines between provincial capitals were buzzing. Emissaries shuttled back and forth, clauses were circulated, trial balloons floated. By the end of May, as the chorus of appeals became louder, the decision was made. The prime minister would call the premiers to Ottawa for supper on 2 June. If there was progress, they would go into public session and continue talking the next day. Three years after the meeting at Langevin, the circle had closed. With less than three weeks to go, the nation-builders would try again to pick up the pieces. Once more, into the Meech.

Why the delay? Why had it been left so long? Later, Mulroney revealed that it had all been part of the plan. From the middle of May, before the Charest report, before the Bouchard resignation, he had planned an eleventh-hour meeting. He had gathered his closest advisers — Murray, Spector, Paul Tellier, clerk of the privy council — and shared his strategy. "I told them when it would be," said the prime minister. "I told them a month ago when we were going to start meeting. It's like an election campaign, you've got to count backwards. You've got to pick your date and work backwards from it.

"And I said, 'That's the day I'm going to roll all the dice.'"

Seven Days in Ottawa

SUNDAY, 3 JUNE 1990

ONCE AGAIN, THE PREMIERS AND THE PRIME MINISTER GATHERED TO DIS-
cuss the constitution. Once again, they would attempt to save the
crumbling accord. This time they would meet for supper at the Canadian Museum of Civilization in Hull. From their bright fifth-floor
room in the curatorial wing, they would face the Ottawa River,
swelled by the late spring runoff. They would see the oxidized copper
roofs of the Château Laurier, the gothic Parliament Buildings and the
Supreme Court perched on the lip of the escarpment. On this sun-
splashed, windblown evening, the view was inspirational, even romantic.

As the nation-builders spilled from their dark sedans before
throngs of journalists, they seemed weary of their mission. Clyde
Wells was resolute. He would listen but he intended to insist on
changes to the accord. Gary Filmon was hopeful. He talked about a
will to find a solution. Grant Devine was practical. He was willing to
take any solution. Joe Ghiz was philosophical. It was wrong that the
fate of twenty-six million Canadians should rest on the shoulders of
eleven politicians, but, well, that was the way it was. Robert
Bourassa was dispassionate. He said the situation was serious. He was
applauded by a clutch of fellow provincial Liberals, members of a
party committee studying the options should the accord fail. Their
presence was a subtle reminder of Quebec's determination.

By the time the first ministers went upstairs to the dining room, it
was a little after seven o'clock. Three years to the day, on the other
side of the river, they had laboured all night and watched the sun rise.
Today, they would labour all evening and watch the sun set.

The venue of the meeting, like the timing of it, was portentous. The Museum of Civilization is in Quebec, and by choosing it the government made a statement of sorts. The building's exterior, of contoured limestone, reflects the land itself. The Great Hall soars, dwarfing the totem poles carved by natives on the West Coast. If Canada's first peoples were not invited to the table upstairs, at least their legacy was visible downstairs. Even the name would give pause to the first ministers: *The Canadian Museum of Civilization*. The exhibits in the museum re-create the beginning of Canadian life. Would this conclave mark its end?

One of the premiers gazed at the panorama and said, "The road to Hull is paved with good intentions." The first ministers, joined only by Lowell Murray, were seated at the table in their usual order. They dined on fresh artichokes and grilled shrimp, roast tenderloin of beef, fiddleheads and roasted potatoes. Two Ontario wines were served. (Bill Vander Zalm, disturbed that there were no wines from British Columbia on the menu, sent aides out the next day to find some in Ottawa. They did, and they bought some at a discount for the premier.) After dinner, the prime minister spoke for about forty-five minutes. As he had at the opening of the meeting at the Langevin Block, he read from newspaper editorials and articles, this time from the *New York Times* and the *Wall Street Journal*. He contended that there would be serious economic consequences for Canada if Meech Lake failed. To reinforce his argument, he produced confidential forecasts from the Bank of Canada on monetary reserves and on the response of the money markets. In particular, he talked about a recent bond issue the Province of Newfoundland had floated on the New York market. Mulroney argued that, because of the uncertainty over Meech Lake, the province would have to offer an interest rate sixty basis points higher than usual on the thirty-year, $150-million issue. He suggested that would cost the provincial treasury $20 million to $30 million more. Wells disagreed. He conceded that nervous investors were demanding a higher yield, which some bond traders were calling "the Meech Lake premium." But Wells said it was only ten to twenty basis points higher and would cost the province only about $10 million over the life of the bond.

After making his economic argument, Mulroney switched to "the bigger picture of Canada," as one premier put it. He repeated what he had said in the House of Commons on 31 May: that the price of failure was too high. The future of Canada turned on Meech Lake.

Given the shrill, apocalyptic tone of Mulroney's warning in recent days, he seemed to be suggesting the country would live or die by the accord. At one point, Mulroney produced a well-thumbed copy of *Where I Stand*, his collection of speeches published in 1983. He wanted to correct Wells, who had quoted from the book in some recent remarks. "The trouble is, Clyde, you read the wrong section of the book," Mulroney said. "You should read this part." He wanted to show that he had always thought it was unconscionable that Quebec was still buying cheap power from Churchill Falls under a forty-year contract Newfoundland had signed in 1969. Wells said little, although he did challenge him on a couple of constitutional points. Relations between the two, while always courteous, were frosty. When Wells had met Mulroney a few days earlier in Ottawa, he found him strained and sometimes incoherent. Now, as Mulroney read, his captive audience was also starting to wonder. David Peterson listened to the prime minister quote himself, scribbled a note and passed it to a colleague: "This is stupid," it said.

Other premiers spoke. Each discussed his "margin of manoeuvrability" and set out his "bottom line." Robert Bourassa, in contrast to Mulroney, did not talk of doomsday scenarios. "Things will be difficult in Quebec, but I will do what I can to prevent a bad reaction," he said. As Frank McKenna put it, "He never tried to use the consequences of failure as reason for passing Meech Lake." Bourassa talked about the economy and the importance of stability, but he did not offend or insult. In manner, as in thought, he was the most consistent of the premiers in this story. While Peterson and Pawley wavered at the Langevin meeting, and while Filmon, McKenna and Wells retreated later on, Bourassa remained firm, calm and measured. What he said now was what he had said precisely three years ago: he wanted the Meech Lake Accord, nothing more, nothing less.

After the sun had dropped from the sky, a summer rainstorm lashed the region. Before midnight, when the first ministers descended with empty hands and troubled expressions, nature's wrath seemed like an omen.

There had been no discussion of the key issues: Senate reform and the distinct-society clause. There was still a variety of proposals on the table: the Charest committee, the New Brunswick companion resolution, papers from Manitoba and Newfoundland. The premiers agreed to meet again in the morning in the Government Conference Centre in Ottawa. Officials and reporters began placing bets on how long the meeting would last. When someone predicted it would break up Thursday at noon, there was laughter.

MONDAY, 4 JUNE 1990

At eleven o'clock, the premiers met around an oval table in a dim, windowless boardroom on the fifth floor of the centre. Over the next week, the room would become a crucible and confessional. Everyone would come to loathe it. Downstairs, a battery of ministers, officials and lawyers, among them the country's leading constitutional experts, set up shop. They called it Camp Meech.

Mulroney presented nothing new in the ninety-minute morning session, which bothered Wells and Filmon, who were told to be patient. On his way into the afternoon meeting, Mulroney promised three times "to crunch" the issue. One of Lowell Murray's favourite neologisms, it entered the constitutional lexicon that week. Mulroney proposed that the dissenting provinces ratify Meech Lake by 23 June, and that the first ministers establish an agenda to discuss a series of constitutional amendments in other areas to be passed later. Of those, Mulroney wanted to address the easy ones first, such as removing unanimity for the territories to become provinces. To Filmon's dismay, his concerns — the Canada clause (recognizing, as he said, Canada's "aboriginal past and multicultural future") and Senate reform — would be among those considered later. In addition, there was no discussion scheduled on the issue of protecting the Charter from the distinct-society clause.

Both at the dinner and in the morning session, Filmon had suggested that the Charest report be the basis of a compromise. Mulroney's proposed schedule, however, made that impossible. "It was pretty evident that in no way would the prime minister embrace the Charest report and in no way would Quebec accept it," he recalls. "The excuse was that Lucien Bouchard's resignation had changed the entire climate." Within the last two weeks, the federal government had shown Filmon and Wells a working document, called "State of Play," that incorporated many of the Charest report's findings. While Bouchard's departure had reduced the government's latitude to make a deal, that document still addressed some of Newfoundland's and Manitoba's concerns, particularly on the distinct-society clause and its relationship to the Charter.

Now Mulroney proposed passing the Meech Lake Accord as it was and making further constitutional amendments later. He suggested that Senate reform be discussed at a full-fledged conference on 17 September, and that a new constitutional agenda be established to consider linguistic minorities, the admission of new provinces and aboriginal rights. The only point still to be decided, said federal officials, was an amending formula for Senate reform. "If we can overcome that, the rest can be resolved. The rest are not deal-breakers." This, though, may have been dissembling. Ottawa was planning for failure. If the conference was going to break up, the federal government would rather it founder on Senate reform than on the distinct-society clause, which could be painted as an attack on Quebec.

When the premiers emerged after the first full day of talks, they were despondent. "I am not the slightest bit optimistic," said Don Getty, who became a barometer of the mood among the nation-builders. "Tomorrow's meeting could be very short." Grant Devine suggested that the first ministers were "close" — where "close" means near the edge. Filmon said the federal government was bargaining in bad faith; it was now an advocate of Meech Lake. Odd, that. At Meech Lake, Brian Mulroney was criticized for acting as a mediator. Now he was criticized for being an advocate.

The strangest moment of the day came when Frank McKenna left the meeting and announced his support for the accord. His halting, sputtering endorsement went virtually unnoticed. The idea for making the long-awaited announcement then was to generate momentum for the talks. "We [McKenna and his advisers] concluded the meeting was a failure," he says. "We had gotten nowhere. I said, 'It is going to crash tomorrow morning. There is no room for compromise.' So I made a decision on the spot. We had no plan or anything. It was totally spontaneous." (Another version suggested that it was not spontaneous, but planned with the federal government to be delivered after Mulroney unveiled his plan.) Regardlesss, McKenna had finally declared himself. After two and half years of misgivings and misapprehensions, he had embraced the accord, even if it was an anti-climax. The first critic had become the first convert. A senior minister from one of the pro-Meech provinces was mystified that McKenna had settled for so little. "Here's the guy who essentially caused all this trouble, and at the end of the day, his agenda was trivial," he said. "You say to yourself, 'McKenna, if that's all you were talking about, why did you even open your mouth?'"

Depressed over the prospects for the conference, McKenna re-

turned to his room in the Château Laurier. "I felt terrible. It was the
worst day of the whole week. It was a suicide mission, but we
wanted to keep the whole thing going." Buchanan and Ghiz asked
him to join them for dinner with the other premiers, as did Peterson
and Wells, but he said he "didn't feel like partying tonight." Mc-
Kenna phoned home and prepared to go before the cameras in the
morning to discuss the future of the country.

TUESDAY, 5 JUNE 1990

The gloom lifted when the premiers began considering a plan presented by Joe Ghiz and proposed by Jack Pickersgill, the former Liberal minister. Before the conference, Pickersgill had suggested a national commission on Senate reform. If there was no reform after
three years, the four western provinces, as well as Newfoundland,
would get four more seats in an expanded Senate. Prince Edward Island would get one, too. (Ghiz wangled an extra seat for his province, a kind of broker's commission.) The first ministers liked the
plan. It would not guarantee reform, but the penalty, the so-called
hammer clause, would be an inducement. If it didn't work, the premiers could go still go home with something.

The premiers, who were now reporting to the media twice a day,
had begun to speak a language of their own. Frank McKenna talked
about a commssion that would "implicate" the people. Instead of an
equal Senate, John Buchanan talked about "an equitable" one.
Devine kept talking about finding "the magic"; McKenna said there
was "no magic." Maybe not magic at that hour, but a little movement. The premiers felt that Bourassa could entertain a compromise
on the Senate to show flexibility, even if some of his advisers thought
that it was better to let Meech Lake fail than to make concessions.

McKenna suggests that, by Tuesday, Filmon began feeling the
heat. "I thought it all changed when Filmon began talking about the
premiers' meeting in Winnipeg this summer. Bourassa said to him,
'You know, Gary, if Meech Lake fails, I don't know what will happen. I probably won't be able to go.' I watched Gary's face and I
sensed for the first time that he came to grips with just how serious
this was. Gary came of age. He knew that this was dead serious business. The atmosphere changed."

Perhaps that was one of the reasons that Filmon began to relax his
insistence on "certainty" that any changes to Meech Lake be made in

a separate agreement to be passed by 23 June. On Tuesday, he made a startling concession. "It's obvious that this companion resolution will not go through by 23 June," he said, his glance turning to Bourassa. "It's obvious to me that we can resolve this question on the basis of trust." *Trust*. Peterson had raised it often, and now Filmon was echoing it. His concession was greeted with relief. As McKenna put it later, "Filmon made the noble gesture. He was going to have to trust his colleagues to do what they said they would. He could not rely on legal certainty, he had to rely on moral certainty."

That night the nation-builders were confident when they left the Government Conference Centre. "I feel so much better about the future of my country," said Getty. "It is kind of a battered country. Meech Lake had a faint heartbeat, and that heart is beating away now, and I love this battered country." While others reinforced Getty's unabashed sentimentality, Filmon and Wells were more guarded. And Sharon Carstairs, who had arrived Monday with Gary Doer, warned that protection for the Charter and a declaration of the Canada clause were the bottom line for her, the deal-breaker.

Still, if Monday was for pessimists, Tuesday was for optimists. "A Good Day" proclaimed the banner headline in the *Ottawa Citizen*.

WEDNESDAY, 6 JUNE 1990

The premiers had been talking for three days but, by bureaucratic protocol, this meeting was still not an official first ministers' conference. There had been no public sessions, no position papers, no texts of speeches. The country knew only what the premiers chose to tell it every morning and every evening, and that was not much. At the end of each day, Stanley Hartt, Mulroney's chief of staff, and Norman Spector, the head of the federal-provincial relations office, spoke to reporters. These briefings, always attributed by journalists to "senior officials" and always held late at night, presented the official, or federal, interpretation of the day's events. The provinces, particularly Quebec, also did a little "spinning" of their own.

As the meeting entered the fourth day, it was apparent the conclave on the fifth floor had taken on the secretiveness of the meetings at Meech Lake and Langevin. The process that had produced Meech Lake was to be the process that would save it. The secrecy did not disturb the federal officials. They cited public-opinon polls showing that Canadians were bothered less by the process of constitutional reform than by its content. But it did bother Clyde Wells, who had been agitating all week for a public session, even a short one. "From the beginning I said to the prime minister that we should not meet in private on Monday morning. We should have a public session. I said this every time that we sat down, and it got so that the prime minister said to me, 'Look, Clyde, I take your point. I will acknowledge publicly that you have always taken this position.' Okay, I was one of eleven. I couldn't impose my position on everyone else."

The situation was aggravated by the length of the meetings. The first ministers, ministers, officials, lawyers and journalists had been marooned for three days and counting. No one seemed to have brought enough clothes. The premiers said they were short of socks and shirts, and enterprising haberdashers actually sent them some. David Peterson joked that when Joe Ghiz saw the response, he complained he was short a suit, and someone provided one. The bureaucrats were getting little sleep as they worked overnight to prepare new texts.

Having reached a tentative deal on the Senate the day before, they had planned to turn to other items. But the agreement on the Senate was coming apart. Bourassa had thought about it overnight, listened to the taunts of the Parti Québécois and the response in the media, and turned cool. He told McKenna and others privately that "it could not work in any circumstance in Quebec." He was worried about preserving Quebec's predominance in the Senate, currently 24 of 104 seats. If the other provinces got more seats in an expanded Senate of 125 seats and his number stayed the same, his proportion would fall from 23 percent to 19 percent. Therefore, whatever proportionate increase the other provinces wanted, he wanted, too, to preserve Quebec's share. Bourassa's demand for more was an echo of the other provinces' demands at Meech Lake. But it was dubious; one of the purposes of Senate reform, from the point of view of the smaller provinces, was to reduce the preponderance of Ontario and Quebec.

Another problem surfaced on Wednesday. There was still no agreement on the Canada clause, which now existed in five versions. In addition, the distinct-society issue was as yet unresolved. The Newfoundland officials — including constitutional scholar and former senator Eugene Forsey — were attempting to clarify the relationship between the distinct society and the Charter. They came up with a wording they thought protected the Charter and conferred no new legislative power. At the end of the day, some premiers thought there had been a breakthrough in the talks. Bill Vander Zalm, again eager to return to British Columbia, announced that he was not booking his room for the next night. "I'll save the taxpayers a little money," he said. "I'll be checking my watch at 1:00 p.m. because that is check-out time." Frank McKenna was emotional. "I can tell you with certainty that the people inside are working in a very loving, generous, civil way to try to do something that will be good for the country," he said. Bourassa declared his position was better understood, that it was a constructive day, in preparation for "the second round." Filmon measured progress in "inches to infinity."

If the views were in conflict, it was understandable. This was becoming the longest campaign of the Constitutional Wars. There was still no settlement, and the federal government was in no rush. "It will take as long as it has to," Mulroney told reporters. "Some of you are on double time right now. I don't see any complaints." Perhaps, during the week, the dollar would plunge or the market would crash. The hope was that the longer the meetings went on, the more likely Newfoundland and Manitoba were to crack. The strategy seemed to be working; Wells and Filmon were reconsidering. As McKenna put it later, "For these two days [Wednesday and Thursday], Wells seemed quite committed to passing the accord, and it was Gary who was expressing a lot of reservations." If this was true, it marked an astonishing reversal for Wells. The loudest critic, the premier with the deepest reservations, now seemed to be yielding, or, in the language of this negotiation, "cratering."

That Wells was even reconsidering — given his insistence on change in the last weeks and months — showed the power of the process. Day in and day out, he faced a wall of opposition. "It tears the hell out of you," he said later. The argument on every issue had three stages. First, the premiers would discuss what was right with the point in question. Then they would argue that Quebec could never accept it. (Bourassa never had to do this himself.) Finally, after Wells and Filmon tried to mount a counterargument, the premiers would say the accord was necessary to save Canada. "If you don't do it, you are going to destroy Canada," they told Wells. It left him isolated and frustrated. "No matter what you think intellectually, or on any other basis, you have to do it to save Canada," he recalls them saying. "That's the way it went. That's no way to build a constitution. It came down to that ultimate threat. How can you say no to that? That's what's wrong with that god-awful process, where people can get away with that in the secrecy of a room. In public they could never do it; they would be cut to pieces." Filmon conceded later that the constant discussion of "the instability and uncertainty" of failure, both in the room and from other business and minority language groups at home, was influential in converting Manitoba. "We began to feel we had squeezed the lemon as much as we could."

Ultimately, this was the triumph of the Group, the power of the Premiers' Club. In Ottawa, not even a Wells seemed able to resist its persuasion. By Wednesday, the premiers were hostages. One popular explanation for the conversion of the dissidents was the "Stockholm Syndrome" — or how Filmon, Wells, Carstairs and Doer came to accept Mulroney's view of the world. No one could offer any other plausible explanation for what seemed like the greatest retreat since Napoleon fled Russia.

THURSDAY, 7 JUNE 1990

The changing mood of the meeting was now as reliable as the ebb and flow of the tides. High tide, low tide — it was all part of the daily rhythm. Downstairs, reporters looked hungrily for news, but found only morsels from self-important officials running around with cellular telephones. Upstairs, the premiers were still wrangling. The word now was that Filmon was prepared to make a deal, providing he could convince his opposition leaders. "Filmon was not opposed to making an arrangement," recalls a provincial minister. "He had a political problem. And everyone understood that, if his political problem could be solved, Manitoba would come on side."

By mid-afternoon, the contours of a proposed deal were emerging on Senate reform and the Canada clause. The distinct-society clause would be handled by a letter signed by legal experts saying that it did not confer new legislative power on Quebec. At about three o'clock, Filmon left to consult with Carstairs and Doer. Wells was there. Later, the four were joined by officials and Roger Tassé. Many of the premiers thought there was a deal. "From us, it [the proposed deal] went out [to Doer and Carstairs] as a done deal: 'This is the most we can do on these issues,'" said McKenna. "It went to them as an offer. And that's when it fell apart." The meeting lasted two or three hours. At one point, Bourassa joined the meeting. He saw their revised wording and knew he did not like it, but he did not say what he would do.

Carstairs and Doer, for their part, did not see the proposed deal as final. They were never told it was a take-it-or-leave-it proposition. In fact, they insisted on a new proposal: entrenchment of the Canada clause before 23 June. Wells added his conditions: a political declaration from the first ministers on protecting the Charter from the distinct-society clause, and a clarification of the spending power. He had dropped immigration and the Supreme Court from his demands. When the two premiers returned, the powder keg blew. Wells stood at the end of the table and delivered the new position that he, Filmon, Doer and Carstairs had agreed on, as well as the earlier Senate proposal. As one premier put it, Wells hit every one of Quebec's sacred cows. "We've had this meeting," Wells said. "Here's what we're prepared to do."

When Bourassa, usually a model of decorum, heard Wells's proposal, he went white and exploded. "If that's the way you feel, fuck you," he said. What set him off, some suggest, was the reference to the distinct society in the Canada clause. Peterson was also angry. "You went out carrying our brief and came back carrying their brief!" he snapped at Wells. "Whose side are you on?" The delicate balance had been shattered. "Obviously, Filmon and Wells did not try to sell it," says McKenna of the deal. "They went in there to try to use them [Carstairs and Filmon] as bargaining power for more. They presented new demands which anyone who knew Meech Lake knew were totally unacceptable. They just trailed the rake through all the burial grounds." Filmon remained silent. Peterson attacked Wells, who continued standing. As one premier noted, it was the only time that week that anyone stood to make a statement.

"Not one of Newfoundland's concerns has been addressed," Wells said. "I'm stripped bare. I've been here for five days and I have nothing. I am naked." He was in tears. He was a proud man, overcome by the strain. "He was very strung out at that point," allows McKenna. Bourassa, who was preparing to leave the talks, then turned to Wells and said, "Clyde, you will destroy any hope of national unity, you will destroy any hope of Senate reform, but you will keep your vanity." There was a few seconds of silence, and Wells responded, his face beet red: "There is no one more committed to bilingualism and francophones than Clyde Wells."

Then Joe Ghiz interjected with what Peterson called the best speech of the week. He took dead aim at the Canada clause, which would have protected multicultural rights. He pointed a finger at Wells and

said, "Are you trying to tell *me*, Clyde Wells, the son of an immigrant who came to this country without a penny in his pocket and
had to sell dry goods in order to survive, are you trying to tell *me*,
someone of Lebanese origin who became premier of a province, and
the proudest person in Canada, that, in Canada, I have got to have a
provision in the constitution to protect *my* rights?"

It was now around seven o'clock. Mulroney called a recess, during
which he tried to defuse the tension. But the damage was almost ir-
reparable. Bourassa left the session but did not tell his colleagues he
was going to announce his departure. It was a preemptive strike. He
knew that everything that had been said around the table, particularly
that the distinct society had been under discussion, would get out. To
dispel fears at home that he might be weakening, he decided to act.
He had shrewdly removed himself from part of the process; he had
raised the stakes by putting one foot out the door. At around 9:30
p.m., Bourassa's press secretary entered the cluttered, cramped
media room and handed out a press release. The one-paragraph statement, in French, read: "Premier Robert Bourassa has told his colleagues, during the meeting, that he will abstain from any further discussion directly or indirectly on the clause in the Meech Lake Accord
recognizing Quebec as a distinct society." The declaration was a
bombshell. Someone observed wryly that it was the first official piece
of paper issued since Sunday's dinner menu.

Upstairs, there was also surprise. The premiers did not know of
Bourassa's move until they saw the statement. This time, Filmon let
fly. "We're all on the edge here. I'm finished with all these pressure
tactics. I'm going back to my hotel. I'll see you tomorrow, if there is
any more point to this." Fearing that Bourassa might leave the building before anyone else, which would make it look as if he was scuttling the talks, Ian Scott rushed to the Quebec delegation and implored them to stay until all the other premiers had gone. They did.
When Bourassa emerged, he told reporters: "Enough is enough." His
colleagues looked shaken. McKenna was ashen-faced; he said Meech
Lake was a roller coaster and he had nearly lost his stomach. Others
took aim at the nitpickers and nay-sayers — read Wells and Filmon
— who were dwelling on trivialities. "I caution you," warned Getty.
"Stop taking shots at Meech Lake because you are starting to hit Canada in the heart. Stop worrying about commas." A stern Buchanan
declared: "It's time for good Canadian common sense, and no time

for legal niceties." The idea was to paint the critics as fussbudgets whining over commas and semicolons, to make their complaints sound picayune.

In the early hours of the next morning, the discrediting of the critics continued. In their midnight briefing, Spector and Hartt offered their version of events: there had been a tentative deal. Filmon had accepted the package on Senate reform, the Canada clause and the distinct-society clause. Carstairs and Doer had rejected it. "Filmon withdrew a proposal that he participated in the writing of," said one of them. "We do not know why he changed his mind. They [the premiers] may send a different salesman tomorrow." The charge enraged Carstairs and Doer (he called it "malicious bullshit"), who thought the federal government was simply trying to undermine their position. McKenna now says he acted impetuously when he came out that night. "I was, rather recklessly, blaming it on Carstairs and Doer. They did not have full information. They were being made fall guys. It was really a breakdown of communication."

Wells recalls, "I took the worst browbeating of the conference that day. [They said] that I was threatening the future of the nation by not agreeing to do what everyone else was doing, that I was holding up the nation. Emotional speeches were directed at me. I let myself get emotional, and I can't forgive myself for that, because I don't think that served any good. I lost my self-control and I regret that." It was, then, he says, that he decided to hold a press conference the next morning.

FRIDAY, 8 JUNE 1990

At 7:30 a.m., Wells breakfasted with three key strategists for Jean Chrétien — Eddie Goldenberg, John Rae and Eric Maldoff. All urged him to make a deal. Carstairs, whom Chrétien had been leaning on all week, was also there. At the meeting, Wells seemed ready to accept even less than he had the night before; he had dropped his insistence on a stronger Canada clause. When Deborah Coyne, his adviser, found out that Wells had reduced his conditions to Senate reform and a political declaration on the Charter, she was outraged. She thought Chrétien had succeeded in winning over Wells, and resented his intervention. The premier, she concluded, was cracking. That morning, Eugene Forsey resigned from the Newfoundland delegation. He thought the process was hollow and wanted to be free to criticize it. Wells later read his letter to the premiers, but postponed the news conference, which would have broken the meeting's solidarity.

Whatever his compromises, Wells was frustrated that he had won nothing. He was tired that morning, and the strain was showing; he snapped at Coyne, who in turn clashed with Neil Finkelstein, a constitutional lawyer who was also advising the government. Wells blames his predicament on a process that allowed first ministers to advance arguments in private they would never use in public. "I couldn't understand how I let myself get sucked into that and stayed for all that length of time," he says. "A kind of collegiality develops, even though there may be strong views expressed, there is a sense of collegiality. No one wants to do things to make life difficult. So you keep going, you make the concession, you agree. A little bit more, a little bit more, a little bit more, and finally you are on that thing and there is no way off it." Wells told Mulroney about his press conference, and Mulroney asked him not to do it. Wells relented. "Collegiality takes over again," he said. "At the PM's request, I agreed to defer it." Wells was, in a sense, validating the old dictum: if you don't want to settle your case, don't come in the room.

Wells went back in the room, but Bourassa did not. His *coup d'audace* had upset some premiers, but Peterson thought it would force the issue. He wanted Quebec to declare its bottom line to break the impasse. As one Ontario official put it, "When they left, we thought it was great news. Suddenly reality would intrude. At last we would get down to it." All week, Bourassa's ambiguity had created problems. When he said a position would cause Quebec "great difficulty," as he often did, he really meant it was unacceptable. "He never appeared to close things off out of politeness," said the official. "He never said, 'It's off the table, Clyde.' People could take that as 'a positive maybe,' when in fact, it meant 'no fucking way.'"

Next, the first ministers discussed the proposal that a group of eminent jurists offer a legal opinion on the Charter and the distinct-society clause in the form of a letter to be appended to the accord. It would try to address the fears of Wells, Filmon and Carstairs that Quebec might use the collective rights of the distinct-society clause to override the rights of individuals. Though the pro-Meech premiers had always said that it could not happen, none would sign the letter. When Bourassa came back to the room, the talk turned again to the Senate. Again, Joe Ghiz presented his proposal, now supported by

McKenna. It would allow all provinces to retain their veto for five years, and if there was no reform by then, some provinces would get more seats. Around the table, it became known as the "asskicker" proposal. (Over the course of the week, there were actually several such schemes, most of which got nowhere. One plan, which would have given seats to Quebec, was called the "asskisser" proposal. One of the more novel ones came from Bill Vander Zalm, who suggested that if there was no reform in five years, all the senators be fired and new senators be appointed or elected to fill their seats. He did not spell out how it would work. Quebec seemed to like it. Bourassa went over to Vander Zalm and exclaimed, "Bill, you're a genius!")

By around six o'clock, Wells was still unsatisfied, even though the proposal would give Newfoundland four more Senate seats. Because a province cannot have fewer seats in the Senate than in the House of Commons, Newfoundland would get another three seats in the House. "That was no inducement to me," he told the first ministers. "What's three seats out of three hundred? One percent! What I want is real input for smaller provinces in the Senate." He did not see his gain as much of a penalty to the larger provinces. Mulroney, who knew almost all the members from Newfoundland were Liberals, thought it was. "Yes, Clyde," he said, "but now I have to deal with three more MPs from Newfoundland." Meanwhile, Quebec was pushing for more seats to maintain its proportion of the Senate. Wells was now convinced that as long as there had to be unanimity, there would never be Senate reform. The Ghiz proposal was now off the table. Wells, followed by Filmon, was ready to walk out.

"Now, I am going to have my press conference," said Wells.

"Oh, don't do that," said Mulroney.

"But I have been deferring it *all day* for you," said Wells.

"Oh, please, *don't* do that," replied Mulroney.

"Prime Minister, I must do that."

"Would you, for the sake of the country, and for me, not do that?"

"Prime Minister, I regret that I have to say no to you."

Wells kept refusing, and Mulroney kept pleading. "Don't do it, Clyde, for the future of the country, don't do it," he said. Then other premiers intervened. "Why can't you not do it?" they asked Wells. "The prime minister has asked you not to do it! How can you say no?" Wells was adamant. "Look, for a week we have been here in secrecy," he replied. "I have objected to it. I told you this morning I would do it." In fact, Newfoundland had prepared 300 copies of an

analysis of its position — in particular, where it had made compromises — that Wells intended to release to the media.

"They kept haranguing me," recalls Wells. "There were a few
more emotional statements from the premiers. They told me that I
had to have it my way, or no way. I was always right. But I had been
abandoning my way all week to the point where there was nothing. I
guess that's when I realized that I was back into what happened the
day before, when I lost control."

Wells tried to remain calm. "I'm prepared to discuss this on the
merits," he said. "But I'm not prepared to participate in a personal
discussion about who's breaking up the country, who doesn't give a
damn. If that's the basis of your discussion, you go ahead, you have
the discussion without me." Then he began gathering up his papers.
"I feel the same way," added Filmon, as he stood up. "This isn't the
right way to do it." Angered that Bourassa had now rejected the Senate plan, Filmon saw no point in staying.

Wells was sitting at the end of the table near the door. When he
rose to leave, Don Getty, who was across from him, pushed his chair
back on its wheels and moved between Wells and the door, effectively blocking it. "Won't you even stay to talk about it?" he asked.
Wells stopped, pivoted, and said, "Yes, I will stay and talk about it.
But I won't be abused personally, as the one to break up the country." Wells stayed. Getty, the former football quarterback, did not
tackle him, as some suggested; he simply performed a strategic block,
as any good linebacker might have.

With Wells in his seat, Peterson asked him, "What is there that you
find wrong with this communiqué [the agreement]? Give us the detail
of what you find wrong." Wells repeated his objections. Then Peterson produced a proposal of his own. He had it ready to offer in the
event the talks collapsed: "the nightmare scenario." He offered to
give up six of Ontario's twenty-four Senate seats, and asked New
Brunswick and Nova Scotia, each of whom had ten seats, to give up
two apiece. The ten seats thus accumulated would be shared among
Newfoundland and the four western provinces. Quebec's share
would remain the same. The federal government knew about the offer. In fact, earlier in the week, Mulroney had raised the prospect of
Ontario making a big concession at the talks, such as giving up its
veto over Senate reform. That did not sit well with Peterson; he and
Ian Scott did not think the largest province in the land should relinquish its say in national institutions. But the premier did ask his offi-

cials to come up with something new. The scheme came from James MacPherson of Osgoode Hall Law School, one of the many experts Peterson had brought with him to Ottawa. When Peterson saw the proposal, he reportedly told MacPherson, "Jim, you may have just saved Canada."

Wells was taken aback. Struck by Peterson's "generosity" with Ontario's seats, he was now convinced that the province would agree to an equal and effective Senate because "Ontario doesn't put its interests ahead of the nation." At the same time, though, he worried that the compromise was necessitated by Quebec's intransigence. He now feared that Quebec would never agree to real Senate reform. "How can I resist?" he says he asked himself. "How can I justify refusing when Ontario was being so magnanimous? How can I hold out? So you get sucked back into that vortex again."

All of a sudden, the chemistry changed. Within minutes, there was a deal. Frank McKenna was puzzled that Wells had accepted Peterson's offer so quickly. "Clyde instantly changed mood again," he recalls, "which I found a little bizarre because two or three hours earlier I had thrown the same proposals out [for discussion]. But there was no interest then." The reaction bewildered McKenna, who could no longer read Wells. "We didn't know whether Clyde wanted to sign Meech Lake or not," he says. "He was giving us strong signals that he wanted to, and then he would go into a complete mood change when he would rail against it. There were times he felt it had been done, and other times he would throw up roadblocks." McKenna was describing a tormented soul who opposed the accord deeply but worried about the consequences of its failure. It is one explanation for the fluctuation in Wells's behaviour.

By Friday at about seven o'clock, there was a deal. The Senate was settled and the Canada clause was delayed to another round. Wells went downstairs, approached Deborah Coyne, and touched her on the elbow. "I think there is an agreement, and I know, Debbie, that you probably won't like it," he said. Coyne, who had spent three years fighting the accord, was crestfallen. She told Wells if he wanted to make a deal, she only wanted to make sure it was the best one. It was a poignant moment.

Earlier, Mulroney had asked McKenna and Wells to draft a provision that would allow the first ministers to review the impact of the distinct-society clause on the Charter. They had been joined by Roger Tassé. McKenna proposed the first ministers review the clause after ten years and "receive such recommendations as may flow from it." As McKenna puts it, Wells wanted stronger language, directing the first ministers to make amendments. "Look, Quebec isn't going to allow that," McKenna pointed out. Wells, says McKenna, replied: "Well, let's put it in and see where it goes anyway." Since Tassé did not object, McKenna thought the federal government agreed with Wells. Still, he saw problems. "I knew Bourassa could not accept Clyde's interpretation, but I really thought Clyde was asking for more than he expected to get, and he [Wells] knew it, too." Wells, for his part, said McKenna raised no objections. The draft of the provision was then sent out to be added to the text, which had to be corrected, translated into legal language, and typed.

Then, the nation-builders, their work done, relaxed. Supper was brought in. Both Peterson and Wells (who had now rejoined his colleagues) wanted to adjourn and return in the morning for the long-delayed public session; they worried that remaining another evening would be misread. Both complained to Mulroney, but he wanted to wait for the whole text. The bar was rolled in. Wells, who is not a teetotaler, did not partake. Rather, he wondered why it was taking so long to add a five-line clause into the agreement. His colleagues, joined by officials, were buoyant. Wells was not. "I didn't feel there was anything to celebrate," he said. "I wasn't sulking. I just didn't want to lose what little control I had left to alcohol." So Wells waited. John Buchanan, a seasoned raconteur, held forth. David Peterson put his feet up and told a joke or two. One of the officials turned to Wells and said, "Now it's your turn, Premier Wells." Wells wasn't feeling festive. "I'll pass for now," he said quietly.

At 11:30 p.m., the officials brought in the agreement, which was called the "final communiqué." It was about five legal-size pages, and the premiers were to initial it that night. It was handed to the premiers, who began reading it. Wells was tired and had a headache. The clause he had drafted was missing. "I think it's me," he recalls. "I can't find it. I feel stupid asking where it is. I go back over it again, and I don't see it. So I ask the prime minister, 'I don't see it. Where is it?' The prime minister says, 'It's not there. I remember, Clyde, you sat down with Roger and drafted it. Where is it?'" Wells asked again: "This is important. Where has it gone?"

Finally, after checking with Tassé, Mulroney explained that the clause was left out because Quebec had not agreed to it, one of those "last-minute glitches." Wells was livid that for three and a half hours no one had told him that, and that he was then presented with a document to initial. Although Mulroney wanted a copy signed by all the premiers for his daughter Caroline's sixteenth birthday on Monday, Wells refused. So did Filmon. McKenna maintains the clause was there, but in different language. It simply called for review after ten years. He was unfazed; Wells was angry. "Clyde went into a tirade, accusing people of treachery and deliberately doing this, that Quebec had done this, that they were dictating everything. It was real bad chemistry then." Wells remembers saying little and returning to his hotel exhausted.

When the session broke up, Bourassa proclaimed a deal was at hand. "The mission is accomplished," he said. "It's a very great day for Canada."

SATURDAY, 9 JUNE 1990

The first ministers argued over a constitution for six days and on the seventh, paused, looked around and continued to argue. God had created the world in less time but, then, a deity does not have to seek unanimity. By Saturday, the psychological strain was growing; the captives were going a little dotty. There were stories of McKenna's imitations of his colleagues, including the prime minister, whose chair he once occupied in his absence; of David Peterson's jokes and anecdotes consuming 10 percent of the time; of premiers abandoning the traditional order of seating, and at one point, mixing up their nameplates to confuse Mulroney; of Joe Ghiz calling Wells "a prick" (probably untrue) and McKenna, in conversation with others, referring to Wells as "a dink" and that "fucking constitutional lawyer" (probably true, despite McKenna's denials). The week had become a filibuster, a dance marathon, a talk fest. Some of the premiers quoted Benjamin Franklin, some quoted the Bible, some talked of their boyhoods. As the country watched, tethered to the talks by an electronic umbilical cord, the first ministers remained behind closed doors. The meeting, it should be noted, was still not formally a first ministers' conference. It might be the longest session in constitution-making, but, officially, it was still a dinner of many courses.

This was the ultimate "roll of the dice." If the boys could be kept at the gaming table long enough, and if the stakes were raised high enough, they would come round. It was, once again, negotiation by exhaustion. At the outset, few observers thought the prime minister would dare do in Ottawa what he had done so effectively at Meech Lake and the Langevin Block. But there he was, in June, hoping history would repeat itself, and it nearly did. Charming, shrewd, mellifluous, he isolated the dissidents and, one by one, brought them to heel. There was, in Mulroney, a little of Lyndon Johnson: the student of human weakness, the merchant of persuasion, the purveyor of favour. That week, he was all of those. His admirers — Devine, Buchanan and Vander Zalm — saluted him. His detractors — Wells and Carstairs — distrusted him. In all this, Mulroney told one first minister, his only desire was the same as that of Sir John A. Macdonald: "I just want to keep the country together for another day, so it could last a week, so it could last a month, so it could last a year."

On that Saturday, though, Mulroney needed all his powers of manipulation. He was faced with a premier who felt disillusioned, humiliated and betrayed. Mulroney knew the deal was coming undone, unravelled by a missing clause. "Wells had already realized, psychologically, how far down he had come," said one of the premier's associates. "The clause was the last straw. It was not that alone, but it gave him a reason to crawl back. Then he started to come out of it." Mulroney knew the importance of the clause. He spent much of the night trying to find out what happened to it. He talked to his officials, and particularly to Tassé, who was horrified that Wells might suspect him of mischief. In fact, the clause had been changed by Spector and others because they knew Quebec would not go along with it. The first ministers would now review not just the impact of the distinct-society clause, but the effect of the entire Charter.

Mulroney's campaign to regain the premier's confidence began when he called him early Saturday from 24 Sussex Drive. With his son Nicholas crying in his ear, he explained that it was all a mistake. Later, on his way into the morning session, the prime minister offered a long apology, in response to a reporter's question, which Wells watched on television from inside. The premier forgave Tassé, but insisted it was no error that Wells was not told that his clause had been dropped from the text.

At the morning session, the matter was discussed for hours. "They got into this honour and this lawyer-and-gentleman shit," said one premier. "Tassé and Wells had a private meeting to express their respect for each other. Then Wells came back and said, 'It couldn't be Tassé who screwed things up because he is too fine a man.'" The point was to pacify the premier. After agreeing to the deal early Friday evening, he had decided later that he would refuse to sign. He would attend the talks, say little, sign nothing. "Having made that decision, for the first time I felt at ease," Wells recalls. "I called my wife, Eleanor, and said, 'I'm finally at peace with myself.'" But, by the time the talks resumed that morning, after Wells had told the premiers of his plans, he came under renewed pressure. The draft document had committed Newfoundland, Manitoba and New Brunswick to seek "approval" of the accord. Wells said no, and announced he would put the accord to a free vote. He would not campaign against it, and he would invite the premiers to address the assembly. "I'm there, I am in the room, but I am not arguing for anything," he recalls thinking. "Whatever you put in the document is fine with me, but I won't endorse it."

His colleagues begged him to reconsider. "Is there anything we can do to rework the clause to make it acceptable to Newfoundland?" Mulroney asked. Over the course of the day, the clause was rewritten. The final communiqué committed Wells (as well as Filmon and McKenna) to submit the accord "for appropriate legislative or public consideration and to use every possible effort to achieve decision prior to 23 June 1990." When it was all over, Wells regretted he had gone that far. He attributes his consent, again, to a willingness to accommodate. "I should have known better," he says. "But you try to agree. It was a compromise clause for all to sign. That was a gross error, but you get into that damn collegiality again. You lose your perspective. Collegiality destroys judgement." Later, he bristled when other premiers misrepresented his conditional approval. "I agreed to it. And, sure enough, everybody said, 'Premier Wells signed the agreement along with everyone else.'"

When they broke in early afternoon, there were still problems. Joe Ghiz, the one with the Master's degree in law, remarked that "there must be two hundred lawyers in there fighting over words." Getty, who was one of four premiers who was not a lawyer, suggested, "If they can't get the right wording, we should kick them out." Even with the lawyers, the agreement fell into place by late afternoon. A national commission would be set up to examine the "Triple E Senate." If there was no progress by 1 July 1995, Quebec would maintain its twenty-four seats, Ontario would lose six, and the four western provinces, Nova Scotia, New Brunswick and Newfoundland would have eight seats each. The provinces and the federal government would agree as soon as possible to discuss amendments to ensure territorial representation on the Supreme Court, strengthen women's rights, and protect minority language rights. Constitutional conferences on aboriginal rights would be held every three years. The Canada clause would be studied by a parliamentary committee. Hearings would begin 16 July 1990, and a report would be issued later in the year. The first ministers would review the process of constitutional reform and the need for mandatory public hearings. On the distinct-society clause, the first ministers would "take note of the public discussion" on the issue, review the advice of experts on its legal impact, and append a legal opinion to the document. That opinion seemed to say the clause did not create new legislative authority for Parliament or the provinces, and did not infringe upon the Charter, but it was later challenged by other legal experts. The letter was not signed by the first ministers and had no legal weight.

There it was, then. A country's salvation on thirteen pages, awaiting the signatures of the first ministers. A declaration of peace in the Seven-Day War, the war to end all Constitutional Wars. The "agreement" came around 8:00 p.m. At about 10:30 p.m. that Saturday, the first ministers assembled downstairs. It was the first time they met in public that week and the last time they would meet in that round. Before they came down, officials, ministers and dignitaries took their places. Jean Charest chatted quietly with a colleague, his report now a historical artifact, his reputation sullied in Quebec. Diane Wilhelmy, the influential Quebec mandarin, embraced other officials, her years of work seemingly complete. Norman Spector, clad in a grey checked suit that looked like the one he wore at the last signing ceremony, accepted congratulations. Sharon Carstairs and Gary Doer hunkered down in the media section. As the room filled up, the premiers pulled up seats at the table, then applauded the prime minister as he took his. There was an air of forced merriment in the hall, as if all of them were giving it one more push, all the while knowing that this stone sled would never reach the top of the hill. In that soaring hall, which had once resounded with the announcement of arrivals and departures of passenger trains, one could almost hear, in this contrived ceremony, a last, hoarse appeal to the country and its leaders: "All aboard!"

Whatever the shaky prospects for the accord, the federal government wanted to clothe it in the vestments of success. Mulroney's entrance had been staged — the premiers were told where to be and when — and his remarks treated the accord as *fait accompli*. For the third time in three years, he proclaimed "a happy day for Canada. The agreement before us will reintegrate Quebec into the constitutional family." He praised all the premiers, who had persevered for seven days "to find a way for Quebeckers to feel truly a part of a united Canada." This would happen "once the accord is adopted." From Mulroney, there was no doubt or pause; the accord was as sure as tomorrow's sunrise. He had it in writing, didn't he?

After he spoke, the first ministers signed the document. Spector dutifully carried it from premier to premier. There were orchestrated standing ovations for Filmon, McKenna, Wells and Bourassa. None was planned for Peterson, and when Wells rose to salute him, he applauded alone for a few seconds. In another calculated gesture, Mulroney asked Wells, who ordinarily would speak last, to speak first, perhaps so that other first ministers would be able to dampen his criticism with their euphoria. In his remarks, drawn from notes written in a large scrawl (he can't see without his glasses), he explained what he had done. "I will take this proposal back — and this is what I have committed to do and this is what my signature means, and it means only that" — to ask his cabinet and caucus to decide on a free vote or a referendum. Later, he reaffirmed his view of Canada. For the first minutes he spoke, Frank McKenna stared ahead stone-faced. Lowell Murray leaned back in his chair, his head bobbing as if it were ready to explode. Robert Bourassa sat expressionless as Wells urged Quebeckers "to place Canada first and Quebec second."

The rest of the premiers were, by turns, folksy, whimsical, sentimental and exuberant. The tone was unusually patriotic, which made it particularly un-Canadian. It was here that the most prominent features of the Premiers' Club — the male bonding, the union of the jocks, the fidelity and fraternity — were on display. With it came the usual hyperbole and a little prevarication. Grant Devine talked about sacrifice and faith. "Every single one of these ministers has paid the political price, but we all won because the nation won." He turned to Peterson, "the big guy over there," and praised his Senate proposal. "David, that was very, very moving, and very generous," he said. "With a chance like that, we can't turn it down."

Joe Ghiz, the peppery Islander, slammed the process but exonerated the first ministers: "We didn't invent it. We inherited it." (Of course, as Devine said, you could get away with anything on television, even allowing people to believe that the amending formula forced premiers to write a constitution in three private, marathon

meetings.) Ghiz, never short on words, threw bouquets at all the premiers and said of Wells, with whom he had had harsh words over the
week, "You are big man! You are a statesman! And we are all proud
of you."

The master of hyperbole was Mulroney. He found new adjectives
for every premier. John Buchanan was "that old and distinguished
friend of ours, who has played such an important leadership role at
first ministers' conferences." Buchanan returned the compliment,
and heaped praise on Bourassa. "You stand tall in the eyes of all Canadians tonight," he said. "You are a most tenacious individual, sir."
Gary Filmon said: "As a child of an immigrant, I've never wanted to
be anything but a Canadian." Frank McKenna, for his part, talked
about his deputy premier, Aldea Landry, as "not only a woman, but
a great Canadian too."

And so it went. After a week of bloodletting, name-calling, crying,
swearing and scheming, they had come downstairs to declare victory
and go home. They talked about each other with fondness, even if
some of them did not mean it, but they were honouring the code of
the Club. When it was all over, they had come away winners. They
had preserved the benefits of the accord, and some had won the prospect of more Senate seats. Even Wells had been brought around,
however briefly, by the power of the group and the horse-trading of
constitutional politics. Then, having cut a deal that sealed their victory, the premiers excoriated the process that had made it all possible,
as if it had been imposed by divine edict.

When the last speakers were through, a federal official with oper-
atic training rose on cue to lead the singing of "O Canada." In the
back, Sharon Carstairs's seat was empty. Unhappy, uninterested and
feeling physically ill, she had quietly left the hall.

Endgame

THE MANITOBANS LEFT OTTAWA QUICKLY, FLYING FROM ONE POLITICAL storm into another. Gary Filmon, who could not abide another night in the capital, picked up Sharon Carstairs and Gary Doer and boarded a government plane for Winnipeg at 3:00 a.m. On the airplane, the three leaders planned strategy. Carstairs and Filmon worried about persuading their caucuses to support the accord; Doer said he did not expect trouble with his. Having agreed to the accord, they resolved to put it through the legislature. That would mean introducing the motion of ratification, holding ten days of public hearings, then more debate and a final vote. They had thirteen days for a process they believed would take at least a month.

The triumvirate had decided to support the deal on the previous Friday afternoon. For Carstairs, in particular, it had been an agonizing decision. While Filmon and Doer had at least endorsed the accord in principle in the past, she had always opposed it. Her opposition was visceral. In the weeks before the Ottawa meeting, when the accord seemed ready to collapse, she had, however, reconsidered her position. She had spent time campaigning with her old friend, Jean Chrétien, whose advice troubled her. Then she received a visit from another friend, a lawyer and human-rights activist she greatly admired, and he, too, made her rethink her position. "I began to ask myself if I was part of the problem, that if I left [the job] it [the process] might become easier," she reflected. The emotional strain brought sleepless nights and drove her to tranquillizers. Carstairs — who says she was sexually abused as a child and is not intellectually bullied — was under enormous pressure to change her mind. She was tormented by this long, arduous fight. Yet, in a startling reversal, having weighed the consequences, she was now prepared to make a pact with the Devil.

The tortuous sequence of events began unfolding in Manitoba soon after the party leaders returned. On Tuesday, 12 June, Filmon rose in the legislature and asked for unanimous consent to introduce the accord for debate without the normal two days' notice. All members appeared to agree, until Elijah Harper, the New Democrat from the northern riding of Rupertsland, cupped his hands to his mouth and shouted: "No." His firm, terse denial became the loudest cry of defiance in the story of the accord. Ultimately, it was its death knell. Harper, a Cree Indian who had once been chief of the Red Sucker Lake band, was laconic and reserved. He often wore his long raven hair in a pony tail. He had gone to the University of Manitoba, and was an analyst in the Department of Northern Affairs before he was elected in 1981. Later he was a cabinet minister. Initially, it was thought he just wanted to make a political statement on the accord that day and would eventually give his consent. "It's about time that aboriginal people be recognized," he said. But he denied consent the next day, and the day after. By week's end, with the tabling of the accord now delayed until 18 June, Filmon began warning the accord might die in Manitoba.

Day after day, Harper held fast. A ceremonial eagle feather, a symbol of the bravery of the warrior, lay on his desk. He quickly became a focus for all aboriginal people who felt betrayed by the accord. When procedural experts and lawyers rushed to his side, it was apparent he intended to kill the accord. In that, he probably had the acquiescence of his fellow legislators, many of whom seemed quite willing to see the accord go down at the hands of the aboriginal people. Suddenly, the issue was not just between Quebec and Canada; it was an aboriginal concern. Carstairs was quietly relieved by the shift in focus. "I had this incredible sense of calm, that it wasn't me any more, it's somebody else," she remembers. "Our first people have said, 'This isn't an English-French issue.' I never thought it was anyway, but I couldn't say it because I'm English."

Carstairs was particularly worried about the lingering antagonism to Quebec and to the accord in the province. It was no accident that the accord never went to public hearings in Manitoba, where 3,500 people had asked to speak; the party leaders were convinced, as they were after Bourassa introduced Bill 178 in 1988, that the hearings would be a forum for prejudice. Hence, they kept the debate in the legislature, where they had some control over what was said. With the province the centre of national attention, they feared that the bigots and the crackpots, rather than the legislators, would be seen to be speaking for Manitoba.

Throughout the next week, as Harper continued to withhold his approval, he and other native leaders who had come to Winnipeg were impervious to threats. The stand-off in the Manitoba legislature reflected their frustration not over the accord itself, which had denied them specific rights, but over a process that had ended in failure since 1987. Harper knew well that the meeting at Meech Lake in April of that year had come only weeks after the last constitutional conference on aboriginal rights had failed, ending a five-year effort to define those rights. That collapsed, principally because the western premiers felt that the concept of native self-government was too ill-defined for inclusion in an entrenched constitution. Yet, just a few weeks later, the premiers embraced a nebulous notion of Quebec as a distinct society, playing down concerns that the concept lacked precise legal definition. When those premiers readily agreed to that and to Quebec's other conditions, it was obvious to the native people that Quebec's agenda had taken precedence over theirs. Now the constitutional priority after Meech Lake was going to be Senate reform, and they were being told to wait again.

Threats about the consequences of failure, which had persuaded the premiers, did not carry much weight with the aboriginal people. The end of the accord would invite economic calamity? We are already poor and unemployed, they said. The end of Meech Lake would kill constitutional change? We are already tired and frustrated by the process, they said. The end of the accord would force Quebec to leave Canada? Quebec has never been a friend of ours, anyway, they said. Whether the answers — or even the questions — were accurate hardly mattered. Harper and his acolytes were ready to bring down the accord, and many Canadians supported them. The native leaders were so confident of their cause that, when Lowell Murray and Norman Spector went to Winnipeg to meet them on 18 June, the discussion lasted only an hour. The natives were not interested in the federal government's six-point plan, which offered a royal commission on native issues and a commitment to recognize native people as a fundamental characteristic of Canada. They could not be persuaded. But by then, Filmon proclaimed that time had run out and blamed it on Mulroney. "They chose to roll the dice, and now they're reaping what they sowed," he said. Mulroney, joined by McKenna and Bourassa, blamed Filmon. They said if the three Manitoba leaders wanted to pass the agreement, they could. "To govern is to choose," volunteered Bourassa.

They were right. The three leaders, if they had been emotionally and intellectually committed to Meech Lake, probably could have found a way to suspend the rules, bring in closure and ratify the accord. They probably could have gone to public hearings, and even if they had not, they could have argued that the all-party task force had already consulted Manitobans. No one doubted their sincerity in bringing back the accord to Manitoba. But that did not mean they had forgotten their ordeal in Ottawa, where their patriotism was called into question. After that, Mulroney could expect commitment, but he could not command enthusiasm. It was no surprise, then, that they watched impassively as Elijah Harper denied the country its battered accord. As long as the three stayed together — and they did — voters had nowhere to go. With no time to hold public hearings, they had a moral, even a legal argument for refusing to circumvent the process. Gary Filmon, Sharon Carstairs and Gary Doer did not plan the strange turn of events in Manitoba, but they felt no anguish over them. Indeed, quite possibly, they felt a perverse pleasure.

Meanwhile, some of the same psychology was at work in Newfoundland. The week in Ottawa had been devastating for Wells. Because his antipathy to the accord was rooted in principle and because, unlike Filmon, he bore his responsibility alone, his distress ran deep. "I watched him becoming shrivelled as a human being as he faced this every day," says Carstairs of the impact of the process in Ottawa. His colleagues say he had sent out mixed signals all week. One day he seemed to want a deal, the next day he did not. "He is a man of principle," says a senior provincial cabinet minister who watched the premier closely. "But he was incapable of acting. It was classic Hamlet. I don't believe he ever wanted to do this, and he should have said so at the beginning."

By all appearances, Wells began to reconsider his opposition to the accord in St. John's in late May. When Lowell Murray went to see him to discuss the Charest report, his willingness to consider new options surprised even some of his own people. He seemed then to be more a lawyer than a crusader, less willing to make the larger ideological arguments against the accord. "Something had broken in the sense that if something could be worked out, he would go for it," says one of his officials. "I thought a vision of the country died that day." Of course, Wells had always promised to accommodate Quebec ("We were prepared to compromise a great deal when we got to Ottawa," he says), but within limits. Newfoundland needed some concessions. By Friday, at seven o'clock, after six days in the hothouse, Wells had agreed to a deal that gave him almost nothing he wanted. He railed that "the damned collegiality" and "the vortex" had broken his will to resist. "In the end, it got to me," he says. "By Thursday and Friday, it had gotten to me. It [the roll of the dice] nearly worked." But late Friday night, after he discovered the missing clause, Wells was retreating from his tentative support for the agreement. He wavered again on Saturday when he agreed "to achieve decision," but by that evening his resolve to resist had begun to revive.

When he returned to Newfoundland on Sunday, where he was greeted by his people as hero, his will became even stronger. Hundreds of Newfoundlanders cheered him, serenading him with "Ode to Newfoundland." Touched, he began crying. He talked confidently about a referendum, which would probably have defeated the accord (he had begun drafting a question on the way home). He even proposed extending the deadline, which he knew would be unacceptable to Quebec. "This was amazing," says one of his officials. "Two days later, he is admitting that the agreement [he nearly signed] had zilch for Newfoundland. He was admitting he was ground down." No doubt if Wells truly wanted the accord to pass, all he had to do was say so. In a referendum, or in a free vote, his influence alone could have determined the outcome. But the man who nearly agreed to a deal and recommended its passage was losing enthusiasm the farther he got from Ottawa. The process had angered and alienated him. He had been wounded in the Seven-Day War, and he had nearly given up the fight. It was only when he regained his strength that he saw how near he had come to capitulating.

Sharon Carstairs noted a change. While Wells never said explicitly that he would recommend the agreement, she thought he would: "I was a little surprised by some of his statements when he got back to Newfoundland. If we hadn't felt as strongly that Wells would go along with it, *we* wouldn't have gone along with it! His reading of this to his own people — that 'I brought it home and I'm not supporting it' — was not quite the reading he gave me, which was that 'I will

take it home as the best deal we could get under the circumstances.'
[It was] not that we agreed to it, not that we supported it, but it was
the best [deal] we could get. And we would vote for it in the legislature." Like his colleagues in Manitoba, Wells could have found a way
to pass the accord. In the end, for reasons of principle, pride or pique,
he chose not to.

Yet, even though Wells had rediscovered his antipathy for the accord and was convinced it would fail in a free vote in his legislature,
he acted in other ways to improve the prospects of its passage. These
acts, it might be argued, were to satisfy the other part of his tormented soul — the side that had briefly triumphed in Ottawa and was
deeply troubled by the consequences of failure. It might explain why,
the day after he had proposed it, he dropped the referendum idea and
the plan to extend the deadline. "I suppose you could say I've
changed my mind," he said on Monday, 12 June, after talking to
Chrétien and Mulroney. "I don't want to put this country in jeopardy
by taking an intransigent position." At the same time, he stressed that
he would not carry on a campaign to reject Meech Lake. His internal
turmoil might explain his decision to adjourn the legislature, to allow
members to consult their constituents, and to invite the other first
ministers to address the House of Assembly. (Peterson, Devine and
McKenna accepted.) It might explain his treatment of the three members of his caucus ("I gave them the highest praise and commendation
in the presence of other members of the caucus") who announced
they would support the accord. All told, could this behaviour suggest
a mercurial man who wanted the accord to pass to allay his fears of its
unknown consequences for Canada, but who did not want to be held
personally responsible for it?

As the accord moved fitfully towards resolution in Manitoba and
Newfoundland, there were developments on other fronts. In New
Brunswick, the legislature approved the accord unanimously on 15
June. McKenna, stung by those who were blaming him for throwing
the nation into this eleventh-hour frenzy, called for unity. "The only
time we fight is when we talk about our damn constitution!" he
raged. The next week, while Elijah Harper was still blocking the resolution in Manitoba, and the House of Assembly had resumed debate
in Newfoundland, the federal Liberals gathered in Calgary for their
leadership convention. Calgary — along with Winnipeg, St. John's
and Ottawa — thus completed the constitutional quadrangle. It was

one of four stages on which the saga played itself out that weekend of 23 June.

From the beginning, the mood of the convention was strained. The country was agonizing over its future, and a once-proud party was turning on itself. Since January, when the leadership race to replace John Turner had opened, the party had resumed its arguing over the accord. Jean Chrétien, who would have preferred to make a deal, declared his candidacy in January and renewed his public opposition to the accord in a scholarly speech at the University of Ottawa. Even Sharon Carstairs, who was consulted on his speech, said it was tougher than she expected. Chrétien let slip that he had checked the text with Pierre Trudeau, which probably did not gain him much support. His two main rivals — Sheila Copps and Paul Martin — supported the accord. As discussion of Meech Lake divided the country that winter and spring, it divided the leadership race. Even when it was obvious the convention would be a coronation for Chrétien, the accord continued to act like a slow poison spreading within the party.

The rifts that had undermined John Turner's leadership had not healed by the time the party met in Calgary. On the night the faithful bade him farewell, the eve of the accord's demise, Turner was eloquent and passionate. "We must never give up this country!" he pleaded, as the crowd roared its approval. "Never, never, never!" It was a fine speech, strong and sometimes sentimental, which recalled his early promise. The next evening, when the candidates spoke, the bitterness bubbled up. Turner and Trudeau, the old adversaries, sat many rows apart. When Chrétien talked about Quebec and Meech Lake — a subject on which Chrétien had been refusing to comment since the Ottawa conference, fearing it would harm his standing — some delegates booed. Geills Turner, her face twisted in disgust, could be seen saying, "Oh, shut up, Jean!" At the end of the convention, party officials had to plead with Turner to join Chrétien and the other candidates on stage.

The mood on the day of the balloting, Saturday, 23 June, was almost surreal. Chrétien's and Martin's supporters argued on the floor of the convention. Some wore black armbands. Jean Lapierre, who had served briefly in Turner's cabinet, and Gilles Rocheleau, another Quebec Liberal MP, announced they were leaving the convention and, eventually, the party. When the results of the first ballot were in, and Chrétien had won, the celebration was muted. Pierre Trudeau,

Keith Davey and others applauded the man who had pursued the leadership since he lost it to Turner in 1984. The question, though, was what value this prize? Could this divided, bankrupt party, its base shattered in Quebec, its leader in apparent disrepute among his own people, its philosophy and *raison d'être* in question, rise again? Could this likable, roughhewn populist put the pieces back together?

In St. John's and Winnipeg and Ottawa, other players had other matters on their minds. In Manitoba, the legislature was finally debating the accord but was expected to adjourn Friday, 22 June, at 12:30 p.m., without a vote. If that happened, the accord would die in Manitoba. Since the previous Sunday, Clyde Wells had more than once raised the prospect that there might be no vote in Newfoundland if there was no vote in Manitoba. On Thursday, at Wells's invitation, Mulroney had flown to St. John's to address the Assembly. Afterwards, he had dinner at the premier's home. Wells says that, while he was not absolutely certain then how the vote would go, he thought the accord would be rejected. He cannot remember if he expressly told Mulroney there would be no vote at all the next day, but he probably did not, although it was clearly on his mind. After dinner, he went back to the legislature, stayed until adjournment and consulted his caucus. The consensus then was even stronger that the debate should be adjourned without a vote if the process faltered in Manitoba. Later he called Filmon and Carstairs, both of whom assured him that their legislature would adjourn the next day without a decision.

Carstairs thinks Lowell Murray and Brian Mulroney were telling Wells and Filmon different things. "We were told that 'Newfoundland is taking the vote at eleven in the morning, and they will vote in favour,'" she says. But when she spoke to Wells that night, after he met with his caucus, he said there would likely be no vote the next morning, and if there was, the accord wouldn't pass. "Wells thought we were going to hold a vote, which was nonsense," she says. "The prime minister was giving him the wrong information." Carstairs advised Wells not to vote until he heard from Manitoba. She reassured him there would be no vote, and promised he would receive a call as soon as the legislature adjourned.

The next day, Friday, 22 June, debate on the accord resumed at 10:00 a.m. in Newfoundland. As Wells tells it, he spoke to John Crosbie, who was in St. John's orchestrating the pro-accord forces, and told him that a vote in Newfoundland, without one in Manitoba, would probably cause "harm and resentment." This was probably a moot point by now. Short of passing the accord, little was likely to help Wells improve his appeal in Quebec, where he was now as popular as Lord Durham. Nonetheless, Crosbie seemed "impressed" by Wells's comments and said he would pass them on to Murray. At 10:30 a.m., Murray returned a call Wells had placed earlier. Again, Wells told him a vote would be "pointless" and "harmful." But Murray said the government was looking at a dozen proposals to get around the problem. The most promising was a request to the Supreme Court to defer the start of the three-year ratification period to 23 September 1987, when Saskatchewan approved the deal, from 23 June, when Quebec had approved it. That would give Manitoba three more months to debate the issue and ratify the accord. This was an arresting proposal from a government that had insisted for months that the deadline was immovable. Upon hearing Murray's proposal, Wells advised waiting. "I told him that, in that case, it would be best to defer the vote in Newfoundland because it was virtually certain to be rejected if the vote were taken at that stage and that would make the reference to the Supreme Court utterly useless," he says. "Senator Murray argued that they felt they would be only able to ask the court for an opinion if the accord had been passed by all provinces other than Manitoba, where there was a commitment by the leaders to cause it to be passed." Here the tone turned icy. Wells disagreed, arguing that the court would decide on the legalities, not on political commitments. "If they can extend the time for Manitoba, they can extend it for Newfoundland," he said. Wells made it clear that the reference would be useful only if Newfoundland adjourned, because a vote "would certainly result in rejection." Murray said he would discuss the matter and get back to him.

At noon, Elijah Harper called Wells and told him he intended to stop the accord. Wells met his caucus an hour later, and it agreed not to take a vote, but directed Wells he could proceed with one, depending on what he heard from Crosbie and Murray.

At 12:26 p.m., in Winnipeg, Harper said no again. The legislators rose to sing the national anthem. Harper said it was "a great day for Canada." The accord was not going to pass in Manitoba before the deadline. Carstairs was talking to reporters outside the chamber when her secretary pulled her away to talk to Wells. "We're not going to vote," Wells said. "Fine," she replied. "It's the best choice you could make. If you're going to be blamed, better to be blamed for not having taken a vote than for defeating it."

By 2:30 p.m., Newfoundland time, Wells had not heard from Murray. Wells placed a call but could not get through, although Murray's secretary said he was there. Moments later, she came back on the line to tell Wells that Murray had left the office without taking his call. Instead, Murray went on television to say that the process had ended in Manitoba but that the federal government would ask the Supreme Court to rule on the legality of deferring the deadline. The senator said the matter now turned on Newfoundland. If it passed there, Manitoba could approve it in the future. If it did not, the accord would die. Wells was incensed. He consulted his caucus, who agreed this put Newfoundland in an untenable position. "We were being pressured to vote against the conscience of the majority of members, or Newfoundland would be blamed by the nation for the failure of the accord if we voted as we believed we should," he says. The caucus decided to adjourn the debate until the high court could rule on extending the deadline.

Wells later described Murray's appearance on television and his offer as "the final manipulation." He had already endured months of neglect, the browbeating in Ottawa and, most recently, Mulroney's remarks on rolling the dice. Those remarks, in a newspaper interview on 12 June, angered the dissident premiers in particular and diminished Mulroney's stature. "I was offended," said Wells. "I felt played like a puppet on a string. Perhaps there is nothing more offensive to a thinking mind than the sense of being manipulated. It is the ultimate violation of the person."

After his caucus meeting, Wells met again with John Crosbie and with Tom Rideout, the province's Conservative opposition leader. He reiterated that he intended to adjourn the House because of Murray's "manipulation." He says Crosbie and Rideout agreed the vote would result in rejection of the accord. Crosbie said he would call Mulroney. He came back later and told Wells that the federal government would consent to adjournment, without a vote being taken, if Wells would agree to state publicly that he would support the accord in the future. "I told Mr. Crosbie that was blackmail and we would not give in to it," the premier says. If there was ever any doubt that Newfoundland would let the accord die, it vanished then. Later that afternoon, when the Tories shouted, "Vote, vote," Wells was so angry that he was tempted to go through with it. "Let's hold the vote," he told his House leader. But then he reconsidered. The House of Assembly voted only to adjourn. Just as there was no vote in Manitoba, there was no vote in Newfoundland. The accord had died, not with a bang, but a whimper. In Ottawa, Murray went before the cameras, his expression pained. Pointing to Wells's signature on the 9 June document as the shutters clicked, he said: "Premier Wells's decision to break his commitment has dashed the one remaining hope to have Meech Lake succeed." Then he repeated the performance in French.

The death of the accord in Newfoundland caused a slanging match between Wells and Mulroney. Mulroney accused Wells of reneging on his commitment. "He cancelled the most fundamental and noble dimension of a democracy," Mulroney said. "The real reason Clyde Wells cancelled the vote is that he was afraid to take a chance on Meech passing." Wells said he was manipulated. Was it an excuse to avoid acting? A victory of indecision? "Who victimized whom by that ordeal?" asked a cabinet minister from a pro-Meech province. "We were the victims, and Wells was the victimizer, because he wouldn't make up his mind. He was looking for a way out at every turn. That's what happened on Friday. He got another chance to avoid a decision."

The critical question was whether the accord would have been approved had a vote been taken. Wells insists it would have been defeated; others suggest it would have passed. Some claim polling by the federal government had shown a shift in popular opinion and the accord would have squeaked through by two votes; another count shows it would have lost by five votes. Wells, who refused to reveal his intentions during the debate, says that he would have voted against it.

In the end, it hardly mattered. Elijah Harper or Clyde Wells or Lowell Murray may have held the dagger, but the country was an accomplice. By Saturday, it was all over. In Quebec City, Robert Bourassa addressed "the nation" of Quebec and reaffirmed his province's status as a distinct society. For him, it was the last insult, a blow upon a bruise. In Ottawa, Brian Mulroney warned that Canadians should not delude themselves that nothing had happened, but neither should they despair. In Calgary, Clyde Wells arrived at the Liberal convention and was greeted warmly by Pierre Trudeau. Later that day, the Liberals elected Donald Johnston, the man who had left the Liberal caucus over Meech Lake, as their new president. His resurrection was seen in some quarters as the unearthing of yet another fossil.

In the hall in Calgary, as in the rest of this country, there was a strange serenity that day. Something had happened and nothing had happened. Perhaps the mood was relief. Perhaps it was uncertainty. Perhaps it was foreboding. For three years, there had been a rising cacophony. Now, after all the shouting, wailing, crying and bawling, after all the recriminations and lamentations, it was as if the radio had suddenly died. On that day, finally, there was silence.

Epilogue

WITH THE DEATH OF THE MEECH LAKE ACCORD, THE CONSTITUTIONAL debate entered what might be called the Phony War. Despite warnings that Canada stood at the abyss, it did not topple on 24 June. Neither the stock market nor the dollar fell; perversely, the dollar climbed to its highest level in ten years and foreign investors increased their holdings of government bonds. The rivers continued to flow and the trains continued to run late. It was the first weekend of the summer, and the country craved tranquillity. To those who said nothing would happen the day after, it looked as if nothing had happened. This, though, was an illusion. Rather than ending the Constitutional Wars, the collapse of the accord renewed them. Metaphorically, it seemed the summer of 1990 was to Canada what the winter of 1940 was to Europe: an interlude of anxiety and inactivity after the formal declaration of war but before the outbreak of real hostilities.

A new creative tension was at work. The government of Quebec, stung by its perceived rejection, began drawing up its own agenda for the powers, rights and roles it deemed necessary to affirm its distinctiveness. It announced that it would no longer negotiate as one of ten provinces but would henceforth bargain only with the federal government. To draft a more comprehensive program — perhaps a provincial constitution — it struck a nonpartisan commission to travel the province, solicit opinion and make recommendations. The provincial government was then expected to frame formal demands and seek new talks with Ottawa. Already, Quebec was signalling its desire for more powers over immigration, telecommunications, manpower training, financial institutions and foreign policy. The blueprint for Quebec's new relationship with Canada might be called independence, sovereignty-association or something else, but it would not be the status quo. Canada was likely to emerge as a far different country, if it was a country at all. In future, Quebec would have to ask for more than it did at Meech Lake; indeed, its new demands would probably make the accord, once its price of acceptance of Canada, look like a bargain.

If Quebeckers knew who they were and where they were going, the rest of Canada wasn't so sure of its direction. As soon as the provinces saw that Quebec was vying for bilateral agreements, they demanded similar treatment. Bill Vander Zalm, finally free of the albatross of the accord, mused about a form of sovereignty-association for British Columbia. Collectively, the western premiers talked about a new form of "fiscal federalism" that would curtail Ottawa's spending power. Only a month earlier, one of those western premiers, Gary Filmon, had complained that the Meech Lake Accord would weaken the central government. This was the post-Meech Canada, and it had not taken long for the premiers to make themselves at home. Freed of the yoke of Meech Lake, the horses were already pulling in different directions. David Peterson, trying to reposition Ontario as the broker of Confederation, saw danger in this and raised the alarm. But as a unified and self-confident Quebec began plotting its future, the rest of Canada fretted about the prospects of a balkanized country surviving in the shadow of a superpower. With greater urgency than ever before, English Canada would now have to determine what it wanted. Its emerging identity would be shaped by its changing demographic character; by the challenges of the international economy, principally the impact of continental free trade and by a mounting debt that threatened the welfare state. The passage to self-definition would be fraught with angst.

As much as Canadians looked ahead in trepidation, they looked back in detachment. There remained questions. Why did Meech Lake fail? Could it have been saved? Could this malaise have been avoided?

From the beginning, the players knew that constitutional reform was a minefield. While there had been good reasons to reopen the question in 1986, there had also been reasons to leave it alone. If the country was unlikely to last a thousand years without constitutional change, as Trudeau boasted it would, it could have lasted another ten years. The constitution may have lacked political legitimacy in Quebec, but few seemed to notice or care; Quebec nationalism was at a nadir in 1986. Bourassa himself admitted there was no need to proceed when he did. Waiting would have had advantages. It would have allowed Quebec to acquire more self-confidence and cultural security, the greatest counterweight to independence. It would also have allowed Canada to adjust to two seminal changes: the Charter of Rights, which was remaking the country's social attitudes, and the free-trade agreement, which would remake its economy. Both were radical departures. The accord would have been another, and it may have been too much for the country to digest.

The process was as questionable as the substance. The assumption was that Canadians should be told as little as possible. The argument that Quebec's proposals were nothing new was a thinly disguised rationalization for negotiating behind closed doors. In reality, there was virtually no public consultation until after the fact, and even then, half the provinces avoided public hearings. In another era, that approach would have been fine. Brian Mulroney talked as if the country could still make constitutions the way the Fathers of Confederation had — in private, in profanity, plied with liquor. "In Charlottetown, the boys arrived in a ship — and spent a long time in places other than the library," he said. "This is the way it was done. This is the way Confederation came about. There was no great public debate; there were no great public hearings. It became a kind of tradition." Canadians may not have been passionate about their constitution, but they resented having one imposed on them. In a sense, the Meech Lake Accord was a revolution from above, a new regime contrived by politicians for politicians. It was constitution-making by stealth. The secrecy could be blamed, in part, on the need for unanimity. The trouble is that an informed electorate expects more in an open, pluralistic democracy. The lesson of the Patriation Round was that Canadians took a proprietary interest in the constitution, particularly the Charter of Rights. They had come to see it as a birthright, and they did not want it weakened.

From the beginning, the first ministers denied that popular impulse. They denied that constitutions must be made differently. Meech Lake was chosen as the sight of the first meeting in order to avoid, as one adviser put it, "having every bloody interest group outside the door." That obsession with secrecy created problems later. Not only did it undermine public faith in the process, it weakened Quebec's credibility. In the final months, when Bourassa claimed repeatedly that he could not compromise because he already had — that his five conditions were a minimum — he was not dissembling. Quebec *had* compromised. The trouble was that it had made its concessions in private and received no political credit for them. While it had never retreated from its five conditions, it had narrowed them considerably over months of interprovincial talks, and again at Meech Lake and Langevin. No one believed Quebec when it said it had been accommodating. The country saw only Bourassa's frown of rejection.

The other problem with the Meech Lake Accord was that it could not be reopened and altered. The other provinces, having committed themselves to the Quebec Round, could not raise other issues. They could not trade kilowatts for cabbages, as one premier said, which, however distasteful, ensured agreement in 1981. Changes to the package — even changes that did not affect Quebec's original demands, or that corrected flaws — could not be introduced. Having foreclosed the possibility of amendments, the framers then warned, in language that threatened to become self-fulfilling prophecy, that the country's future hung in the balance. It was as if they had constructed a castle on sand, refused to reinforce the foundation, then warned of disaster as the waves began to lap at its walls.

At the outset, Quebec was promised that its agenda would be dealt with first, in isolation from other demands. But, at Meech Lake, items were added to the list, such as the requirement of annual constitutional conferences and the right to choose senators. Most important, all provinces got what Quebec got; the Quebec Round became the Provincial Round. Quebec may have expected and accepted that, knowing that other provinces had to have something, but allowing those concessions may have hurt its interests. Quebec's five conditions, though never entirely embraced by English Canada, were part and parcel of a transfer of power from the centre to the regions. In this devolution of power, the federal government was a willing partner. It offered more than Quebec had asked for, while ignoring other regions such as the North. In return, the central government asked for nothing for itself. It was content to herald Quebec's approval of the constitution, which, it was true, was no small achievement. But rather than be hailed as the agent of conciliation, Mulroney was dismissed as the agent of capitulation, the patsy of the provinces.

Even with the mistakes of timing and negotiation, there was still, after the meeting at Meech Lake, time to undo the damage. In fact, there was greater flexibility than people thought. David Peterson and

Howard Pawley had enough doubts about the agreement to force amendments at the Langevin Block. Bourassa had enough room to make concessions on the spending-power and the distinct-society clauses. If Pawley and Peterson had felt strongly about Meech Lake, they could — and should — have pushed for more changes, or killed it then. Instead, Peterson relented ("I lost," he said later), and Pawley deferred final approval by insisting on public hearings. Had the accord collapsed then, it would not have been catastrophic; even Bourassa says he could have walked away from Langevin, as he had walked away from Victoria, with little political fallout. As the premiers could have sought changes, so could the opposition leaders. When John Turner and Ed Broadbent offered their support so readily, they missed an opportunity to use their influence to forge a better agreement. Had Turner done so, he might have saved his leadership. For these reasons, in retrospect, the thirty-three days between Meech Lake and Langevin were critical.

Once the accord was signed, however, it took on a life of its own. After the talks were over, Mulroney said it was better to have tried to accommodate Quebec than not to have tried at all. Mulroney was right in spirit, but wrong in practice. The fact is that he had opened a Pandora's box of frustration and vitriol, setting in motion a train of events he could not control. He and his colleagues had misread the mood of the country and left it worse off than when they started. It was that fear of failure that had inhibited Quebec in the first place. While Bourassa had raised the issue, he wanted to proceed only if he could succeed. But when the accord failed, he ensured that he would be the major beneficiary.

Because the premiers never thought ratification would take three years, they never committed themselves to passing it in three months. They assumed that succeeding governments would find their work as impressive as they had. The demand for unanimity was not their fault, nor was the three-year ratification period, but neither did they take sufficient account of either of them. Some premiers were particularly culpable. In New Brunswick, Richard Hatfield did not pass the accord before he called an election he was sure to lose. His successor, Frank McKenna, then delayed it for two and a half years. Had New Brunswick passed it, Manitoba would likely have been the lone hold-out by the summer of 1988. "I have to share responsibility and it weighs heavily on me," says a rueful McKenna. "I don't think any of us has done a great deal of honour to the country."

In Manitoba, Pawley dawdled. He had subtly linked the accord to free trade. He, too, could have passed it before his government fell. Gary Filmon and, later, Gary Doer found their own reasons for delaying the accord.

Bourassa, who showed a strength and consistency that made him the most compelling of the premiers, had cause to feel betrayed. In theory, he could say that the accord was passed by the House of Commons, supported by all three party leaders, ratified by eight provinces with 96 percent of the population and celebrated on three different occasions. He could say that two premiers had renounced their predecessors' signatures, and one of the provinces actually rescinded its ratification. He could lament all this, and, to a degree, he would be right. But Bourassa was also responsible for the collapse of Meech Lake. When he refused a moderate court ruling on Quebec's sign law, having broken his promise to allow bilingual signs and rejected the proposed allternatives, he dealt the accord a grievous blow. The premier could have chosen another course, particularly in 1986. Bourassa, *un homme de la situation*, chose not to.

Of course, there were a host of other reasons for the failure of Meech Lake. The federal government did not sell the accord effectively, fearing, it seemed, that Canadians would reject it if they knew too much about it. Ottawa ignored the dissident premiers, shunned its friends in other provinces, and created a crisis that forced eleventh-hour talks, which, ultimately, helped kill the deal. In a larger sense, the public animosity towards the Conservative government undermined its credibility. The accord became a lightning rod. When Canadians were angry over regional disparity, budgetary cutbacks, unemployment, interest rates or the goods and services tax, they aimed at the government and hit Meech Lake. Most of all, they blamed the head of that government, and the accord's principal advocate, Brian Mulroney.

The story of Meech Lake is the story of "if," the longest word in the English language. If the accord had been negotiated more wisely, if it had stuck to Quebec's five conditions, if it had been ratified more quickly and accepted more readily, if Richard Hatfield had won and Clyde Wells had lost, if there had been no Bill 178 and no Sault Ste. Marie, if Lucien Bouchard had not quit, if there had been less time, if there had been more time . . . All these conditions helped drain Meech Lake, but there were other forces at work.

Meech Lake showed how hard it is to achieve constitutional change in a large, diverse country. After all, everything seemed to be in place for constitutional reform in 1986. Here was a new federalist government in Quebec, a new government in Ottawa with a national majority, a circle of new premiers with no baggage from the past, and a short, modest list of proposals. What could go wrong?

Part of the reason for its ephemeral success — and its enduring failure — was that Meech Lake was an accommodation among politicians who had interests to protect and constituencies to serve. Throughout it all, politics mattered more than principle. Everyone had good reasons to support or to oppose the accord. Brian Mulroney, his government flagging in the polls in 1987, wanted to consolidate his electoral base in Quebec. He coveted a deal and was prepared to relinquish powers to get one. Robert Bourassa wanted to strengthen Quebec, assert his nationalist credentials and contain his separatist opposition. He deftly used the threat of the Parti Québécois to his advantage, whether it was refusing concessions on the accord or concessions on minority language rights. Other premiers had their own agendas. Howard Pawley did not want to open the constitutional question because of the politics of language, and Gary Filmon wanted to ignore it because of the politics of minority government. The western premiers, particularly Bill Vander Zalm and Don Getty, demanded something on Senate reform at Meech Lake because they could not go back empty-handed. Similarly, Brian Peckford wanted a favour on fisheries; he thought he needed it for home consumption. David Peterson wanted protection for women and ethnic Canadians because they were a vocal element of his constituency. Each, in his way, acted to protect his interests. But others who had no advocate at the table — such as aboriginal people or northern Canadians — were ignored. Tony Penikett, the government leader of the Yukon, called the process "Kafkaesque" for condemning his constituents to constitutional limbo without a trial. "We never even got a hearing," he says. "What was the evidence? What was the charge?"

No wonder the first ministers wanted to take the agreement and run. With so many constituencies making so many demands, how could everyone be satisfied? Meech Lake began falling apart when first those groups, and then those regions, began clamouring for their share. Western Canada, as much as the North, wondered how it would ever get Senate reform with unanimity. Eastern Canada wondered about the strength of the federal government to keep it afloat.

Ethnic Canadians wondered why they, too, were not a fundamental part of Canada. Aboriginal people saw Quebec's agenda addressed before theirs. Perhaps the strongest impulse in this debate was a sense that Quebec was being treated differently, that Quebec was "special," that it had disproportionate influence in Canada. That wave of discontent revived old fears and doubts. After watching the province of Quebec repeatedly select the national government and the prime minister, support a free-trade agreement and reject its own view of bilingualism, the rest of the country began to wonder. It asked, more in confusion than in prejudice, where it left them. Could a prime minister ever come from Atlantic Canada or western Canada? Could Quebec ever understand English Canada's own cultural insecurity, and why it might be threatened by free trade? Could Quebec understand how English Canada had accepted bilingualism, an idea it had never really liked but still tolerated? As much as English Canada misunderstood Quebec, and it did, Quebec misunderstood English Canada. It was predictable that Meech Lake would come to represent the flashpoint in a clash of wills. Finally, after years of taunts and threats, it happened: English Canada's maximum met French Canada's minimum. When the thin flame touched the combustible gas, the country caught fire.

Some suggest this crisis was inevitable, with or without Meech Lake. The determinist school argues that the accord would not have prevented a showdown between Quebec and Canada, only delayed it. Quebec, the theory goes, had been seeking more powers for thirty years. If the flashpoint had not come this decade, it would have come in the next one. The powers Quebec did not get in the accord, it would have demanded later as a distinct society. This argument, in itself, is plausible. In fact, Bourassa had already spoken of a second round in which Quebec would seek new powers. As leverage to justify his demands, he or any other moderate premier could always point to more militant opposition. Such was the reality of a two-party system in a province where no government had served more than two consecutive terms since the 1950s.

The collapse of the Meech Lake Accord makes this prospect even more likely. Clear-eyed supporters of the accord knew that the process would never end and hoped only that the accord would bind Quebec more closely to Canada and fulfil some of its aspirations, at least temporarily. It would, for better or for worse, buy time. Canada might be a piece of poetry, impossible and unrealistic, but at least

Meech Lake would write one more stanza. The hope was that in the process Quebec would grow, become more prosperous, feel comfortable within Canada. This was the optimist's reason for passing Meech Lake; it was also the pragmatist's argument. Perhaps Sir John A. Macdonald had it right. Perhaps Meech Lake would preserve Canada for another week, so it could last another month, and another year.

Whatever the reasons for its failure, the Meech Lake Accord was a watershed in the experience of a moderate, decent people who had lost their way and, perhaps, their will. It was the longest and bloodiest of the Constitutional Wars, and probably the last of its kind. Canadians will still quarrel, since questioning their good fortune seems to be part of their national character. But the cause of the conflict, and the consequences of its resolution, will be different in the future. The fight will no longer be over a power here or there, and the prize will no longer be a placated Quebec. This time, the battle will be over a new, different — and, some would argue, better — arrangement. Rather than bickering over the nation-state of the nineteenth century, the new debate will address the superstate of the twenty-first century.

On 24 June 1990, thousands of Québécois marched in the streets of Montreal. It was St. Jean-Baptiste Day, honouring the patron saint of French Canada, and the city was awash in Fleurs-de-Lis. The crowd watched the parade, the first since 1969. It seemed that every ten years Quebec and Canada take another step in their search for country and constitution. In 1960, it was the election of Jean Lesage and the launching of the Quiet Revolution; in 1970, the October Crisis; in 1980, the referendum; in 1990, the end of the Meech Lake Accord. On that day, there was no mourning. People chanted, "Meech Lake is dead; Quebec lives!" There was no anger, no violence, just a sense that something was over and something was beginning. *A la prochaine.* They knew the circle had closed. They knew the moment was at hand. Most of all, they knew that "next time" was now.

Endnotes

This book was compiled from more than a hundred interviews, with all the premiers, two opposition leaders, and active and former politicians at both levels of government. In addition, I interviewed officials in both Ottawa and the provinces, as well as constitutional experts. Some of the interviews were on the record; some were not. Wherever possible, those interviewed for each chapter are listed. To honour confidentiality, some names have been omitted. Secondary sources are also listed here.

PROLOGUE

The paraphrase of Machiavelli's dictum appeared in a memorandum written by senior bureaucrat Michael Kirby in 1981, cited in Lenard Cohen, Patrick Smith and Paul Warwick, *The Vision and the Game: Making the Canadian Constitution* (Calgary: Detselig Enterprises Ltd., 1987).

CHAPTER 1

The meeting at Meech Lake was reconstructed from interviews with all ten premiers who were in the room, and the only two officials present, Norman Spector and Oryssia Lennie. Other material was provided by provincial officials and ministers. There are no official minutes of this meeting.

CHAPTER 2

This chapter was drawn largely from interviews with all the premiers, their friends and colleagues. For more on Robert Bourassa, see L. Ian MacDonald, *From Bourassa to Bourassa* (Montreal: Harvest House, 1984). On William Vander Zalm, see Gary Mason and Keith Baldrey, *Fantasyland: Inside the Reign of Bill Vander Zalm* (Toronto: McGraw-Hill Ryerson, 1989).

CHAPTER 3

Several books have been written on the Patriation Round. The best is by Michael Valpy and Robert Sheppard, *The National Deal: The Fight for a Canadian Constitution* (Toronto: Fleet, 1982). Also, see David Milne, *The Canadian Constitution: From Patriation to Meech Lake* (Toronto: James Lorimer & Company, 1989); Edward McWhinney, *Canada and the Constitution 1979–1982* (Toronto: University of Toronto Press, 1982). For Mulroney's speeches, see Brian Mulroney, *Where I Stand* (Toronto: McClelland & Stewart, 1983). For a full-length biography, see L. Ian MacDonald, *The Making of the Prime Minister* (Toronto: McClelland & Stewart, 1984). Also see Rae Murphy, Robert Chodos and Nick Auf der Maur, *Brian Mulroney: The Boy from Baie Comeau* (Toronto: James Lorimer & Company, 1984).

CHAPTER 4

For the official report on the Mont Gabriel Conference and the text of Gil Rémillard's keynote address, see Peter Leslie, *Rebuilding the Relationship: Quebec and its Confederation Partners* (Kingston: Institute of Intergovernmental Affairs, Queen's University, 1987). For background on federal-provincial relations, the institute's annual publication on "The State of the Federation" is useful. The Quebec Liberal Party's constitutional position is spelled out in "Mastering our Future" in 1985. Also helpful in understanding the evolution of the position is "A New Canadian Federation," published in 1980.

CHAPTER 5

The meeting at the Langevin Block was reconstructed from interviews with all premiers and the two officials in the room, as well as federal and provincial officials. The quotation on page **112**, "that bastard Trudeau" appeared in an adaptation of this book in *Saturday Night,* June 1990. On 2 May 1990, in Sherbrooke, Quebec, Robert

Bourassa told reporters that he had checked his notes "and nothing confirms" the quotation. He said he attacked the opponents of Meech Lake but denied making personal attacks. "It amazes me that three years later on the basis of hearsay, journalists are coming to these conclusions," he said. The quotation was drawn from a personal memo dictated by one of the premiers two days after the meeting at Langevin. It has been confirmed by two others who were in the room. As one of them put it, "He said it and everyone at the table heard it."

CHAPTER 6

This chapter was drawn from interviews with Ian Scott, Peter Meekison, Ron Watts, Peter Leslie, Bryan Schwartz, Eugene Forsey, Norman Spector and Lowell Murray. The two best sources on the substance of the accord are Peter Hogg, *The Meech Lake Constitutional Accord Annotated* (Toronto: Carswell, 1988); and Bryan Schwartz, *Fathoming Meech Lake* (Winnipeg: Legal Research Institute of the University of Manitoba, 1987). Other useful commentary on the accord can be found in Roger Gibbins, ed., *Meech Lake and Canada, Perspectives from the West* (Edmonton: Academic Printing and Publishing, 1988); Michael Behiels, ed., *The Meech Lake Primer* (Ottawa: University of Ottawa Press, 1989); K. E. Swinton and C. J. Rogerson, *Competing Constitutional Visions: The Meech Lake Accord* (Toronto: Carswell, 1988).

CHAPTER 7

Interviews with John Turner, Donald Johnston, Michèle Tremblay, John Nunziata, Sergio Marchi, André Ouellet, Marc Lalonde, Tom Axworthy, Lloyd Axworthy, Charles Caccia, Robert Kaplan, Keith Davey, Eric Maldoff, Serge Joyal, Michel Robert, Jerry Grafstein. (Raymond Garneau, a key player, refused to be interviewed.) The Liberal party resolution that was passed in November 1986 can be found in "Policy Resolutions," the 1986 Convention of the Liberal Party of Canada, Nov. 27–30, Ottawa. The party's amendments are in the report of the House of Commons Committee on 9 September 1987. For some of Turner's early thoughts on federalism, see John Turner, *Politics of Purpose* (Toronto: McClelland & Stewart, 1968).

For background on Turner's life and career, see Jack Cahill, *John Turner: The Long Run* (Toronto: McClelland & Stewart, 1984).

CHAPTER 8

Interviews with Jacques Hébert, Allan Blakeney, Claude Morin, Mitchell Sharp, Tom Axworthy, Marc Lalonde, Charles Caccia, Robert Kaplan, Roy McMurtry, John Roberts. For background information on Trudeau, see Richard Gwyn, *The Northern Magus: Pierre Trudeau and Canadians*, (Toronto: McClelland & Stewart, 1980); Michel Vastel, *Pierre Trudeau, le Québécois* (Montreal: Les Editions de L'Homme, 1989); Patrick Gossage, *Close to the Charisma* (Toronto: McClelland & Stewart, 1986). For background on his own thoughts, see Pierre Trudeau, *Federalism and French Canadians* (Toronto: Macmillan, 1968). Trudeau's essay is in the Toronto *Star*, 27 May 1987. Other sources were transcripts of interviews with "The Journal," 28 May 1987 and "Morningside," 29 May 1987. His testimony before both parliamenary committees can be found in *Pierre Trudeau Speaks out on Meech Lake,* edited by Donald Johnston (Toronto: General Paperbacks, 1990). See also Pierre Trudeau and Tom Axworthy, eds., *Towards a Just Society: The Trudeau Years* (Toronto: Viking, 1990).

CHAPTER 9

Interviews with Frank McKenna, Clyde Wells, Gary Filmon, Sharon Carstairs, Gary Doer, John Stewart, Howard Pawley, Roland Penner. Both the pledge to act "as soon as possible" and the deadline of 31 December 1988 are in the political accord accompanying the legal text. In Filmon's speech on 16 December, he also talked about a companion accord that would raise other issues later.

CHAPTER 10

For the Manitoba position, see the final report of the Manitoba Task Force on Meech Lake, 1989. For the New Brunswick position, see the Select Committee on the 1987 Constitutional Accord, Final Report, 1987. The quotation "a roll of the dice" is from an interview Mulroney gave to the *Globe and Mail,* 12 June 1990. Page 213: "His office was flooded with calls and letters and flowers." By July 1990, Wells had received 30,000 letters.

CHAPTER 11

"If that's the way you feel, fuck you" (page **243**) is cited in *Maclean's,* 18 June 1990, p. 20. The magazine claims two premiers confirmed the exchange. Wells says, "It never occurred — total and complete fabrication."

CHAPTER 12

Interviews with Carstairs, Wells, Filmon and McKenna. See Wells's statement on the events of the final days on 3 July 1990, issued by Office of the Premier, St. John's. Also, Brian Mulroney's interview on "The Journal," 29 June 1990.

A Constitutional Chronology

1 9 8 0

20 May Quebeckers reject sovereignty-association in a provincial referendum.

13 Sept. First ministers' meeting in Ottawa ends in failure, after four days of talks.

6 Oct. Government tables patriation resolution in the House.

1 9 8 1

2 Nov. First ministers' conference on the constitution begins.

5 Nov. Agreement is reached on patriating the BNA Act with a charter of rights; Quebec Premier René Lévesque dissents.

1 9 8 2

17 April Canada Act proclaimed by Queen Elizabeth II with agreement of all provinces except Quebec.

1 9 8 4

30 June Pierre Trudeau leaves office and John Turner is sworn in as prime minister.

4 Sept. Conservatives, under Brian Mulroney, win a federal election.

6 Dec.	Mulroney and Lévesque discuss future constitutional talks.

1 9 8 5

3 March	Quebec Liberals set out five conditions for accepting the 1982 constitution.
20 June	Lévesque announces his retirement.
2 Dec.	Liberals, under Robert Bourassa, win Quebec election.

1 9 8 6

9 May	Gil Rémillard outlines Quebec's proposals at Mont Gabriel, Quebec.
4 July	Mulroney announces a new drive for talks with Quebec, led by Senator Lowell Murray.
21 July	Mulroney sends letter to premiers asking for help bringing Quebec into the constitution.
12 Aug.	Edmonton Declaration issued by premiers' conference; premiers agree to deal only with Quebec's issues.

1 9 8 7

5–6 March	First full federal-provincial meeting on Quebec's demands.
17 March	Mulroney invites premiers to Meech Lake at the end of April.
30 April	First ministers' conference at Meech Lake leads to an agreement to amend the constitution.
11 May	Meech Lake agreement is debated in the House of Commons.
25 May	Final day of hearings in Quebec City on the agreement.
27 May	Trudeau attacks Meech Lake in the media.
3 June	Second first ministers' meeting at the Langevin Block brings unanimous agreement on the amendment, known as 1987 Constitutional Accord.

23 June	Quebec National Assembly ratifies the accord.
27 Aug.	Trudeau attacks accord before Joint Senate-Commons Committee.
28 Aug.	Premiers' conference agrees not to reopen accord.
21 Sept.	Senate-Commons Committee recommends adoption without changes.
23 Sept.	Saskatchewan ratifies the accord.
13 Oct.	Liberals, led by Frank McKenna, sweep New Brunswick election.
26 Oct.	House of Commons approves the accord.
7 Dec.	Alberta ratifies the accord.

1 9 8 8

30 March	Pierre Trudeau appears before Senate committee.
18 April	Liberal-dominated Senate introduces series of amendments to the accord.
25 April	Saskatchewan approves a bill that overrides French language rights but offers some services to francophones.
26 April	Gary Filmon's Conservatives win a minority in the Manitoba election.
13 May	Prince Edward Island ratifies the accord.
25 May	Nova Scotia ratifies the accord.
22 June	Alberta introduces a bill to overturn the act that had provided for French language rights in province.
22 June	Commons again ratifies Meech, turning down Senate changes.
29 June	British Columbia and Ontario ratify the accord.
7 July	Newfoundland ratifies the accord.
21 July	Manitoba says it will hold hearings on the accord.
19 Aug.	Premiers' conference authorizes Alberta premier Don Getty to investigate Senate reform.

31 Aug.	Commons passes free-trade legislation.
29 Sept.	New Brunswick begins hearings on the accord.
21 Nov.	Tories win the federal election.
15 Dec.	Supreme Court strikes down Quebec's French-only sign law.
16 Dec.	Manitoba government introduces a Meech Lake resolution. Filmon speaks.
18 Dec.	Bourassa announces he will use the Charter's notwithstanding clause to override the judgement restricting French-only signs.
19 Dec.	Filmon withdraws Meech Lake from the Manitoba legislature.
20 Dec.	McKenna calls for protection of minority language rights and removal of the notwithstanding clause.

1 9 8 9

20 April	Meech opponent Clyde Wells and his Liberal party are elected in Newfoundland; he threatens to rescind the accord unless his demands are met.
9–10 Nov.	Meeting of first ministers in Ottawa fails to resolve the impasse.

1 9 9 0

20 March	Book edited by Trudeau is published; it attacks Meech and Mulroney.
21 March	McKenna announces details of companion resolution.
22 March	On national television, Mulroney announces McKenna's proposal will be studied by a special Commons committee.
5 April	Quebec National Assembly passes a resolution that it be approved unchanged.
6 April	Newfoundland rescinds approval of the accord.

17 May	Special committee report urges that a companion resolution of additional reforms follow the Meech Lake accord.
22 May	Federal environment minister Lucien Bouchard quits the Tories, saying the committee's recommendations would weaken Meech.
3 June	First ministers gather for dinner in Hull.
9 June	Tentative deal is struck to save the accord after seven days of closed-door meetings of first ministers in Ottawa. Wells dissents.
12 June	Manitoba NDP member Elijah Harper blocks attempts to introduce a Meech Lake resolution to the House of Assembly
15 June	Accord is passed by the New Brunswick legislature.
20 June	Commons introduces a resolution encouraging Newfoundland and Manitoba to pass the accord.
22 June	Newfoundland and Manitoba legislatures adjourn without voting on the Meech Lake Accord. Accord dies.
23 June	Jean Chrétien chosen federal Liberal leader.

The Meech Lake Communiqué April 30, 1987

At their meeting today at Meech Lake, the Prime Minister and the ten Premiers agreed to ask officials to transform into a constitutional text the agreement in principle found in the attached document.

First Ministers also agreed to hold a constitutional conference within weeks to approve a formal text intended to allow Quebec to resume its place as a full participant in Canada's constitutional development.

Quebec's Distinct Society

(1) The Constitution of Canada shall be interpreted in a manner consistent with

  a) the recognition that the existence of French-speaking Canada, centred in but not limited to Quebec, and English-speaking Canada, concentrated outside Quebec but also present in Quebec, constitutes a fundamental characteristic of Canada; and

  b) the recognition that Quebec constitutes within Canada a distinct society.

(2) Parliament and the provincial legislatures, in the exercise of their respective powers, are committed to preserving the fundamental characteristic of Canada referred to in paragraph (1)(a).

(3) The role of the legislature and Government of Quebec to preserve and promote the distinct identity of Quebec referred to in paragraph (1)(b) is affirmed.

Immigration

— Provide under the Constitution that the Government of Canada shall negotiate an immigration agreement appropriate to the needs and circumstances of a province that so requests and that, once concluded, the agreement may be entrenched at the request of the province;

— such agreements must recognize the federal government's power to set national standards and objectives relating to immigration, such as the ability to determine general categories of immigrants, to establish overall levels of immigration and prescribe categories of inadmissible persons;

— under the foregoing provisions, conclude in the first instance an agreement with Quebec that would:

- incorporate the principles of the Cullen-Couture Agreement on the selection abroad and in Canada of independent immigrants, visitors for medical treatment, students and temporary workers, and on the selection of refugees abroad and economic criteria for family reunification and assisted relatives;

- guarantee that Quebec will receive a number of immigrants, including refugees, within the annual total established by the federal government for all of Canada proportionate to its share of the population of Canada, with the right to exceed that figure by 5% for demographic reasons; and

- provide an undertaking by Canada to withdraw services (except citizenship services) for the reception and integration (including linguistic and cultural) of all foreign nations wishing to settle in Quebec where services are to be provided by Quebec, with such withdrawal to be accompanied by reasonable compensation:

— nothing in the foregoing should be construed as preventing the negotiation of similar agreements with other provinces.

Supreme Court of Canada

— Entrench the Supreme Court and the requirement that at least three of the nine justices appointed be from the civil bar;

— provide that, where there is a vacancy on the Supreme Court, the federal government shall appoint a person from a list of candidates proposed by the provinces and who is acceptable to the federal government.

Spending Power

— Stipulate that Canada must provide reasonable compensation to any province that does not participate in a future national shared-cost program in an area of exclusive provincial jurisdiction if that province undertakes its own initiative on programs compatible with national objectives.

Amending Formula

— Maintain the current general amending formula set out in section 38, which requires the consent of Parliament and at least two-thirds of the provinces representing at least fifty percent of the population;

— guarantee reasonable compensation in all cases where a province opts out of an amendment transferring provincial jurisdiction to Parliament;

— because opting out of constitutional amendments to matters set out in section 42 of the Constitution Act, 1982 is not possible, require the consent of Parliament and all the provinces for such amendments.

Second Round

— Require that a First Ministers' Conference on the Constitution be held not less than once per year and that the first be held within twelve months of proclamation of this amendment but not later than the end of 1988;

— entrench in the Constitution the following items on the agenda:

1) Senate reform including:
   - — the functions and role of the Senate
   - — the powers of the Senate
   - — the method of selection of Senators
   - — the distribution of Senate seats

2) fisheries roles and responsibilities; and

3) other agreed upon matters

— entrench in the Constitution the annual First Ministers' Conference on the Economy now held under the terms of the February 1985 Memorandum of Agreement;

— until constitutional amendments regarding the Senate are accomplished the federal government shall appoint persons from lists of candidates provided by provinces where vacancies occur and who are acceptable to the federal government.

The 1987 Constitutional Accord

WHEREAS first ministers, assembled in Ottawa, have arrived at a unanimous accord on constitutional amendments that would bring about the full and active participation of Quebec in Canada's constitutional evolution, would recognize the principle of equality of all the provinces, would provide new arrangements to foster greater harmony and cooperation between the Government of Canada and the governments of the provinces and would require that annual first ministers' conferences on the state of the Canadian economy and such other matters as may be appropriate be convened and that annual constitutional conferences composed of first ministers be convened commencing not later than December 31, 1988;

AND WHEREAS first ministers have also reached unanimous agreement on certain additional commitments in relation to some of those amendments;

NOW THEREFORE the Prime Minister of Canada and the first ministers of the provinces commit themselves and the governments they represent to the following:

1. The Prime Minister of Canada will lay or cause to be laid before the Senate and House of Commons, and the first ministers of the provinces will lay or cause to be laid before their legislative assemblies, as soon as possible, a resolution, in the form appended hereto, to authorize a proclamation to be issued by the Governor General under the Great Seal of Canada to amend the Constitution of Canada.

2. The Government of Canada will, as soon as possible, conclude an agreement with the Government of Quebec that would
   (a) incorporate the principles of the Cullen-Couture agreement on the selection abroad and in Canada of independent immigrants, visitors for medical treatment, students and temporary work-

ers, and on the selection of refugees abroad and economic criteria for family reunification and assisted relatives,

(b) guarantee that Quebec will receive a number of immigrants,
including refugees, within the annual total established by the
federal government for all of Canada proportionate to its share
of the population of Canada, with the right to exceed that figure by five per cent for demographic reasons, and

(c) provide an undertaking by Canada to withdraw services (except citizenship services) for the reception and integration (including linguistic and cultural) of all foreign nationals wishing
to settle in Quebec where services are to be provided by
Quebec, with such withdrawal to be accompanied by reasonable compensation, and the Government of Canada and the
Government of Quebec will take the necessary steps to give the
agreement the force of law under the proposed amendment
relating to such agreements.

3. Nothing in this Accord should be construed as preventing the negotiation of similar agreements with other provinces relating to
immigration and the temporary admission of aliens.

4. Until the proposed amendment relating to appointments to the
Senate comes into force, any person summoned to fill a vacancy in
the Senate shall be chosen from among persons whose names have
been submitted by the government of the province to which the
vacancy relates and must be acceptable to the Queen's Privy Council for Canada.

MOTION FOR A RESOLUTION TO
AUTHORIZE AN AMENDMENT TO THE
CONSTITUTION OF CANADA

WHEREAS the *Constitution Act, 1982* came into force on April 17, 1982,
following an agreement between Canada and all the provinces except
Quebec;

AND WHEREAS the Government of Quebec has established a set of
five proposals for constitutional change and has stated that amendments
to give effect to those proposals would enable Quebec to resume a full
role in the constitutional councils of Canada;

AND WHEREAS the amendment proposed in the schedule hereto sets
out the basis on which Quebec's five constitutional proposals may be
met;

AND WHEREAS the amendment proposed in the schedule hereto also recognizes the principle of the equality of all the provinces, provides new arrangements to foster greater harmony and cooperation between the Government of Canada and the governments of the provinces and requires that conferences be convened to consider important constitutional, economic and other issues;

AND WHEREAS certain portions of the amendment proposed in the schedule hereto relate to matters referred to in section 41 of the *Constitution Act, 1982;*

AND WHEREAS section 41 of the *Constitution Act, 1982* provides that an amendment to the Constitution of Canada may be made by proclamation issued by the Governor General under the Great Seal of Canada where so authorized by resolutions of the Senate and the House of Commons and of the legislative assembly of each province;

NOW THEREFORE the (Senate) (House of Commons) (legislative assembly) resolves that an amendment to the Constitution of Canada be authorized to be made by proclamation issued by Her Excellency the Governor General under the Great Seal of Canada in accordance with the schedule hereto.

INDEX